Dickson Lam's *Paper Sons* combines memoir and cultural history, the quest for an absent father and the struggle for social justice, and naming traditions in graffiti and in Chinese culture. Violence marks the story at every turn—from Mao to Malcolm X, from the projects in San Francisco to the lynching of Asians during the California Gold Rush. After one of his former students at the June Jordan School of Equity is gunned down on a street corner, Lam is compelled to tell a mosaic of stories. What does it take, in this social context, to become a person who respects himself and holds hope for those coming up through a culture of exclusion and violence? Lam writes with a depth of hard-won understandings both political and psychological. This is an important book, beautifully crafted, rich in poetic images and juxtapositions, that offers insight and compassion for a nation struggling to make sense of its immigrant nature. I congratulate Dickson Lam on this fine work.

—ALISON HAWTHORNE DEMING, contest judge
for Autumn House's 2017 Nonfiction Prize

From China to Hong Kong to San Francisco's North Beach projects, Dickson Lam's *Paper Sons* (and daughters) navigates the mysteries and betrayals of deleted and recovered memory, of tagging crews and migrant parents, of generational secrets. Dickson Lam's unforgettable characters blaze like falling stars and illumine a world. *Paper Sons*, written in short pieces like a document torn and reassembled, is also the story of a determined younger brother who reclaims the truth, and the fierce, protective sister who shows him the way.

—JAYNE ANNE PHILLIPS, National Book Award Finalist

Raw, monstrous, white-knuckled recollections of love-hate, hate-love, abuse, regression, repression, and all the darkness and light any foolish-brave memoirist could possibly summon forth. It rings true to anyone who has gulped deeply from that well of pain. Highly recommended!

—ANDREW X. PHAM, author of *Catfish and Mandala:
A Two-Wheeled Voyage Through the Landscape and Memory of Vietnam*

This moving memoir about coming-of-age in the hardscrabble streets of San Francisco while coming to terms with a dysfunctional family sheds fresh light on the Asian American immigrant experience. Dickson Lam presents an unflinching and poignant portrayal of his troubled father and the emotional toll of being a father figure to inner-city youth. Charting a heart-wrenching journey of strength and forgiveness, *Paper Sons* is an exhilarating debut.

—RIGOBERTO GONZÁLEZ, author of
Butterfly Boy: Memories of a Chicano Mariposa

Dickson Lam's *Paper Sons* is a groundbreaking memoir about growing up Chinese American, about working-class kids of color in the Bay Area, about the sorrows and survival of his troubled family. Through his roles as a son, a student, a teacher, and a writer, Lam creates three-dimensional portraits of people who have too often been silenced in our culture, and he rings immense sympathy even to those who have hurt or disappointed him, particularly his father. This is a moving and necessary work, and I thoroughly agree with one of his students, "You're a deep man, Mr. Lam."

—DAVID MURA, author of *Turning Japanese: Memoirs of a Sansei*

With *Paper Sons*, Dickson Lam dissects his own life as a vehicle for understanding what it is to be a good man in this world. *Paper Sons* isn't just a memoir, it's a triumph. Dickson Lam yanks you into his heart and sews up his chest behind you. The only thing breaking out is this debut.

—MAT JOHNSON, author of *Pym* and *Loving Day*

* * * * *

PAPER SONS

DICKSON LAM

PAPER SONS

A MEMOIR

DICKSON LAM

Autumn House Press

Pittsburgh

 Autumn House Press receives state arts funding support through a grant from the Pennsylvania Council on the Arts, a state agency funded by the Commonwealth of Pennsylvania, and the National Endowment for the Arts, a federal agency.

Cover Art: Cafe Racer/Shutterstock.com
Book and cover design: TG Design

ISBN: 978-1-938769-28-3
Library of Congress Control Number: 2017958366

*For my sister
and
my students*

*My aunt haunts me—her ghost drawn to me…I alone devote
pages of paper to her….I do not think she always means me
well. I am telling on her….*
—MAXINE HONG KINGSTON

* * * * *

*You must take your opponent into a deep dark forest
where 2 + 2 = 5, and the path out is only wide enough for one.*
—MIKHAIL TAL

* * * * *

CONTENTS

PART I

CHAPTER I

KING

Two months after my student Javon King was killed, I boarded a plane to see my father. The last time I visited my dad in Minnesota I was fourteen, the same age Javon was when he first entered my classroom, a small kid who wore his hat backwards, afro leaking out the sides. While standing on a crowded corner, he was gunned down, the fatal shots fired from a bus. I blamed myself for why he was there that day and not at school.

Javon was part of our inaugural class of a hundred freshmen. I'd joined with a handful of gung ho teachers to start a school in San Francisco, my hometown. We were a diverse school, half Latino, a quarter Black, a quarter Asian and white, the white students mostly from Russian immigrant families. The name of our school contained our mission: June Jordan School for Equity. How we got that name probably tells you more. We left it up to the students. We gave them three candidates they could name the school after, unsung activists we admired, civil rights leader Ella Baker, labor organizer Philip Vera Cruz, and poet June Jordan. Once the students heard a spoken word recitation of Jordan's "Owed to Eminem," it was a wrap. The first lines of the diss poem: "I'm the Slim Lady the real Slim Lady / the real Slim Lady just a little ole lady."

We were an alternative school. We didn't have a principal; we had co-directors. We didn't have counselors; we had advisors, and each of us had to take on that role, responsible for a caseload of fifteen students. I'd added the phone numbers of my advisees' parents into my cell phone, and I'm sure they had mine added on theirs.

Originally, Javon wasn't my advisee. I wasn't even his teacher, and boy, was I grateful. He was the school's biggest headache. His nickname was Waga. Sounded like baby talk to me. He'd skipped a grade back in elementary school, his proof he was a genius.

That first year of our school, San Francisco State University housed us, our classrooms on the same floor as college classes, but within a few months, we received enough complaints that we feared we'd get the boot. When we'd investigate a complaint, the trail inevitably led back to Javon.

He dribbled a basketball in the hallway, disrupting a professor's class. He took a groundskeeper's golf cart for a joyride across campus. He stumbled upon a wheelchair in the gym and rode laps around the court, even though the owner of the chair, an SF State professor, shouted and hobbled after him on crutches.

My advisees, in comparison, were angels. The biggest headache I had was one being too clingy. This student, wearing her usual gray hoodie, would slip me letters before school, during passing period, and after school. She mostly wrote about typical freshmen anxiety, not making friends, that type of thing. She was Chinese and signed the letters Mui Mui, Little Sister. One teacher suggested I set boundaries. I couldn't, though. The student's family resembled mine growing up—a family that relied on an absent (migrant?) father to make ends meet. Her dad would visit from Hong Kong once a year during Christmas, and that's when the student wrote the longest letters. Nothing in her writing merited a call to CPS, but from the way she'd act—she'd clam up whenever she tried to talk about her dad—I'd expected a bombshell.

Fine, I told her, you can call me Goh Goh, Older Brother.

It was a reversal of roles. I was the youngest in my family, and my mother had raised us under a clear hierarchy. She was at the top, infallible. My father, Bah Ba, came second, and he wasn't around enough to dispute this. Next in line was Goh Goh, then Ga Jeh, my older sister. I had a title too, Sai Lo, Littler Brother, but my siblings simply called me by my first name. I wasn't allowed to address them by theirs. First name privileges were a one-way street: older to younger. Another privilege they had—kicking my ass. I was taught not to fight back. "Who told you to be the youngest?" my mother would say.

My sister and I, as teenagers, rarely communicated. It seemed the only time we spoke was to fight over the phone. She'd storm into the room, yelling at me to get off, throwing around the word "urgent," as if lives were at stake. Then she'd get on the phone, and all she'd do was sweet talk some boy or talk about whether or not she should sweet talk some boy.

Later, as adults, Ga Jeh and I would commiserate over failed relationships. We'd end our conversations with "I love you." No one said that in our family growing up, which I hadn't had a problem with. In fact, it'd been a source of cultural pride: we're not into that touchy-feely crap! But now my sister had gotten in the habit of telling us that she loved us. My brother and mother wouldn't reciprocate her I love yous. I, on the other hand, went along. I couldn't leave my sis hanging. We were closer than we'd ever been, though when it came to discussing our father, Ga Jeh and I still weren't able to confront the past together.

OVERLAP

I got sucked into Javon's orbit when an advisee confided to me that Javon had stolen a teacher's wallet. I reported this to the staff, and they nominated me to squeeze a confession out of Javon. When there was a pressing student issue and the co-directors weren't around, I became the default dean.

I had Javon sit by my desk in the main office. All the teacher desks were located in this room, abutting and facing each other, the close proximity meant to foster a family-like atmosphere. We even divided students and teachers into families, clusters of students who would share the same teachers, but one veteran teacher complained about all this rhetoric of family. "I got my own," she said. "I don't need another one."

Javon rose from his chair. "I gotta be somewhere," he said as though he had a pressing appointment.

"It can wait. Sit."

Javon fell back in his chair, still wearing his backpack, which featured a cartoon image of three girls with humongous eyes.

"Who's that on your bag?" I asked him.

"Powerpuff Girls."

"Boys like that show too, huh?"

"I know what you're trying to say, Mr. Lam. That's sexist."

"You like this school?"

"Not really."

"I can help you transfer."

"To where?"

"How about Balboa?"

"Hell, nah. I'll stay here."

"Three different students have told me—and they put this in writing—that they saw you steal Ms. Mana's wallet." I only had the one statement from my advisee, but three testimonies sounded indisputable. I understood deceit was an effective strategy for an interrogator. As a young teenager, my friends and I had stolen frequently from a baseball card shop until the owner offered us jobs. He handed us index cards and told us to jot down our contact info. We raced to finish the cards. "Print neatly," he said. We shoved each other aside to hand him our index cards, to get picked for an interview. I was chosen first. The owner brought me to his office in the back. He closed the door and said an eyewitness claimed we were the kids responsible for the missing Ken Griffey Jr. rookie card. If I didn't confess, the owner said—he flapped the index card in front of me—he'd call my mother.

"Man, some students are trying to set me up," Javon said. "That's why I hate this school."

"What do you think the other teachers are going to say when I show them the student statements?"

"I didn't do anything."

"They're going to kick you out."

"Oh well."

I placed a piece of lined paper on the desk with a pen. "If you won't own up to it, take responsibility, you'll be out of here. You think your mom's gonna be happy about that?"

He slouched into the seat.

"Think it over." I opened the door, and before I could close it behind me, Javon said, "What I got to write?"

In addition to the confession, Javon wrote a letter of apology to Ms. Mana and served as her helper after school to make amends. To keep our eye on Javon, we gave him two new advisors, myself and one of the co-directors, a double-team approach. We met with him and his mother every Friday morning to continually check in about his progress. His mom would show up on her way to work, dressed in a hospital uniform. For a short period, Javon moved in with his father, and he'd be the one to attend the Friday meetings. The extra attention paid off. Javon raised his grades and quit his reckless behavior, but he remained the class clown, at least in my class.

Though I'd agreed to transfer him into my Humanities class, a course combining English and history, I'd wanted to block the move, worried that Javon would drive me nuts. I was already struggling.

I couldn't get my students to focus. They'd chat like it was the lunchroom.

I could've sought guidance from seasoned teachers, but I had too much pride for that. I wasn't a rookie, so I didn't have that excuse. Twenty-seven, fourth year of teaching, and I still hadn't grown into an authority figure. I sure didn't dress like one. I'd wear baggy corduroys and cargo pants, oversized plaid shirts designed by hip-hop clothing brands. I'd rock Tims to my classroom. This was my version of dressing up.

At the first school I taught at, Urban Academy in New York City, my attire was even more casual: jeans and a T-shirt, the school even more alternative than June Jordan. Students chilled on couches in the hallway. I'd wear a baseball hat, not on my head—I'd take it off when I entered the building—but I'd snap the strap of the hat around a belt loop in my jeans, the hat hanging against my thigh, the same way it had back when I was a teenager, when teachers had forced me to take it off.

I didn't feel that removed from my June Jordan students. Not only because I was still in my twenties, or grew up in 'Frisco like them, but because our lives overlapped. I taught students related to old homies. Some of the connections I would learn about later, but some I knew then. One advisee's family had lived in the same public housing project that I had grown up in. Her older brother had schooled me in a pickup game. And more recently, during a spring break from teaching, I'd hung with her brother in Miami, along with several other dudes from my old projects.

Another student had a cousin, Keino, who'd been killed. He and I hadn't been tight—he was still in middle school when I was in high school—but we'd kicked it a number of times, at the basketball gym and in the mornings at the bus stop in front of his school. Though he was from a different turf, most of the dudes I was running with back then claimed that same set. Keino and his middle school crew were the younger version of us. We'd all refer to each other as "cousin."

The student, a thirteen-year-old girl, would come into my room to talk about Keino. She recounted the gory details of his death. He'd been in a van, shots to the face, an AK-47, close range—closed casket. I'd heard the story before, from someone who was in that van, but hearing it again from my student, someone I was entrusted to nurture, made me feel responsible for Keino's death. Not his murder but for the weight of it, at least on my student.

Whatever feelings I had didn't change anything. My student dropped out of school, and I never heard from her again.

LAMINATOR

Javon would run around my room, gossiping, dancing, pulling pranks on other students, slapping a kid on the nape of his neck and darting off. I'd grab him by his Powerpuff Girls backpack and drag him back to his seat. Throwing Javon down into his chair, I felt fatherly.

One of the co-directors, Shane, observed my class for an evaluation. Together, we'd partnered to advise Javon. She was one of the original founders of the school, a white woman with freckles in her early thirties. Shane was that rare blend, a visionary who had no ego about doing the dirty work. She'd roll up her sleeves right alongside us. It was her who gave me the nickname: "Laminator."

After Shane observed my class, we met in her office. "The students like you," she said, "but they're not respecting you." Students had been talking over me, out of their seat, side conversations galore. I had to reinvent my teacher persona, become firmer, serious, a different kind of man. I wasn't sure I knew how.

We came up with a plan for Javon in my classroom. I stuck him in the corner. With fewer distractions, he got his work done. His last major assignment for me was a research paper on the Black Panthers. I'd lent him a stack of my Panther books: *Seize the Time, A Taste of Power, Revolutionary Suicide*. It wasn't a stellar paper, but it was solid, and he was proud of it. I showed it to his mother, evidence that he (I) had turned things around.

In the last month of the school year, regular classes ended and we began Intersession, a three-week-long experiential program. Students had several PE-related courses to choose from, and Javon signed up for "Go Wild," an outdoors course with Shane. They went on a backpacking trip, hiking through redwoods to a cascading waterfall. On another excursion, Javon stepped up to be a leader, guiding his group through an orienteering activity. His indefatigable energy was bottled in the classroom, but in the outdoors, that same energy was prized. When I saw him after his overnight trip, he said, "Next year, you guys gotta make Intersession year-round, Lam." This is how I want to end Javon's story, with him thinking of his future.

BUS DRIVER

In high school, I wasn't a troublemaker in class like Javon, but I also needed a kick in the ass. I was a graffiti writer, and I'd cut school to hop the city bus all around San Francisco. I'd sit in the window seat of the last row, unloosen the cap of my marker, and slide the window open, so the smell of ink wouldn't reach the driver. I'd hit up my name, RANK, on the white panel that ran vertically alongside the window, the letters to my name written top to bottom, a totem pole of letters. I knew all the bus routes, which ones went to which bus yard, how you could shut down the engine of a diesel city bus by flipping a secret switch located on the backside of the vehicle. I'd return to school to nap while my tags stamped on buses zigzagged around the city.

Bus drivers were our adversaries. We tagged when they weren't looking in the rearview mirror, when they'd lean into a turn, spinning the steering wheel, their eyes fixed on the road. Sometimes we'd get lucky, and a driver would have their mirror aimed away from us. When a driver caught us in the act, usually they'd just shout until we got off. But once, a driver called me up to the front like he was inviting me to sit down in his living room. We were the only ones left on the bus. He gave me a you-could-be-doing-more-with-your-life talk, which somehow didn't come across as corny.

Another driver stopped the bus and charged at me and my homeboy sitting in the back. The two of us each squeezed through a window and jumped. But the driver wasn't deterred. He gave chase, on some superhero shit. He abandoned his bus, along with his passengers, in the middle of a one-lane street, cars honking, traffic stalled. I turned back after a couple of blocks. The driver was gaining. I didn't think I had the stamina to elude him. As soon as I turned the next corner, I stopped while my friend continued. I leaned against the wall, creeping to the edge of the corner, listening for the footsteps of the approaching driver. When he drew close, when I could hear him panting, I slipped past him, speeding off in the opposite direction.

The man my mother had an affair with was also a bus driver. Their relationship started back when I was in elementary school. Willie, a Filipino guy, would come over during his lunch breaks while my father was working in the kitchen of a restaurant in Chinatown. Willie would have on sunglasses, dressed in a brown uniform. My mom would put on makeup before he arrived, heavy blush and blue eye shadow.

They'd go in her room and lock the door. Just looking at photo albums, my mom would say. She had a stack of albums in her closet. There were two types, ones that contained pictures of our family, and ones that contained pictures of her vacations with Willie. He was careful never to be photographed, always the photographer. They'd take trips to Disneyland, Hawaii, and, once, Paris. My mom carried a small wallet, and on the front cover was a picture of her in a bikini, kneeling on the beach, a yellow flower in her hair.

She'd somehow convinced my father that she was going on these trips with friends from her ESL class. In the beginning, I also believed her. As I got older, I began to see through the lies, but I played along like my brother and sister and kept my mouth shut.

It wasn't difficult. Bah Ba never probed or protested, as though his wife taking off was *his* vacation. While my mother was gone, which couldn't have added up to more than a week or two a year, we were left alone with our father. One morning, my sister confided to me that she had cried herself to sleep.

I told her I'd done the same. I figured we both really missed our mom. We weren't used to spending so many hours with our father. Usually he'd be out playing mahjong—he was a gambler—and our home was simply his pit stop. He'd change clothes after work, drink a beer or some Hennessy, make his presence felt through burps and unapologetic farts, and then take off before dinner. We wouldn't even bother to keep a chair at the dinner table for him. He was an old-school kind of father: bringing home the bacon was his sole obligation.

Back then, I didn't harbor a grudge against Bah Ba. I'd sit in the chair closest to the front door, waiting for him to come home from work. When he appeared, I'd hurl myself at him. I'd inhale his scent: flour and grease mixed with nicotine. My hugs weren't entirely selfless. I was trying to set myself apart from the rest of my family. Goh Goh was too cool for such displays. Ga Jeh used to sit on Bah Ba's lap, but with middle school on the horizon, maybe she thought she was too old for that. My mom kept our father at arm's length, though she'd suffocate us with hugs. I became the only one to hug my dad, the last to give up hope, the last to understand that he was already on his way out.

To be fair, it wasn't always mahjong that kept my father out at night. Once, he enrolled in a culinary course at a local community college's satellite campus. He'd come home with American cook-books, and I'd look over his shoulder as he perused the recipes. Perhaps he had aspirations of a better-paying job.

My father may have also spent his nights frequenting strip clubs. On his desk, tucked away underneath old envelopes, I discovered several coins stamped with naked women and the name of a strip club in North Beach. "Your father's not a pervert," my mom said. "Some guys from work probably dragged him there."

When Willie and my mother would return from her room—really, my parents' room—Willie's shades would hang from his collar. He had beady eyes, and the pockmarks on his cheeks made me uncomfortable. Looking at his face was like staring at a scar.

He wouldn't leave immediately. They'd sip coffee in the kitchen. My mom would speak to Willie in "broken" English, inflected with the giddiness of a teenager. Sometimes, he'd have her sit on his lap. He'd call my mother by her Chinese name, Laih Fong, but he'd mispronounce it, unable to use the correct tones. From his lips, my mother's name sounded like some sort of Ching-Chong Chinese.

I was set up for a variation of the Oedipus complex: Willie, the father I had to kill. It wasn't lost on me as a graffiti writer that Willie drove the buses that I treasured. I'd cut class to mark them, some of which I knew he would later drive. I'd tag RANK on the windows, on the ceiling, and on the back wall. The final stroke of my name, the front leg of my *K* a slash.

TWO TRANSFERS

After my sophomore year in high school, I decided to transfer schools, from McAteer to Galileo. Gal was just a few blocks from my house. More of my friends went there, but that's not why my mom signed the paperwork. She'd been shocked by my low grades, finally seeing my report card in the mail. Up to then, I'd been beating her to the mailbox and tossing my report cards in the dumpster. She had no clue I'd been fucking up, and nobody from McAteer gave a shit. No phone call home or notice in the mail about my absences. In Geometry class, I amassed sixty-four absences, though miraculously, I passed.

The teacher was a white dude with a gray afro, an ex-hippie who showed us slides of his tie-dyed shirt days. On the day of the final, right before the bell rang for class to begin, the guy sitting next to me told me the final was the same as the study sheet, multiple-choice questions, but I didn't have the sheet. I'd skipped the review day. The guy handed me his study sheet so I could scribble the answers on my desk. It turned out there were two versions of the final. One, exactly the same as the study sheet; the other, same questions but in a different order. The other guy received the jumbled version, and I received the replica. I filled out the answers in seconds, but I tried to play it smooth. Waited half an hour to turn it in. Half an hour of watching the guy next to me struggle through the questions, drawing triangles, hexagons, parallelograms, shapes that bewildered him.

After I turned in my test, I was given the second part. I'd have to show my work. There were no answers to select from. Our final grade in the course would be the average of these two tests. Never mind everything else that had been done or not done in the semester. I figured I already had an A on the first part, so I didn't get flustered with the second test, though I knew I couldn't solve any of the problems. I rested my head on the desk and knocked out until the bell rang. I passed the second test forward, blank except my name. That's how I managed a C in Geometry.

When my mom discovered my grades, which included a couple of Fs, along with all my absences, she threw a couple of plates at the wall, finger jabbed my temple, less of a stab than a push, but eventually she acquiesced to my transfer of schools. It offered her hope.

In the second year of June Jordan, we left the college campus and moved into a building in the Excelsior, a neighborhood closer to where most of our students lived. We also needed more room. We were doubling in size. At SF State, we had classrooms on three different floors, some on this end, some down that wing, the main office, somewhere in between. The lack of contiguous space resulted in a dismembered school.

Before we began the second year, we had to set up schedules for our students. In our new main office, a former woodshop, we crowded around a group of tables pushed together. On the tables were piles of index cards, each with the name of a student and their gender, ethnicity, and skill-level noted in the corner of the card. We were to manually program our students' class schedules to ensure balanced groupings. Losing Javon to another teacher was not a total accident.

At a typical high school, students get a new set of teachers every year, but at our school, we wanted students to remain with the same teacher for two years, for continuity's sake. Our classes were also intended to be mixed-age, half sophomores, half freshmen, a balance of old and new. Because we only had freshmen in the first year of the school, my returning students couldn't all return with me. I had to make room for the next freshmen class. Half of my returning sophomores were to be handed over to a new teacher, Ms. Luna.

Our new class list contained blank slots for freshmen, which we were to fill using the index cards, but the sophomores had already been assigned. Javon was on Luna's list.

"If you see any red flags," another teacher said, "we can still make some switches."

"Any advice about my group?" Ms. Luna asked me.

When I saw her list, I knew I should've fought to keep some of my students, particularly Javon, who I'd invested so much time in, but I chickened out. If I had a repeat of the year before, I would've quit teaching, a failure. I had a better shot at being a new man with new kids. I exchanged my old students for new ones like I was trading in a bad poker hand.

"You'll be fine," I told Ms. Luna.

She must have detected something in my voice, because she laughed. "You sure about that?"

Luna was a strict teacher, but my students turned out to be a handful, even for her. She'd kick Javon out often. He'd head to my classroom, which was the standard procedure—kids going to their advisor. Javon, as a sophomore, had gotten rid of the Powerpuff Girls backpack. Now he rocked buttoned shirts and wore a gold earring.

I'd be in the middle of class and wouldn't have time to check in with him. I'd sit him in the corner and tell him to write an explanation of what happened, but I'd rarely discuss it with him afterwards. I'd just send him off to his next class. I had new students to worry about.

As the fall semester wore on, Javon's grades plummeted. Shane asked how it happened that Javon was no longer my student. "All that progress you made with him last year," she said.

"The foreign languages messed up the scheduling," I said. "I couldn't figure a way around it."

Our last resort with Javon was to switch him into another family, hoping a new advisor and new set of teachers might work some magic. It didn't. He continued to blow off assignments. That by itself we could work with, but Javon was also getting sent out of class regularly, within the first minutes of class. It seemed intentional on his part.

At a staff meeting, we voted for Javon to leave the school. "If we keep him," I said at the meeting, "what message are we sending to the rest of the students?"

I volunteered to meet with Javon and his mother. It was a delicate matter. We didn't have the power to kick out a kid. If a student hadn't committed a serious offense, a transfer had to be voluntary. We laid out the reasons why Javon would be better served at a different school, and Javon was all in.

"Teachers here be on you 24/7," he said. "They be doing too much."

His mom, though, wasn't budging. She countered, and rightly so, that our school provided more support. Why would she give that up?

To convince her, I drew on my own high school experiences, not of being a student who'd gotten his act together after switching schools—that wasn't my story—but of knowing how to appeal to a desperate mother. "You do the same things," I said, "you get the same results. It's clear to me, and I think to you too, if Javon stays here, he'll just fail another semester of classes. He needs a fresh start, a wake-up call." What I said wasn't total bullshit. I really thought it was the best choice for Javon. Sometimes people need to be jolted into changing. But what was also true, and what I couldn't admit to anyone else, was that I wanted him to leave. His presence reminded me of my cowardice.

The next semester, Javon was placed at a vocational school. I didn't know how things were going for him, but for me, things were looking up. I'd transformed as a teacher. Instead of yelling to get the class's attention, I developed a stern gaze. I'd imagine myself as their parent. I'd make the disappointed face of a father and cross my arms, or the face of an angry mom about to open a can of whu-pass. Once, I got too into character. A boy made a subtle sexual remark about a girl in the class, and I popped him upside the head.

During that spring semester, to boost teacher morale, Shane made appreciation posters for each of us. In the middle was our photo, surrounding by quotes from students. On my poster, one student remarked, "I don't know what got into Mr. Lam this year, but he don't play no more."

The next time I heard about Javon was near the end of that school year. I was on a panel in another teacher's classroom, and we were discussing how a student had just done on her presentation. All sophomores had to develop a presentation and defend it to a panel, consisting of two teachers, a student, and a parent. Our job was to grill them with questions. If they passed, they'd move on to Senior Institute, what we called our mixed-age junior- and senior-level program. The oral defense was a grueling experience for a fifteen-year-old, but passing was cause for celebration. They'd run around the hallways hollering for joy. Some parents would get their kids flowers or balloons. If Javon had remained with us, he would've also presented his portfolio. Maybe I would've been scoring his oral defense at that moment. Maybe his mom would've brought him a lei.

As we were about to announce that the student, dressed in a

business suit, had passed her defense, a cell phone rang. It came from the panel. The student panelist stepped out to take the call.

"What?" he shouted. He rushed back into the room. "They killed Waga." He grabbed his backpack and took off, still on his phone.

The next to leave was the student who had presented, tears easing down her cheeks. Then her mother trailing after her. The other teacher collected the paperwork, numb like me. She left as though unsure what else she was supposed to do. I remained in the empty science room staring at a bent spout.

I would read about Javon in the paper. Minutes before he was shot, he was hanging out on a corner in Hunter's Point near his home with a group of other kids. A city bus approached. On it was a rival crew. The camera on the bus showed the kids passing a backpack between each other, arming themselves. The driver was clueless. Passengers who knew it was about to go down warned the driver not to stop, but he didn't heed their pleas. He pulled over to the bus stop. Some kids near Javon, seeing enemies onboard, began firing at the bus.

It's unclear if these guys were Javon's friends, acquaintances, or if he just happened to be in the same vicinity as these kids. "We know nothing," the homicide inspector stated, but in the very next line, perhaps in an attempt to rationalize tragedy, the inspector added that Javon had once been arrested as an "associate of Westmob," the same turf that the kids who had fired those first shots presumably claimed, though the inspector didn't offer details of Javon's earlier arrest. Had he been charged with directly participating in a crime, or had his arrest been a matter of guilt by association?

Whatever the precise relationship between Javon and the boys nearby, the facts remained. The kids on the bus returned fire, and Javon, unarmed, was the only one killed. Though the article acknowledged that Javon was a student at John O' Connell High School, the quoted district spokeswoman referred to Javon as a student at June Jordan: "He was a very easygoing guy who was excelling at math at June Jordan. He wanted to be an engineer."

FOUR GUNS

I've had a gun pointed at me four times, all as a teenager. All after I'd transferred high schools. Three of the four stemmed from adventures on the city bus.

The first time, I was with a tagging crew, a racially diverse bunch, vandals of all stripes. We were on a bus that had made a stop, and some of us were talking shit through the window to a group of Latino dudes hanging near the bus shelter, maybe late teenagers, dressed in khakis. As the bus was pulling from the curb, one of the Latino guys reached in his waistband, pulled out a gun, and waved it at us. We dropped to the gum-stained ribbed floor as the bus rode away.

The second time was at my doorstep.

My apartment was on the ground floor of our housing project, and it opened up to the courtyard. I was kicking it with Rob. We were inseparable. He lived two floors up, and he'd stop by my house, sometimes for dinner but mostly just to shoot the shit.

I'd transferred into his high school, and I'd met most of my friends through him. Rob was the kind of kid everyone noticed. Had the height and talent of a basketball star, though he could never cut the grades to play for the school. Other kids buddied up to him. Some cowered. Adults treated him like a top prospect. The spotlight clung to him, and if I stood close enough, I could feel the light's warmth, if not its gaze.

That night I was standing in front of my door, which was slightly ajar behind me. Through the opening, my mother could be seen washing dishes at the sink.

Rob had just got paid, a wad of twenties. He opened the bills up into a fan, practically shoving them in my face. The money had been given to him by his father. His pops worked at a car dealership and lived in the East Bay with a new wife and a newborn daughter, who Rob refused to acknowledge as a sister. From time to time, Rob would swing by his dad's job, a two-hour bus ride from our house, and guilt his father into giving him some dough.

None of my family drama was new to Rob. When I told him that my dad lived in Minnesota but paid our bills, he said, "Shit, that ain't nothing but child support." When I explained my parents were still married and that Willie was my mother's secret boyfriend, a guy who'd take her on vacations, Rob praised my mom as a pimpstress.

He stuck the wad of bills into his jean pocket, took out a comb, and began to pick out his afro. He had gray strands sprinkled throughout, though you'd only noticed up close. I'd asked him about the gray hairs once, but all he would say was, "That's what happens when you fuck as much as I do. Grown man shit."

Two men were passing by the courtyard. I didn't recognize them, but I didn't think much about it. Relatives or friends of neighbors would often visit. The men approached us like they wanted to know the time. One took out a gun. The other patted us down. They grabbed Rob's cash. I had nothing in my sweatpants.

Quietly, the one with the pistol told Rob to walk away, and he told me to get back in the house. I went inside and closed the door. My mom didn't hear a thing. She was on the phone with Willie.

The third time someone aimed a gun at me I had a bat in my hand.

An hour before, a friend of mine, a short Latino kid who was growing out his frizzy hair into a 'fro, bumped into another kid as they both rushed to board the bus. My friend could've just apologized, but he acted bold. "Watch where the fuck you're going," he said. I suspected he was only doing the tough-guy routine because the other kid was Chinese, and he thought he could get away with it. So when fifteen of that guy's friends also got on the bus, I thought, I'm not getting my ass kicked for this shit. And the other guy we were with, Jesse, felt the same. "Dumb move," he said.

The Chinese kids wore leather jackets and cheap loafers. Hair with bleached tips. FOBs. We didn't call them Fresh off the Boat to clown them for being an immigrant. We used the term as a lazy label for a Chinese gang. They didn't even have to be a gang per se. They just had to mob deep and speak Chinese. They were not unlike my brother and his friends. They'd cuss in Chinese and call each other "nigga."

At some point during the ride I realized that the Asian kid my friend had bumped into was someone I used to know. He was actually Vietnamese and had hung out at my house once, back in sixth grade, along with a group of other Asian kids. It took me a minute to recall his name. We made eye contact, but he didn't acknowledge me, so I left it alone. When our stop came, Jesse and I made sure we were first to the rear door. I leapt off the bus, and our friend got yanked back by his backpack, the door closing on him.

He met us later at Jesse's house. The beatdown lasted only until the next stop, when the driver kicked all of them off. Our friend with the 'fro had the collar of his shirt ripped, and he kept asking us to feel his head for bumps. The story would've ended there if not for Martín, Jesse's cousin, who happened to be over that day. He paced around with a bat preaching payback. We sunk low on the couch. Above us was a painting of two Native Americans sitting on horses in front of a stream. They appeared dignified, even the horses.

The four of us were all the remaining members of NSK, Notorious Sick Kings, a tagging crew we were trying to revitalize, and Martín appealed to this in his Knute Rockne speech. Something about these moments defining us. How did we want our crew to be known? As punk cowards?

As a general rule of thumb, I had avoided fighting. I'd punked out every time I was challenged except once when a guy dared me to meet him by the track at lunch, and I'd only called his bluff because I knew he was more of a punk than me and wouldn't show. The times I had fought were when the other dude threw the first punch. I'd swing out of reflex. Give me the opportunity to make the first move and I'd wilt.

But I'd decided—enough. I wanted to become someone I could respect, someone courageous. Not Rob's sidekick. I put myself on a point system. I'd gotten the idea from a self-help book my sister was reading. One point for taking a risk, doing something out of the ordinary: not running off the bus when the driver stood up and screamed at me to stop tagging, asking a girl on the street for her number. One point deducted if I wimped out.

I picked up the other aluminum bat and felt the grip.

"I don't know," the kid with the 'fro said. "My head kinda hurts."

"Fuck that," I said and we rushed out.

Two stragglers were at the bus stop. One was the Vietnamese kid. They saw us coming and broke with the quickness. They had a block head start, but I almost caught them. I got close enough that I could see the black label sticking up from the Vietnamese kid's leather jacket. They ducked into a corner store, and I waited for my friends before entering. I was winded and unsure what to do next. We bum-rushed the store, each down a different aisle, but our foes had somehow vanished, as though they'd snuck through a secret portal. I swung my bat at a shelf, packages of ramen noodles, cans of vegetables. The cashier screamed something about the police. On the way out, I swung at the wooden door. I should've peeked outside first.

A cop behind his opened car door had his gun drawn on me.

The last time, it was Rob pointing a pistol at me, horsing around.

It was a tiny weapon, a deuce-five. He'd borrowed it for protection. Some Samoans were coming by the rec center looking for him. The origins of the beef were comical.

Rob and I had been riding in a van driven by another friend when Rob, sitting in the front seat, decided it would be funny to toss his Slurpee into the bus in the next lane. When we were younger, we'd throw water balloons at tourists, and though we'd given that up as too juvenile for sixteen-year-olds, Rob occasionally, for old times' sake, would still do his specialty—hurling a large cup of ketchup at tourists. He'd fill the cup to the rim, ripping through dozens of packets at Wendy's.

Rob flung the Slurpee through the bus window, and the slushy contents splattered on the passengers, the bus packed with students from another school. The plan was to hit the gas and take off, but we got stuck at the light, the bus and its riders next to us. All we could do was laugh. I found out later that the passenger who had taken the brunt of the Slurpee was a guy who was apparently known as Not-the-Kind-of-Motherfucker-You-Should-Fuck-With. Also on the bus was a group of taggers, one of whom identified Rob as the culprit.

Rob carried the deuce-five around but kept a low profile until things blew over. When he first got his hands on the pistol, he showed it to me in the closed-in stairwell that led to his apartment.

"Don't worry," he said, "it ain't loaded."

I grabbed the gun and chased him up the stairs, too scared to pull the trigger. He took the gun from me, and we swapped roles. I ran down the staircase and pretended to be shot in the back. Upon turning around and seeing that my assailant was none other than my partner in crime, I made an exaggerated face of disbelief. I took an invisible bullet to the chest, then another, and another. I fell to my knees, but he kept shooting.

WAGA

We held a memorial service for Javon in the auditorium. Around our necks, hung on a lanyard, was a laminated picture of Javon, him in a jersey with a backward hat. Friends shared stories, what they remembered most about Waga, how they first met, silly things he did. A trio consisting of two students and a teacher performed a rap song directed at Javon, looking down at us from heaven.

On the way to the auditorium, a student, sobbing, had shouted at me and a group of teachers, "You guys did this. If you never kicked him out, this wouldn't have happened."

"That ain't true," her friend, holding her, said. "Don't mind her. She don't mean that."

The sobbing student's accusation hit me as more honest than the speech I'd prepared for the memorial. What I said had little specifically to do with Javon. You could've lifted the bulk of the speech and recycled it for another untimely student death. I steered clear of emotions. Students were wailing outside the auditorium, and I didn't want to feel what they felt. I avoided eye contact with Javon's mother and sister sitting in the front row. Facing them, at the foot of the stage, was a cluster of wreaths.

I told the audience Javon wouldn't have the chance to pursue his dream of becoming a mechanical engineer, but we were still here to pursue ours. Use this tragedy as fuel. That was the way to honor Javon. Give his death meaning. "What are you going to do different now with your life?" I asked.

As I went down the aisle to sit down, Shane grabbed my hand. "I'm glad someone said that," she said.

She and I had been responsible for looking after Javon together, but unbeknownst to her, or anyone else, I'd abandoned Waga, unwilling to deal with the child that I'd been given.

MIGRANT

When I was ten, my father moved out. Ostensibly, it was for our benefit. He left for Minnesota, two thousand miles away. Took a job that paid double what he'd been making, same line of work, a dim sum chef. His salary at his job in San Francisco—which I recall from school free lunch applications—was $200 a week. The annual difference between the two jobs: $10,400—the number it took for Bah Ba to leave us.

I try and contextualize my father's decision. I adjust for inflation. All the numbers double, but nothing changes.

Feeding a family of five with only a couple of hundred bucks a week couldn't have been easy. He was our sole source of income. My mom was a housewife, which she made sure I wrote down on school forms under "Mother's Occupation." My mom had two sources of pride, and they both had to do with appearances: the way she looked, and the way her house looked.

Behind the closet door in the hallway hung her shoe rack, a wall of red heels. Sometimes we'd leave the house, and before we could make it to the bus stop, my mother would scrutinize her heels and realize that this red pair didn't go well with her outfit at all. We'd turn back home for her to switch shoes, another set of red heels, the distinction too subtle for my eyes. And these trips, mind you, were only to pick up groceries in Chinatown.

When I got older, my mother would send me off with money to buy cosmetic products for her at Neiman Marcus. They were handing out gift samples with purchases, a bag of makeup goodies. She'd already gone the day before and didn't want to be seen again. Someone there might get the wrong idea.

At home, my mother was a cleaning fanatic. Swept and mopped the floor every night. Dirt was her adversary. A folded tablecloth hung over the washing machine. A lace doily draped over the top of our couch. Hand towels rested on the top of the floor speakers. Leftover vinyl flooring had been cut to fit the top of our wood-paneled television in the living room. We had to keep the remote in its original packaging, a cardboard case with a cellophane window over the buttons. My mother had fashioned a home resistant to aging.

As a child growing up in Hong Kong, my mother hadn't lived with her father, either; he'd been a migrant worker of sorts, his job far enough that he had to live apart from his family but close enough that he could still visit on his day off.

I want to believe that in Chinese culture, a father living away from his family is nothing new, a noble sacrifice born out of economic necessity. Hadn't the first Chinese arrived in America as migrant workers? They'd been living in an impoverished country, unable to feed their family, so who could blame them for leaving? They were promised riches. California was Gold Mountain. Working as miners, farmers, railroad workers, they maintained ties to their family through remittances. Their hairstyle was also a claim to their homeland—queues, proof of their allegiance to the Son of Heaven, a wish for a return home.

Many, however, would never see their families again. Stuck in Gold Mountain, they'd become scapegoats for white unemployment. Massacres across the West. Two out of every three lynched in California in those days were Asian. Chinese immigrant fathers, living in an openly hostile country, still continued to support their family overseas, though they hadn't seen them in years. It was understood: The bond of father-child and husband-wife couldn't be destroyed by distance. An ocean couldn't separate a family.

Even today, migrant work is common among Chinese. In China, millions flock from the countryside to factories in coastal cities. That's where the jobs are, hundreds of miles away. Sweatshop conditions prevail, maybe a buck an hour sewing jeans that'll be exported to the States. Sometimes it's the father who leaves the family, sometimes the mother. Half the time it's both. Factory workers live in dormitory housing and typically visit home once a year, during Lunar New Year, a reverse migration of millions. With luggage on their backs, they brave the stampede to railway stations. They squeeze into packed trains. The journey to see their children in the countryside may take several days by a combination of train, boat, and bus. It's the largest human migration in the world, fathers and mothers returning home to their children.

My father would visit us once a year from Minnesota. Not for the holidays but for a mandatory meeting. It was a stipulation of our lease, an "annual reexamination." Adults in the household had to sit down with the manager of the housing projects to verify income and who lived in the unit. My parents had to pretend they were a couple that had slept in the same bed for the past year. The lies sheltered us.

For years, I told myself that Bah Ba was forced to leave the restaurant he worked at in Chinatown because it was closing. But my dates were off. Hong Kong Tea House closed its doors five years *after* Bah Ba moved. If he'd continued to live with us until Tea House shut down, he would've watched my brother and sister grow into adulthood. Technically, through his annual visits, my father saw all of us grow into adulthood. Each visit gave him a snapshot of us, and if compiled together, he had a flipbook of memories. But these memories lacked substance.

Bah Ba would spend the bulk of his visits sitting at a mah-jong table—it was like old times. During one trip, Bah Ba came home to the smell of vinegar. In my mother's hand was an old sock stuffed with tobacco leaves that had just been boiled in vinegar. She pressed the sock against my fingertips, a little-known home remedy for ringworm. I squirmed as the scalding vinegar from the leaves soaked into my skin. Bah Ba glanced over at us but didn't say a word. Didn't ask what the odor was about, the sock, or what was wrong with my fingers. He walked straight past.

My dad didn't always turn his back from fathering. He used to kick my brother's ass. I'd wished he had done the same to me. Any type of intimacy with my dad would've pleased me as a kid.

After I'd reconnected with him as an adult, he explained in an email, "I was so rough with your brother when he was little. I felt powerless with my own temper. Finally I retreated to staying away from dealing with the day to day raising the kids part so to control my outburst."

He didn't mention his cruelty to my mother. One night when she refused his advances, he threw her onto the kitchen floor and tried to drag her to their bedroom. To teach her a lesson, he pissed all over the bathroom floor and laughed when she got on her knees and scrubbed.

Perhaps living with us reminded him too much of himself. Minnesota offered a fresh start. Its snowy winters gave everything a layer of white softness, the sidewalk, the bark of a tree, even the sharp tips of a fence.

KISS ME

I was over at my mom's house. I was still getting used to calling it that. I used to call it Willie's house or my mom's boyfriend's house, but now they were married. Her name was on the deed.

I was in the kitchen, telling my mother and sister about Javon. Ga Jeh had been staying at their house temporarily since she broke up with her boyfriend. The guy didn't tell her, until after they had gotten serious, that he had kids and that he was still married, at least on paper, the divorce not yet finalized.

"Javon was only fifteen," I said.

"So sad," my mother said, but she didn't skip a beat as she washed dishes, her back to us. "What do you two want for dinner?"

I sat hunched over the kitchen table. You'd never know it was designed in the mold of a Chinese antique, a dragon pattern hand carved on the sides of the rosewood table. My mother had the table draped with three layers of tablecloth, her reason having something to do with making it easier to clean. The design of the top table-cloth was rows of circles, each row a different color. It was a strain on the eyes when combined with the objects on the table: Hello Kitty place mats, crystal necklaces, gold purses, and a red sequin clutch. Also on the table was a boom box, the same one that had rested on my father's nightstand in our old apartment, the same one he had carried onto the airplane when we immigrated to the States. My mother would use the radio to listen to the Chinese station. Sitting on top of the stereo was a small pillow in the shape of a pair of lips. "Kiss Me," it read. I covered my face with my hands.

"You can't control these things," Ga Jeh said. "It's not your fault."

I pulled my hands away. My lips were salty. My sister grabbed my hand. She had a tattoo on her forearm, a tiger emerging from a lush jungle. I took the tissue she handed me.

HOW SHOULD WE VIEW MAO?

The week after Javon was struck down I had to grade a stack of papers evaluating the life of Mao Zedong. Ruling China for nearly thirty years, Mao was more than a father figure; he was the "Sun in the Sky."

We'd been studying him for the last month, and the students had written essays responding to the essential question of our unit: How Should We View Mao? The question was mine, but it wasn't original. I'd stolen it from my mentor teacher at a school in New York. His versions: How Should We View Lincoln? How Should We View Columbus? The question could be recycled and used for any controversial figure.

I'd proposed the Mao unit to the other Humanities teachers. We worked on a consensus model, having to agree on all units and assessments. Two hundred students focused on the same topics, the same questions. One teacher had objected to my proposal. "The question isn't controversial enough," he said. "Mao was an Asian Hitler. What's there left to say?" We aimed for questions that provoked a range of perspectives, that made students wrestle with moral ambiguity.

"Not everyone sees Mao that way," I said.

"I highly doubt we can find legitimate scholars who'd argue otherwise."

At our next Humanities meeting, I brought a pile of books, some condemning Mao, some defending him, one arguing there was a good Mao and a bad Mao, supporting the standpoint of Mao's successor Deng Xiaoping, who declared Mao was seventy percent right and thirty percent wrong, as if the character of a man could be determined by neat percentages.

I'd grown up thinking Mao was a vile tyrant. That's the way my mother saw him. Both of my parents' families had fled from China to Hong Kong before the communists took over. My mom's family had immigrated seeking work. Bah Ba's family had sought refuge.

They were landlords, the wealthiest in their village, and they wanted no part of land redistribution, which the communists had promised upon victory. The problem was that Bah Ba's grandma, my Tai Mah, wasn't allowed to leave the mainland with the rest of the family due to immigration restrictions. Her opportunity to flee wouldn't come until several years later. She had to remain in the village, the last Lam.

When Mao came into power, as expected, he targeted landlords. They'd exploited peasants for thousands of years, charging exorbitant rents. Peasants had little left to feed their families. In desperate times, many would sell a child into slavery to stave off the entire family dying of hunger. In the new China, landlords were to be stripped of their power and riches.

Anytime I'd bring up Mao, my mother would never fail to mention my Tai Mah. The communists tied her up, a rope around her chest. They led her through the village while peasants hurled insults and spat on her. She stood trial on her knees. The verdict: guilty. As punishment, she was made to stand in the brutal sun with a humiliating sign hung around her neck, her fingers forced into a medieval contraption. Sticks tightened around each digit, slowly crushing them. Her nails snapped off one by one. My Tai Mah screamed in agony as villagers threw stones and shouted epithets.

I showed my students a dramatization of this. It was an old propaganda film from Communist China, but its depiction of a landlord being tied up and having rocks thrown at him was similar to my Tai Mah's story, if less sadistic. To complicate this portrayal, I passed around a book that depicted sculpted scenes comparing the life of peasants with the life of their landlords. In one scene, a mother who could not pay her rent is dragged from her baby to the landlord's house. He'd take the baby's milk for himself.

I asked the students: How should we respond to abuse? Do victimizers deserve compassion?

A MAN OF FEW WORDS

I called my father in Minnesota. I could count on one hand the number of times I'd phoned him in my life. I called him at work. I didn't want to wait until he got home, scared I'd change my mind.

It was summer break, and death was on my mind. My aunt had passed away a month after Javon. I'd stood with my father next to his Ga Jeh's casket. Bah Ba wore a suit a size too big. Each time I saw him he'd grown frailer. He had shaved off his moustache, and he'd dyed his graying hair a not-subtle jet black. Funerals were the only times we got together. In the last year, he had lost his father, mother, and now his sister. He was the new elder of his family, and Bah Ba swore he'd be the next to go.

He sent us an email after my aunt's funeral:

Hello,

Thanks very much for the Father's Day gift. It's a precious memory for me since we do not meet each other very often.

Since your mother and me divorced, I felt hopeless, but I am happy now, because you are closer with me, at least I feel some hope, I still have my children around me, cheer me, encourage me which make me so comfort, and all my dirty mind was gone.

From my bottom of heart, I wish you all well, finally, I am proud because all my children were in the funeral of your Aunt. I think she is proud too!

Dad, thanks very much and may God bless you and family!

* * * * * *

Bah Ba hadn't spoken much English to us growing up, and even in Cantonese, he was a man of few words. His only communication with me: curt replies or grunts. Bah Ba had few reasons to use English, the bulk of his days confined to the kitchen of a Chinese restaurant, yet he could compose an email in English that expressed feelings he shied away from in Chinese.

My mother notes that Bah Ba was not uneducated. He completed high school in Hong Kong, studying English three hours every afternoon. A couple of years after immigrating to the States, Bah Ba went to the Chinatown campus of the local community college and took an ESL placement test. Based on his results, he was told he couldn't register. His score was too high. A perfect hundred. All of the ESL classes offered would be too easy. Bah Ba's writing was strong enough that when my mother showed Willie a postcard that my father had sent from a trip back to Hong Kong, Willie said, "Your husband's a good writer." Willie was himself an immigrant, but he'd arrived as a teenager, his Filipino accent hardly noticeable.

Bah Ba's postcard was written in English, presumably not for the sake of my mother, who he'd always speak to in Cantonese, but for me, my brother, and my sister. Goh Goh and Ga Jeh would've only been able to comprehend some of the Chinese characters, and I none of them. I don't remember the postcard, reading it or ever seeing it. Perhaps even as a child I wasn't able to reconcile an articulate or heartfelt Bah Ba with the father I knew.

I could've replied to Bah Ba's email. Said something supportive but measured. That would've been my predictable response, but at the rate Bah Ba and I were going, our relationship would remain stagnant forever. I'd bury him as a stranger. I didn't want to chicken out from another challenge.

"On Wah, *haih mh haih goh dou?*" I asked the guy at the restaurant for my father. It might have been the first time I spoke his Chinese name.

Bah Ba came to the phone. "*Wei?*"

"It's Dickson."

"*Meh yeh sih?*"

"I was thinking about visiting."

"You have time?"

"I got the whole summer."

"*Houh a.*" And then as though I didn't understand, he added, "Good."

* * * * *

PART II

CHAPTER 2

AN UNRELIABLE NARRATOR

ALLEY

My first memory of my father: he slammed the front door on me, leaving my three-year-old ass out in the dark alleyway. I had nothing on but tighty-whities. My mom had just put them on me when Bah Ba burst into the bathroom. He'd grabbed me by my wrist and pushed me into the alley, then shut the door. Maybe he was pissed because he'd stepped on one of my toys, who knows.

I could hear my mother pleading with my father while I stood silent in front of our apartment on the edge of Chinatown, our first home in the States. We lived at the dead end of the alley, near the dumpster, far from the streetlamp.

At some point, my mother opened the door and swept me into her arms. She brushed off my feet and gave them a warm squeeze. She turned around, but my father was nowhere to be seen.

TOILET

Or maybe my first memory of Bah Ba was when he dropped me
into a toilet. We were in the bathroom of Tea House. Bah Ba was
on one knee and held me over the toilet by my armpits.

His face began to twitch, his grip softened. He sneezed. You
wouldn't expect my father to instinctively cover his mouth. He
wasn't big on etiquette. My father liked to hock a loogie the way
some men like to grab their balls, habitually and unabashedly. But
on this occasion, he had manners. What befuddles me is not that
he covered his mouth but that he had to use both hands.

My butt splashed into the murky pool, my arms and legs flail-
ing about. Bah Ba pulled me up and wiped me off with toilet paper.
Before we left the bathroom, he said, "*Mouh wah bei leih* Ma *tang.*"
Don't tell your mother.

DRUNK

Bah Ba was sitting on the linoleum floor in the hallway, jubilant,
singing Cantonese songs, and laughing to himself. I sat next to
him. His head swayed from side to side, his beard stubble brushing
against my cheek. I put his head on my bony shoulder. We looked
at the mirror and laughed. He staggered toward my mother in the
kitchen, but she scowled and pushed him away. She left him laid
out on the kitchen floor, singing himself to sleep.

The next morning, he told me he didn't remember a thing.

EAR PICKER

My most cherished father-son moments were when my father
cleaned out my earwax. It was Bah Ba's only duty at home. I'd tell
him when it was time, tugging my ear. He'd rinse the metal ear
pick, and I'd pull a napkin from the tin dispenser, a freebie from
his restaurant. I'd unfold the napkin on the kitchen table, then lay
my head next to the napkin, ear to the table, listening to the wood.

Bah Ba would place his hand firmly on my head as he used the cold pick to scrape and dig. He never rushed. Whatever he scooped out, he placed on the napkin. The higher the mound of wax, the better—a marker of time spent with my father. But to get a large pile, I had to wait for the buildup. As a result, these sessions were few and far between.

Once, I waited too long. A ball of earwax had formed, and Bah Ba was unable to dig it out. My mom had to take me to the doctor. What the doc pulled out was the size of a marble.

RED BEAN SOUP

I was turning six, and for my school birthday party, Bah Ba told me he planned something special: red bean soup. I never liked that concoction. Who wants soup served cold? I didn't protest, however. I had never had *his* red bean soup. I assumed my father had a natural gift for the culinary arts. Perhaps he'd developed his craft at a young age, a prodigy.

I'd discover later that when Bah Ba arrived in the States from Hong Kong at the age of thirty-one, four years before the party, he had no kitchen experience, but he lied about this to the owner of Tea House. It was my grandfather's idea. He told his son-in-law not to worry, he would train him. Gung Gung was the head chef at the popular dim sum restaurant in San Francisco. His wife, my Poh Poh, also worked alongside him in the kitchen. All the workers, the cooks, the women pushing metal carts with stacks of bamboo steamers, the hosts and hostesses dressed in suits, they all addressed my grandfather as Sifu.

A couple of months after my aforementioned birthday party, Gung Gung appeared in the *New York Times*. In the Travel section, there was a food guide of San Francisco's Chinatown, and Tea House was described as "arguably the best dim sum restaurant in the country." The article credits my grandfather by name, since he was the head chef. Not surprisingly, no mention of Bah Ba. Eventually, my father would leave Tea House for a restaurant in Minnesota, enticed by the opportunity to become a head dim sum chef himself, a sifu, like his father-in-law.

Another kid in my class also had the same birthday as me. I'd have my celebration first, then he'd have his. The kid's name was Irvin, a Hong Kongnese-sounding name. Hong Kong parents often chose uncommon English names, selecting first names that sounded like last names, and they loved picking names with "-son" as a suffix: Anson, Carson, Eason, Hanson, Henson, Wenson. My parents named my brother Jackson. Girls got off lucky. My sister was named Cindy. Bah Ba chose Dickson for me in the hopes I'd become rich like the owner of a shop called Dickson Watch and Jewellery.

Other kids had a field day with my name. Dickson. Dick. Son. Son of a dick. Dickey Boy. Substitute teachers unknowingly added to the list when they read my name on the attendance sheet as Dickinson or Dickerson. They'd add letters for some inexplicable reason as though Dickson was not a legitimate name.

The night before the party, I snuck a peek at the soup in the fridge. I lifted the lid of the large pot. A cloudy brown pool. Under the surface, dark beans, not red but almost purple. It looked like the surface of an alien planet. I closed the lid, scared to dip my finger in for a taste. I went to bed and wrapped the blankets tight around my body like a cocoon.

At school, I returned from recess and saw my mother and father chatting with Ms. Hong. Bah Ba was dressed in jeans and a casual shirt, the same thing every day. It was strange seeing him here. The only place I'd see him outside of home was at a Chinese restaurant. My mom, on the other hand, was a regular at the school, though not in my class. She'd volunteer in the morning to stamp the hands of kids who, like me, qualified for free lunch.

"Sit down," Ms. Hong said to the class. "You are in for a treat. Dickson's dad brought something he made himself."

"Dickey Boy, what's in the pot?" Melvin whispered. He was a pudgy Chinese kid with a deep tan.

"Red bean soup," I said.

"I hate that stuff."

Bah Ba poured the soup into a row of paper cups. Kids rose and squinted. They recognized the soup, the class being predominately Chinese. Ms. Hong, anticipating the grumbles, pointed out that the red in the soup symbolized good luck and happiness. Two volunteers handed out the cups. Bah Ba had his arm around my mother's shoulder. The picture struck me as odd, my mother leaning into him.

I stared at a bean floating in my cup. I scooped it out and chewed it. I pushed the cup aside. Only a few kids were still dipping their spoons into their cups.

"OK class," Ms. Hong said, "say thank you to Mr. and Mrs. Lam."

"Thank you," the class said in unison.

My mother and Bah Ba slightly bowed their heads in appreciation and came over to me. "Happy Birthday," my mother said, using her kiddy voice that she loved to use in public. "We both go to work."

"What do you do, Mrs. Lam?" Ms. Hong said.

"Call me Ms. Lee." My mother's body straightened up. "I take care of three kids. Some people say, 'you're so beautiful, you don't know how to clean house,' but I sweep, I mop, I cook, I wash dishes. I give him a bath. Yeah, sure." My mother rubbed the top of my head and hugged me. Bah Ba grabbed my shoulder and pulled me in for a light squeeze. He took my mother's hand and with his other arm carried the empty pot.

Out they went, and in came Irvin's mother. His mother's hair was permed, and she wore a business outfit. She looked like someone's boss. As she placed Irvin's cake on the table, some of the boys oohed and aahed. A Superman cake. The Man of Steel had his left fist raised, his red cape flapping behind him. He was the real deal, even had the cowlick. Above him read "Happy Birthday Irvin!" as though Irvin and Supes were homies.

The students rushed to get their plates. I didn't understand the hurry. I grabbed a slice and sat down. I took a small bite. Nothing super about the cake, but my classmates scarfed it down. They became animated, laughing, almost dancing in their chairs. I stuck my fork in the middle of my slice and twirled it until a crater formed, as if a meteor had struck it. To others, it would appear I'd tried to devour the cake.

RED BEAN SOUP STORY

In middle school, by which point Bah Ba had moved out, I used the Red Bean Soup story to paint my father as the clueless immigrant, to distance myself from him and really from all Chinese immigrants. They were FOBs, dressed in knockoff clothes from Chinatown, fluent in "broken" English, an ugly reflection.

I broke from my backward views in high school after I got into Malcolm X. Saw the Spike Lee flick on opening weekend with Rob, then read Malcolm's autobiography and all his speeches I could find. Sometimes, if I couldn't get anyone to cut school with me, I'd play hooky to read in the main library. Sitting next to old men and homeless dudes reading newspapers on rods, I'd pour through a stack of books, J.A. Rogers' *World's Great Men of Color,* autobiographies from Black Panthers, heirs to Malcolm X. The Panthers were how I got interested in Mao, his "Little Red Book" required reading for members. Malcolm preached pride, loving yourself and where you came from. It was hard to mock my father after that.

Perhaps the seeds for my political awakening were planted a few years earlier by my older brother. I shared a room with Goh Goh, and he'd blast Boogie Down Productions, Public Enemy, Paris, and Poor Righteous Teachers, all of whom sampled Malcolm X speeches and rapped about Black unity. My brother took the moniker China MC. Even made a rap video for a class assignment. It begins with him sporting a Starter parka and a bandana tied around his head. He carries a briefcase, which he clutches as though the contents are top secret. He kicks his first verse, and we learn through a flashback that he'd stolen the briefcase from a government safe. The files inside contain the hidden Asian American history that, if revealed, would free us from oppression and being mired in self-hatred. For the rest of the video, shot at his high school, a government goon squad chases Goh Goh through hallways, stairwells, the courtyard, the gym, with, of course, timely pauses for his raps. In those days, my brother would say, "I'm just a product of my environment, baby," a reference to how we lived in the projects, though he never actually hung out in our neighborhood.

The Red Bean Soup story in high school ceased being a public story to poke fun at my dad and became a story I'd tell myself, the last defense against completely writing off my father. Bah Ba had made the soup and managed to come to my party, though he never did the same for my brother or sister. It was the only day I could remember he'd taken off work. No small sacrifice. Bah Ba worked an under-the-table job without personal or vacation days.

RED BEAN SOUP REDUX

I gave my students at June Jordan a writing prompt about a childhood experience. They asked for an example, and I told them the first story that came to mind that wouldn't be a downer, the Red Bean Soup story.

"If he skipped work for your party," one student said, "why didn't he do the same for your brother or sister?"

I sought my mother's opinion. "*Yauh mouh gaau choh?*" she said. How can you have it so wrong? "Your Bah Ba made the soup, but he never came to your school. If he was there, why did *I* carry that pot on the bus? That thing was heavy. I had to walk up three flights with it to get to your classroom."

Her version sounded more credible than mine. Even when Bah

Ba was sick, he'd muster the energy for Tea House. No work, no check.

My version was most likely false, but I continued to tell it.

TWO DRIVERS AND NOT AN OLD SHOE

My mother's first memory of my father was at a nightclub in a fancy hotel. Bah Ba saw my mother sitting by herself, and he asked her for a dance. They spent the night dancing to Elvis, Tom Jones, and the Beach Boys. She thought my dad was "handsome" and had a "sense of humor." A few years later when they had my sister, they named her after this club, The Scene, which they pronounced "De Seen." They switched the order of the two syllables: "Cindy."

When they became a couple, Bah Ba began to ask my mother to cover his shift at his father's gift shop. "In the morning," she says, "I work at the store. Only by myself." Bah Ba would leave to play mahjong, and my mother would never mention the gambling to my father's parents.

She wasn't happy about their relationship, but she accepted it. My mother married my father when she was twenty-one. She only had an elementary education. Anything more required money. As a teenager, she had worked in a factory, assembling Christmas light bulbs.

My mom had bigger dreams of being a singer/movie star. When she was eleven, she read commercials on the radio. At fifteen, behind her grandmother's back, my mother managed to land a gig on television singing classical Chinese songs. The first song she sang was about a woman waiting on her husband to come home, wishing his love was like the trunk of a palm tree, his love never branching off. My great-grandmother saw my mom singing on television and made her quit. Showbiz was for sluts.

For my mother, marrying into my father's family was marrying up. When she'd walk around with Bah Ba, friends of his father would see him and call him *wohng ji*. Prince. Bah Ba's family owned several tourist shops, their most notable one being the store where my mother covered for my father. It was located on the ground floor of the then newly-built Hyatt Regency, the first overseas Hyatt.

I've seen a black-and-white photo of Bah Ba in that store. He's wearing a three-piece suit and tie, posing for the camera in front of shelves of folded clothes. His hair parted neatly to the side, he stands regal over a checkered floor, a fist against his hip, his hand resting on the edge of the glass counter.

After they married, my father attempted a new venture. He picked up a job as a chauffeur, shuttling around Japanese business-men. Then it occurred to him, why not go into business for him-self? He'd be a self-made man, not a son chained to his father. He pawned the gold jewelry my mother received as wedding gifts—necklaces, bracelets, rings—and with the money, he purchased a taxicab. The cab would sit idle, my mother says, parked in front of where he played mahjong.

On another occasion my mom contradicts herself. She says he did have passengers. Many were prostitutes. They'd hop in his cab, and he'd take them from one john to the next. They felt relaxed enough around my father to share tales from work. Bah Ba might've been the only man in their lives they told these stories to. My father, the affable driver.

Willie drove the 30 Stockton. That's how he and my mother met. Simple hellos led to longer chats. One day, Willie convinced her to stay on past her stop. "Sightseeing," he said to my mother, who was sitting in the passenger seat behind him. There's no rush for her to go home. We were at school—I was in the first grade at the time—and my father was at work.

Willie described to my mother the last stop on his route, the Palace of Fine Arts. "There's a lagoon. Swans. Ducks." He kept the descriptions simple, nothing about the rotunda or the Greek columns. Didn't want to confuse my mother, a recent immigrant.

During the ride, Willie played the role of interviewer, and my mom did most of the talking.

My mother refers to that day as their first date. She tells me she wasn't used to having a conversation like this with a man. By man, she means my father.

When my mom first considered divorce, she was pregnant with me. That night, she felt nauseated, had thrown up. My two-year-old sister had a high fever while my three-year-old brother ran circles around our small apartment. My mother pleaded with Bah Ba to stay home this time, to help watch the kids, but he took off to gamble.

Even if my mother wanted to divorce my father then, the laws in Hong Kong made it difficult for women. In 1970, a year before my parents married, the divorce rate was fifty times less there than in the States. Before a woman could petition for divorce, she had to live two years apart from her husband. That's if the divorce was mutual. If it wasn't, she had to live five years apart. She'd have to make it on her own. The lives of her kids would be in limbo. No child support. Not until the divorce was finalized, however long that took.

A quicker solution occurred to my mother: take her kids and immigrate to America. Leave her husband behind. It was *her* father who was sponsoring them, not his. Gung Gung had caught a break and landed a head chef job in America. My mother told her father the plan, but he advised her, "Maybe when he comes here, he won't play mahjong as much. San Francisco isn't like Hong Kong. No one stays out as late. Give him a chance."

The biggest change my father made in America might've been the drinking. It got worse.

Willie's first job in the States was picking grapes in Delano. A year after he quit, Filipino farmworkers in that town went on strike, protesting poor pay and working conditions. Eight days after the Filipinos began the Delano Grape Strike, Mexican farmworkers, led by Cesar Chavez and Dolores Huerta, joined in, recognizing their common struggle; hence, when the two merged forces, they named themselves United Farm Workers.

When Willie met my mother, he was also married. He had a child, a daughter. He told my mom about his rocky marriage to his white wife who was also an alcoholic. Now he was looking to get out. My mother had been thinking the same about her marriage.

After Bah Ba moved to Minnesota, my mother came clean to us. Willie was her boyfriend, and she planned to divorce my father, but only after Willie divorced his wife. Then they'd marry. I was skeptical. It sounded like an episode from a daytime talk show: Men Who String Along Their Mistresses.

But true to his word, Willie did divorce his wife. It was my mother who was unwilling to pull the trigger. She was raised to believe divorce meant disgrace, at least for women. A divorced woman became an "old shoe," spurned by even her own family.

My mother's parents knew about Willie. If it came down to a divorce, they were clear: they'd take my father's side. My mom, however, cites economic reasons, not cultural ones, for her reluctance to divorce my father.

"Your father made $800 a month. Then all take home give me. If divorce, child support maybe only half give me. Not enough for everything, and then how I can take care of three kids?"

My mother didn't consider the obvious option—get a job. She'd say she already had one, taking care of three kids and keeping the house spotless.

Whatever her reasons, she had no intentions of divorcing my father, and perhaps never did. She wanted to live life on her terms. She would not be an old shoe, yet she would not be miserable, either. To pull this off, she needed our help. When she was vacationing with Willie, Bah Ba would call, and we had to follow the script. Mom was on a trip with her friends from her ESL class, we'd say. Lying became second nature, the lies I told my father, the lies I told myself: My mother was not cheating on my father. They were separated, some unspoken arrangement. I was not an accomplice.

ASLEEP

Here's what I ignored when I booked a ticket to visit my father: Back when we were kids, when Bah Ba was still living with us, on the nights my mom was on vacation with Willie, perhaps frolicking down Main Street in Disneyland, while my brother and I were asleep in our room across the hallway, my dad would sneak into my sister's room. Drunk. His fingers slithering across her body. The first time, Ga Jeh was eleven.

Knowing this hadn't deterred me from reconnecting with Bah Ba, and it also hadn't stopped my sister from doing the same.

CROSS THE LINE

I'd confessed what my dad had done to my sister, though not the details, to a room full of students and staff. I was teaching at Dewey Academy in Oakland, the job I had before June Jordan, two years before my trip to Minnesota.

That afternoon we were crammed together in the cafeteria, teachers and a hundred high school students, all standing on one side of the room, waiting for John, the facilitator, to read a statement. If it applied to us, we had to cross an imaginary line. It seemed silly. Our students had enrolled in Dewey, a second-chance school, to make up credits, and instead of completing assignments, they were asked to participate in an activity with imaginary lines, as if they were elementary kids. We'd been told that the school district had contracted with an outside organization, Challenge Day, to provide a program that would be a "celebration of diversity." The veteran teachers had smelled bullshit and opted out. Standing in the cafeteria, trying to locate an imaginary line, I saw now why those veteran teachers had been so cynical.

John had a tribal tattoo wrapped around his arm. The guy had a deep tan like he was from an island, and he wore a red T-shirt that read, "Be the Change." He'd begun the day by gathering the staff in a huddle. The more we shared about ourselves, he'd said, the more the students will open up. "When I introduce a new activity," John had said in a gruff voice, "I want you to jump and holler 'Yeah!'"

The first statements John had read were pointless. Statements about race, gender, and age. We didn't need John to tell us our demographics. I figured these were warm-ups. He hadn't asked about family, which didn't bother me. I thought I'd come to terms with all the shit in my family. No more lies. My parents had divorced, and now we were forming an honest relationship with Bah Ba. He'd come back into our lives when my brother had a son. Being a grandfather—my dad's second chance. He'd invited us to spend last Christmas in Toronto with his side of the family for the first time. They welcomed us, relatives whose names we had to learn, the aunts, Bah Ba's younger sisters, fighting each other to show us around. Two aunts drove me and Ga Jeh to Niagara Falls. They treated us to dinner at a revolving restaurant atop a tower. Below us, the Falls was lit up with colors, like something out of Vegas or a theme park. Our father was like yours, the aunts said. Not a great dad or husband. Never around. He cheated on your grandmother. That's why she left him. For many years, we were angry at your Yeh Yeh. But life is too short for grudges. We brought Yeh Yeh here from Hong Kong—we couldn't let our dad die alone. The past is the past.

I'm sure John read a long list of statements, but there's only three that stick out.

"Cross the line if you have ever been awakened by gunshots."

A flock of students crossed the checkered floor. Sunlight entered through the windows lined with wire mesh, and the light landed across the floor in the shape of small diamonds.

When I was still living in the projects, one night, I heard bullets rattling off from a submachine gun. The sparks flashed through the blinds in my room. A neighbor was enjoying his new toy.

I shuffled across the line. I could feel the eyes of other teachers on me. None of them had crossed.

"Take a look," John said, "at who's standing next to you."

"Everybody's on this side," JB said, revealing his gold fronts. I'd thought JB was his nickname, or that it stood for something, but according to the school attendance sheet, his name really was just those two letters. His white do-rag contrasted with his dark skin. He held a baseball hat, which I had to remind him to take off every day in class. I thought we'd gotten closer when he showed me a picture of his four-month-old daughter, but our skirmishes in class continued.

I had a tough time getting respect when I began working at Dewey. Most were juniors and seniors, and they initially thought I was a student. I had no facial hair. I'd cut off my moustache for my then-girlfriend. She didn't like the way it'd prick her.

The school year was nearing its end, and by now I'd won over most of the students, JB being the exception. Even Rodney had warmed to me. At the start of the year, I'd caught him drawing a picture of me as a monkey. His grandpa lectured him at the parent conference, saying the drawing was racist, that he'd grown up in the South hearing whites refer to Blacks as monkeys. He told me that Rodney subconsciously saw himself in me. "Your facial features are similar," he said, "and we always thought Rodney had Asian eyes."

The conference changed nothing. Rodney continued to torment me, heckling "Rookie" long past when others had stopped. I had to keep kicking him out of class. Finally, I tried an unconventional tactic—basketball. I wasn't confident I'd beat him. He was taller by a couple of inches, and my shot was erratic, my dribbling clumsy, but I prided myself on defense. I knew if I could block Rodney's shot, he'd respect me.

A small crowd formed on the basketball court outside. We'd barely begun, and I already blocked his shot three times. Students on the sidelines laughed and pointed at Rodney. I could tell he was humiliated, even though he smiled.

We slapped hands at the end, but soon Rodney acted up in class again.

A student named Antonio spoke up. "You better listen to Lam, before he takes you out to the court and swats your shit again."

Rodney sunk in his seat.

The whole class laughed at him, and I knew I'd never have to kick him out of class again. He began doing his work and became the star debater. I taped a picture of us by my desk, to remind me that people can change.

"Cross the line if you have lost a friend due to gun violence."

Students dragged their feet across the line, silent except for the smacking of gum. They turned to face us. They reflected the diversity of the school: mostly Black and Latino, a scattering of Southeast Asians, and the lone white student at our school—Carmelina. She pulled a girl in for a hug and gave her a tissue. Some students accused Carmelina of "acting Black." That'd set her off. She'd snap her head and launch into a spiel about her Italian heritage.

The boys who crossed stood arm's length from the nearest person. Some of them stared through the window at cars passing by. Some stared at the ceiling tiles. A couple of boys chuckled in the rear, and John glared at them, putting a finger to his lips.

Antonio looked straight ahead. He had golden skin, a short 'fro, and thick eyebrows. Strange to see him so motionless, so quiet. He was a talkative kid, loved to argue about politics. So much that I'd brought him to a local radio station that wanted to hear what youth thought about the Iraq war.

JB shook his watch, which was decorated with fake diamonds.

"Man," he mumbled, "ain't it time to cross back already?"

I thought of Randy and crossed. Earlier that week, I got a call from Rob that Randy had been murdered. He was from the same turf as Keino, about the same age, another lost cousin. We hadn't hung out since high school, but I remembered the time we slap boxed in an empty basketball gym. He switched into a martial arts stance, and I knew I was in trouble. I'd forgotten he'd taken tae kwon do lessons for years. A roundhouse kick came at my rib cage. I blocked it with my palm, and I felt confident, dropping my hands, but this strike was a setup. He didn't bring that leg back; instead he recoiled at the knee and snapped another kick at my head. It landed across my cheek, a loud smack.

"Oh shit," he said. "Sorry, Dickson."

I laughed and thought it was the coolest shit I'd ever seen. I held onto my cheek and told some of the fellas outside. Randy demonstrated his double kick again. I'd felt embarrassed not knowing martial arts—I was the Asian one.

The friends I'd hung with in high school were the main reason I became a teacher. Many of them never attended college. I'd wanted to reverse the trend of failing schools, failing students.

A student buried her head in the shoulder of a friend. I tried not to cry by using the old make-like-you-got-something-in-your-eye trick. I thought I had it down because of the way I'd rub my fingertips as though I'd found an eyelash.

"Cross the line," John said, "if you have been touched inappropriately as a child. Or know someone who has been."

No one moved. It was silent long enough I wasn't sure if anyone would, but some began to trickle over to the other side.

I was surprised I hadn't immediately thought of Ga Jeh. It was just a year ago that she'd confided in me about what Bah Ba had done. I was lying in bed watching a basketball game when I picked up her call. She didn't tell me what exactly happened, just that it did, several times when our dad was living with us. Her tone was calming, like she was at work, at the concierge desk addressing a customer.

"I'm going to talk to him about it," she said. "I just thought you should know, but don't say anything to Mom. She'll go crazy. No need to freak out about this, OK?" She was still trying to take care of her little brother.

She'd given me her old car, a red Honda Civic, lowered with tinted windows, red racing rims, a silver joystick for a gearshift, the exhaust loud enough to set off car alarms—a real rice rocket, souped-up by some guy she'd been dating years ago. I'd thought she cared for it more than anything. Before she handed me the keys, she gave me a long to-do list for the car. Use disinfectant wipes immediately to wipe away bird poop. Use this cleaner for the racing air filter. Use premium gas. Take the car up to Mom's house to hand-wash it. Bring your own oil for an oil change. Always put up the sunshade.

The first week I drove it, I got into an accident and scraped the fender. I thought Ga Jeh would have a fit, but the only thing she wanted to know was if I was all right.

Before Ga Jeh had called me that night about Bah Ba, she'd also phoned our brother, revealing her secret to him as well, but she wasn't dissuading us from connecting with our pops. In fact, she was still insisting that we chip in for our dad's dentures because he had no health insurance. When our dad invited us to Toronto a few months later, Ga Jeh was the first to accept. I assumed she'd forgiven him or, if not forgiven, was at least willing to accept him into her life. Who was I to persuade her otherwise?

"We all have a balloon," John said, "that we fill up with our hurt. If we don't deal with that hurt, one day the balloon pops, and everything in it spills onto others."

We sat in small groups to debrief the day. I bit my lip, and it helped to focus my mind away from my sister.

"For the last activity," John told us, "we want to hear from you on the mic."

I was never drawn to public speaking. I stuttered at times and wasn't confident in my pronunciation, but sometimes in college, I'd be asked to speak at a rally. There weren't many Asian guys involved in leftist campus politics, and back then I was a sucker for the argument: "If you don't do it, no one will." I had tended to ramble, forgetting my point. That's when I'd throw in a "fuck," and the crowd would cheer.

"You can say anything about how you feel," John said, "or about what you've learned today."

I thought about that damn balloon, and I raised my hand. We'd heard how hurt could translate into anger, how hurt explained why kids lashed out, but no one had said anything about how to deal with the hurt, only to be aware of it.

I walked to the microphone, past clusters of small groups. I heard some students cheering my name, but I kept my eyes on the floor, so I wouldn't trip over anything.

John put his hand on my shoulder. "What's on your mind, bro?"

I grabbed the microphone, but I wished I had thought more about what I was going to say. Couldn't throw in a "fuck" with these students. I could hear my breath on the microphone over the speakers.

"My father moved out when I was ten, and I grew up feeling like he didn't care about me. I started to hate him, and that filled my balloon. But I'm telling y'all, you don't want to live with that hate. Let it go. It'll turn you crazy. You'll do things you'll regret, drop out, get locked up. I forgave my dad, and just like that, all the air left my balloon. I woke up a new person. I forgave my dad for not being there. I forgave him for being a jerk to my mom. I forgave him for what he did to my sister—"

I couldn't continue. I leaned forward, my hands on my knees. The microphone dropped, and I heard the thud over the speakers. I began bawling.

I saw my sister as a child in her bed and Bah Ba next to her. The image of my sister and father moved forward like a video as though someone had hit the play button. Bah Ba tugged at Ga Jeh's pajama pants, and I felt the sensation as though it was me under his hand. I could smell his breath, nicotine and Hennessy. My legs got weak. A gentle push would've tipped me over. I closed my eyes and felt myself being drawn into a dark place I didn't have the strength to resist.

A hand rubbed my back, then an arm lifted me up, but I was limp.

"It's your favorite student," Antonio said.

Another arm helped me up. "No," Carmelina said, "I'm his favorite student. Tell him, Lam."

Other students surrounded me, ready to help. I picked up the microphone. I don't even know if I made any sense at that point, but I remembered why I'd gotten up to speak in the first place.

I spoke through tears to finish what I had planned to say, "If you don't want to forgive for the sake of the other person, do it for yourself."

I heard the crowd clap as I walked back to my seat. I grabbed the Kleenex box to blow my nose and sat down. I looked up and saw JB.

He shook my hand and pulled me up for a hug. "You're a deep man, Mr. Lam."

It wasn't until I was back in my classroom packing up at the end of the day that I realized I had lied to my students. How could I have forgiven Bah Ba if I hadn't dealt with what he'd done? That's why the image felt fresh. I was seeing it for the first time.

Maybe Ga Jeh hadn't forgiven our father. Perhaps like me, she'd hidden the images from herself. We hadn't talked about any of this since she'd revealed it to me. I wasn't sure the exact nature of the abuse, and I wasn't trying to find out.

I told myself I'd call Ga Jeh as soon as I finished grading the set of papers I was taking home, but I didn't. Admitting to myself what Bah Ba had done was one thing, broaching the topic with my sister was another. Should I initiate a conversation, force her to confront the past, or keep quiet, let the past stay buried? I didn't know the best way to help my sister with her balloon, how to keep it from popping—I was still a rookie.

In the two years leading up to my trip to Minnesota, I slipped back into forgetting. I covered up what I didn't want to see as easily as one might toss a throw over a stain on the couch.

GOOD OL' POPS

After I returned from my visit to Bah Ba, I told my sister that I'd encouraged our father to retire in San Francisco, to be closer to us. She wrote me this in response:

> We need to talk, you and me. I don't know how I'm feeling about our good ol' pops. I know how he's "trying" to be a father and a grandfather, but I still feel a lot of anger towards him. I sent him an email asking him why he did what he did, and he never responded! I know I need to see a psychiatrist, but I don't think it's going to help. You forgive him or you don't. And I'm not stable enough to forgive him. I still have to interact with him. I don't like talking to him or seeing him. I try to put those feelings aside, but it's very hard.

* * * * *

I met Ga Jeh at her apartment. She'd just moved in. The place was sparse. Sitting on one of the shelves of her skinny bookshelf was a small brush painting of a panda. I'd bought it for her on a trip to China. In the corner of the room was a papasan chair, a holdover from the apartment she'd shared with her most recent ex. Their dogs would sleep in the chair, or rather, *his* dogs, a greyhound and a bulldog. They were the reason why it had taken her so long to leave the crummy boyfriend. She was ready to say bye forever, but saying that to the dogs, that proved more difficult. Now the chair was all she had of them.

"If Bah Ba moves back," my sister said, "I'm moving out of the

Bay. I still feel like he's a threat."

Her last three encounters with our father had been during funerals. They barely had to talk. And during our visit to Toronto, our interactions with Bah Ba had been buffered by uncles, aunts, cousins, and grandparents. Living in the same city as Bah Ba, Ga Jeh would be expected to regularly share meals with him, to *yahm cha* together on weekends, to invite her abuser over to her house.

"If I'd known how you really felt about Bah Ba," I said, "I would never have gone."

"Sometimes I feel bad," she said, "sometimes I don't give a shit." She blew her nose. "Sometimes I want to kill myself."

I hugged her, and a river of tears followed. I'd spent years listening to teenagers, hearing their family dramas, listening for the quiet signs of abuse. I'd been trained to do this. I'd even had to call CPS once on behalf of a student, yet when it came to my own sister, I'd found it easy to look the other way, to bury any questions about how she might truly feel.

I'd sold out my sister, so I could play out a father-son fantasy.

"I never want to see him again," Ga Jeh said.

"I don't either."

TAPE

Two years later, Bah Ba had retired in San Francisco, and I was refusing any contact with him. Ga Jeh had skipped town, like she'd vowed, moving down to San Diego. I was living in Daly City, just south of San Francisco, in an in-law apartment with my girlfriend at the time, L.

Dressed for a jog that morning in shorts and a soccer jersey, she was rummaging through the TV cabinet in our bedroom for her iPod. "What's this?" She held a videotape for me to inspect.

My cheeks warmed. The last time she discovered an old videocassette, it was *Luke's Freak Show*, basically a guy with a camcorder trailing behind any large ass he could find, on the streets, in a hotel lobby, at a Mickey D's. L's gripe wasn't on feminist grounds—objectification, exploitation, nothing like that. She was pissed I might still have a thing for Black women, not that she had anything against Black women. L was a community organizer who was all about intersectionality and coalition building. She just didn't want to be stuck in a relationship with a guy who not only secretly preferred someone who didn't look like her, a Filipina, but who also secretly preferred someone who didn't look like himself. "This is some self-hate shit right here," L had said when she found that Luke tape.

"That's not even my tape," I'd said. "I love Asian women." She didn't say another word. Just picked up her overnight bag and strolled out of the apartment in her wedge heels, the bag hung on the crook of her elbow, a cigarette held between her fingers.

The spine on the home video L now held in her hand read: "L.A. 1988." The handwriting was mine. I was sitting on the edge of the bed, and I leaned back on my arms. "I forgot all about that," I said. "My dad took us to Disneyland. I must've been in middle school."

"I thought your dad was never around."

"He wasn't."

She held the tape as though weighing it. "Your pops—at least the way you've described him—doesn't sound like a family vacation kind of guy."

"It was a one-time thing," I said.

She sat on my lap and placed the video next to us on the bed. Rocking side to side, she sang a song in Spanish while redoing her ponytail. Half the songs on her iPod were songs in Spanish. She'd spent a year studying in Mexico, and relished any chance to speak Spanish, whether it was translating for a client at her nonprofit job or just somebody at a taqueria. To her, she struck just the right balance between her Pinay pride and her appreciation for Mexican culture, while the way I juggled being Chinese with an appreciation for Blackness was unhealthy. Not enough self-love in my recipe, according to her. This was one of many things we'd argue about. Though we loved each other deeply, deeper than each of us had ever loved, we were always on the verge of breaking up. We'd started couples therapy to try and save the relationship.

I knew L was waiting for a real explanation of the tape, but if there was one thing I didn't want to talk about, it was my dad. L knew my reasons, but she didn't understand how raw my feelings were, how I couldn't stop daydreaming about strangling my father. To say this desire aloud was to admit weakness.

I pulled L's body close, her back against my chest.

She wiggled free. "Tell me about this trip with your dad."

I rubbed the inside of her thigh. It didn't seem a terrible strategy to try and fuck my way out of the conversation.

"Dime," she said, tapping my hand on her thigh.

I grabbed the tape, turned it over a couple of times, and slid it out of its sleeve. Nothing written on the face label. I told L about the only scene I remembered on the video, the one I had recorded.

I'd set up the camcorder on a table by the hotel pool. My mom wades in the shallow end with a swimming cap. My sister leans on a kickboard, drifting. I pretend she's sinking. I grab a lifesaver. "I'll save you," I say, and I toss the ring at Ga Jeh, attempting to encircle her with it like a lasso. It knocks her across the head instead. She screams.

My father's not present in this scene. If he was poolside off-camera, I don't recall it. I can't picture Bah Ba in swimming trunks. I have no image of his naked torso, only the surgical scar across his belly button from an operation he had before I was born. The surgery to repair a hole in his intestine forced him to postpone his wedding with my mother until the following year. Bah Ba never actually appears anywhere in the entire videotape. For the rest of the video, my father was always behind the lens, the one charged with recording us. A year after this trip to Disneyland, my mother talked Willie into taking us again, as though to upstage my father.

My mom disagrees with my version. She says I have the order

wrong. Willie was the one to take me first, and instead of keeping it a secret, she bragged to my father on the phone about the fun we had, substituting friends from her ESL class in the story for Willie. Bah Ba felt slighted he wasn't invited to our first family vacation and insisted we go with him. Maybe it was my father who wanted to upstage the earlier Disneyland trip. Either way, I remembered Disneyland with Willie, not my father.

"You always say he didn't care about you," L said, "but your dad took you to fucking Disneyland."

"And that proves he was a great guy?"

"No, it proves you keep hiding shit from me." It was true. When we began dating, I gave her a spotty timeline of my parents failed marriage, misleading her into believing that my parents had already separated when my mom began seeing Willie. I was reluctant to declare my mother a cheater. I wanted one parent I could respect. When L discovered the truth, she labeled me a "mama's boy" who was unable to see his mom for who she was, not a victim but a master manipulator who I had let off the hook for the dysfunctions in my family.

I shifted my weight, as though suddenly L was heavy on my lap. "OK, what else do you want to know?"

She pulled a piece of lint stuck to my buzz cut. "Any other vacations with your father?" she asked jokingly.

"There was one other time." I recalled during the winter break of my freshman year of high school I, along with my mother and sister, had visited Bah Ba in Minnesota. My brother couldn't get off work. He was a busboy at Bah Ba's old restaurant, Tea House.

My father at that time had a house in a Twin Cities suburb. It wasn't huge, but it had felt roomy, at least for one person. I'd slept on the sofa, firm as a showroom sofa, as though Bah Ba had been waiting to break it in. The only other thing in the living room was a flimsy stereo system. If I pushed a button too hard, the whole unit would sway.

I dug around in his basement one day while he was at work and found a stash of *Playboy* magazines. Actually, I didn't really dig, and it wasn't a stash. They were stacked on a table in plain view, but I wasn't supposed to be down there.

Most days we ate lunch at his restaurant, the kind rented out for banquets. My sister and I would stuff our plates with fried chicken wings at the buffet and grab a glass of soda at the bar. We used the bar gun like we owned the place. Bah Ba had only one day off, so he and I shared few moments: him standing in the doorway marveling at the graphics of the video game I was playing, him sitting down with me to watch *Do the Right Thing*, then getting up when he realized it was a serious flick and not a comedy. I shot hoops at a gym with his boss's son. His neighbor took me sledding. I felt snow on my fingertips for the first time. The snot in my nose froze. All this had made me feel I had a place in my father's world, but now that I had turned my back on him, I wanted to dispose of these memories. I felt guilty even having happy memories of that winter trip. Ga Jeh's version of that visit may not have been as fond.

L leapt off me. "If we're going to make this work," she said. "You gotta start being honest about your family." She shook out her wrist, adjusting her turquoise bracelet.

"I'm sorry I can't remember every little detail," I said sarcastically.

"The only details you remember are the ones your mom wants you to remember. Your father was horrible; she was a hero." L was being preemptive. She'd grown up witnessing her father take his mother's side over his wife's, and L swore she'd never marry into that same dynamic, but here she was, in a relationship with a mama's boy. She needed me to convince her otherwise, to hear me speak with a little compassion for my father, utter some gratitude for his years of hard work, say something that didn't sound like I was parroting my mother.

How I wish I could've explained to L—if I'd had the words for this then—that the reason I couldn't say one good thing about my father had nothing to do with my mom deluding me. I was trying to delude myself, trying to erase positive memories of my father because it was far easier to disown him if I saw him as a total villain. Acknowledging the truth—his sacrifices for me—would lead me to pity Bah Ba, one step closer to changing my mind about him, one step closer to betraying my sister again.

I said none of this to L.

"You don't know what you're talking about," I replied. "My father *was* horrible. And no one asked for your fucking opinion about my family. Key words there—My. Family. Worry about your own."

L put on her jogging shoes and dashed out of the apartment. When I reached the front door—she'd left it open, maybe so I'd follow—she'd already turned the corner. I shut the door and lay back on the bed. I pulled the blanket over me. An image of a tiger at night spread across it, a gift from the mother of a student, a single mother, or was it a mother who'd remarried? I was bad at keeping track of those things.

I picked up the tape. Why did I even have this damn thing? It had survived five moves in six years. Not once had I considered tossing it, and yet, I hadn't watched it a single time either.

I swung open the TV cabinet and stuck the tape in the VCR.

Wherever we're at is noisy and crowded. The camera struggles to remain steady as it trails me, my sister, and my mother. I have a stick of a body. That's apparent, even with my white and red wide-striped polo. My mother's hair flows down so low, I can hardly see her slim body. She has on tennis shoes, not the heels I would've expected. My sister is wearing jeans and a sweater, which seems out of place in LA. She stops at a vendor and laughs at something with my mom. I recognized the place. It's the Alley, an area near downtown LA with tons of small shops selling designer knockoffs.

Bah Ba mumbles, trying to direct us to make a left, but we don't listen or are unable to hear him through the crowd. The camera held by my father pans around, but when it pans back to us, we're gone, subsumed by shoppers. He calls for us, not angry or in desperation, but lackadaisically.

CHAPTER 3

APARTMENT 171

NORTH BEACH POSSE

What Bah Ba did to Ga Jeh colors my memories of my childhood apartment in the North Beach housing projects. I was five when we moved in, twenty-five when I moved out.

On the day we moved in, we picked bedrooms. Ga Jeh chose the room that happened to face the most foot traffic. Goh Goh and I chose the room that faced a narrow strip of lawn. Our apartment was on the ground floor, and Bah Ba, worried about Peeping Toms, made me and my brother swap rooms with our sister. I guess my brother and I understood because I don't remember us putting up a fight. We misplaced the fear, outside our home instead of inside it.

The name of our housing project, North Beach, was misleading. North Beach was up the hill. We were closer to Fisherman's

Wharf. Our backyard was Alcatraz, crab stands, and sea lions down at the pier sunbathing. A salty breeze wandered our streets. Right smack between the two blocks of our housing projects was a cable car terminal; its tracks humming nonstop. A horde of tourists would gather, cameras dangling from their necks. They'd stroll through the middle of our turf like it wasn't shit. Our buildings didn't intimidate, just three floors high. Across the street from the terminal were four-star hotels. Tourists were an occupying army, dressed in shorts and long socks, armed with maps and smiles. We'd launch water balloons at them from the walkways, aiming for the ones with a camera.

Once in a while a tourist would get robbed. We'd stumble upon an empty suitcase near a stairwell. Pizza delivery guys, after getting stuck up, would refuse to deliver to our doors; we had to meet them at the corner. They'd keep their engine running, windows rolled up. When I'd walk up to the car, they'd scan around to make sure it wasn't a setup. Not because I was imposing, but because I wasn't. Sending the innocent-looking one was the oldest trick in the book. They'd lower their window, and I'd slip them bills like a drug deal.

Each project building had a similar layout, comprised of three sections that surrounded a courtyard and a parking lot that opened up to Francisco Street. All the windows on the first floor had burglar bars that formed concentric diamonds. On the raised curbs that led into the parking lots, old men would sit and drink out of a paper bag. Or sometimes they'd sit out there just to sit. It was their porch. One with a graying beard, who'd limp around with his cane, had a dog, a Jack Russell mix who'd bark at me from a block away. Hanging out on the sidewalk would be younger guys, at the same spots day in and day out, spitting on the ground to pass the time. Sometimes it might be one dude by himself, lingering for hours, as though he had a phobia of home.

My project building was on the far end, the only one without a parking lot, a larger courtyard in its place. Unlike the other project buildings, none of our front doors faced the courtyard. We all had our back to it. And that's what we called the courtyard: The Back. My apartment faced Columbus Avenue. Across the street were Tower Records and the Consulate of Indonesia. A few feet from my doorstep was a community garden, and in that small space in between, that's what we called the courtyard.

In elementary school, I'd walk from my house down Francisco Street to the school bus stop and back after school. In third grade, I'd begun doing this alone. My brother was in middle school, and sometimes my sister preferred to travel on her own from school with her friends.

One day I was walking home by myself from the bus stop when some kid about my age with shiny curly hair came straight up to me and punched me. I pushed him away but not with much strength. He laughed and raised his arms in victory, strutting over to his friend standing nearby. Another time, a teenage boy grabbed me by the shoulders and shoved me towards a girl, pretending I was a stuffed animal that he wanted to give her. The day the basketball court opened after months of renovation to the playground, I was the first to show up but was soon crowded off by a large group of kids. One of them punted my ball over the chain-link fence. He didn't take pleasure in it. More like he was doing me a favor. Better the ball than me.

There were as many Asians as Blacks in our housing projects, but it hadn't seemed that way growing up. If you had driven by, you'd be hard pressed to find anyone hanging out who wasn't Black.

I began to act like a tourist, wary of Black kids. I swore that I wouldn't be caught off guard again, but this was no solution. Say the next time a kid tried to bully me, and I was ready for it, what was I really going to do? I was too proud to run, too cowardly to fight.

One afternoon, I was coming home with Ga Jeh. As she was opening the door to our apartment, we heard kids singsonging our names—"Dick-son and Cin-dy, Cin-dy and Dick-son." I saw the tops of two heads on the second floor walkway hiding behind the concrete railing. They reminded me of dark roasted coffee beans. It was Abdullah and Sameerah. They lived two doors down from us. They were much smaller. Ga Jeh was in the fifth grade, and I was in the third, but 'Dullah was only in kindergarten, and his sister was a year younger, though she was much taller than him.

We went inside, and I sat down to take my shoes off. No one else was home. Our dad was at work, our mother was probably doing some grocery shopping, and Goh Goh was just now getting off from school.

My sister leaned back against the front door, her hand on the doorknob, her lips pressed tight. She wore overalls, and her bangs fell below her eyebrows. 'Dullah and Sameerah were still singsonging our names. Ga Jeh didn't lock the door. We had four locks, including two chain locks, which Bah Ba had installed, one high, one low. It was also Bah Ba who'd installed the wire mesh that guarded all our windows, as if the thick steel bars weren't enough protection. "A burglar will need weeks to cut through," he'd told me. I wondered how we'd escape in a fire.

Ga Jeh opened the door and stepped out into the courtyard. "Sa-meer-ah and 'Dul-lah, 'Dul-lah and Sa-meer-ah!"

The two of them upstairs erupted in laughter, and my sister slammed the door.

"Let's go in the living room," I told her. I figured the best thing to do was ignore them.

Ga Jeh stomped past me to the sink and reached behind the cutting board, thick and circular, a piece of wood that seemed sliced directly from a tree trunk. My sister held my mother's cleaver.

"Grab a knife!" she said, raising the cleaver in the air as if it were Excalibur.

She was nuts. My mother wouldn't let me handle a steak knife.

"You're going to be a scaredy-cat your whole life?" she said. She got in my face and gave me an eye-level glare.

I saw myself in her dark brown pupils, trapped in their spheres.

"Pick. One. Up. Now."

I proceeded to the dish rack—my mom always told me to listen to my Ga Jeh—and found the chef's knife in the back. My image was distorted in the blade as I flipped it back and forth.

Ga Jeh shook the cleaver at me. "After this, they won't bug us." She was too small for the knife, which only made her appear more menacing. She wasn't unfamiliar with knives. My mother let her help in the kitchen, chopping garlic or vegetables.

"They'll run," Ga Jeh said. "Watch."

I tilted my knife up.

"Look crazy. Like you'll really do it." She stuck her tongue out and made an ugly face.

I narrowed my eyebrows, trying to slant them like the angry faces I doodled in class.

She looked confused. "Just stay behind me."

It was hard to act wild carrying the knife. My clumsy hands would knock over glasses of soda onto the living room carpet. I didn't want to slip with a knife while I was pretending to slash someone.

Ga Jeh put her hand on the doorknob and turned back to me.

I nodded, tightening my grip on the knife.

She yanked the door open, and it banged against the wall. She burst out of the kitchen onto the courtyard. Her ponytail flapped behind her. I leaped through the door, stumbling forward when I landed.

Ga Jeh waved the cleaver toward the patchy sky. Sunlight gleamed off the knife. 'Dullah and Sameerah leaned over the railing on the second floor, but they didn't flee. They observed us from above like we were animals in a zoo, so focused on us that they hadn't realized we were racing to the staircase at the end of the floor to confront them. From their vantage point, it might've appeared we were about to run past them.

My sister let out a high-pitched shriek. The force of it sent them running. I screamed, trying to match my sister's intensity.

She was sprinting, but the point was to frighten them, not catch them. I didn't recognize this volatile Ga Jeh. I thought of her as more Hello Kitty than anything else.

I realize now that this took place after the abuse began. It could have been my father that sent my sister charging, knife raised.

We skipped steps up the staircase. The plastic beads in Sameerah's hair clicked as she ran. She trailed behind 'Dullah. Years later, me and 'Dullah would run after buses we'd just missed. His face would harden and nothing seemed more important than his next step. We'd catch up with the bus, and tourists would clap when we got on.

They jumped into the stairwell that led to the third floor. We followed, though our mother had warned us not to wander around in our building. I smelled urine trapped inside the stairwell. A dried-up stream snaked down the steps. The words North Beach Posse were written in a block font on the wall.

The third floor presented three choices. North Beach was a labyrinth. One path led to a walkway wrapping around our side of the projects, another to the next project complex, and the last walkway led to a dead-end around the corner.

"Which way?" I asked.

Ga Jeh ran toward the next project building, and I tried to keep pace. Shards of glass peppered the floor, broken bottles. My sister peeked over the railing when we reached the next building. A steady stream of cars flowed below. I looked into the stairwell. No sign of our prey. Mission accomplished.

When we came home and returned the knives to the kitchen, I remember thinking that my sister had discovered the secret of life. When you get picked on, grab a knife. Charge after your tormentors, and they won't do it again. It was a simple recipe, except we didn't count on their mother.

Cassandra pounded on our front door. "Open up!" The walls shook with each thump. I felt the vibrations against my chest. We hid in our parents' room. Lights off. Door locked. The knocking would cease for a minute or two only to begin again. "I know you're in there!"

When the knocking eventually stopped, Ga Jeh and I remained still, worried it was a trap. Silence offered no comfort.

COURTYARD

I was fourteen when I started hanging out with the neighborhood kids. I concocted a scheme to get them to invite me to play basketball.

One afternoon, I heard what sounded like a basketball game in the courtyard—strange because there was no basketball court there. I moved to the kitchen to get a better listen. I turned on the television in the kitchen and lowered the volume.

"Don't sit so close to the TV," my mother said. She picked up the plastic-wrapped remote and raised the volume.

I slid open the window and heard the dribbling of the ball, then a clank. The voices I recognized. Jim, Rob, and 'Dullah. I'd gone to middle school with Jim and Rob. They were a year younger, still in middle school. We'd say, "what's up" to each other, but that was it. These three were among the few kids in North Beach I knew on a first-name basis. I'd gone to a mostly Asian and white elementary school, and although my middle school had been more diverse, I'd arrived scared of Black kids. Ga Jeh, who was going into her last year at that middle school, had warned me that Black kids were bullies. I opened her yearbook and searched for Black faces. "Is he a bully? How about him?"

"Stop being dumb," she said. "I don't know *all* of them."

Three years of middle school, and I had few friends, of any color, to show for it.

I eavesdropped on Jim, Rob, and 'Dullah for the length of two cartoon episodes. If I was another type of kid, I would've just sauntered over and joined their game, but I was a freshman in high school who ate lunch by himself, out in the bleachers by the track. I'd hide in the bathroom during passing periods because I didn't want to be seen roaming around alone. Living a loser life was one thing—coming straight home from school because I didn't have shit else to do—but I liked to think that I still had scruples. I was not about to make a fool of myself and beg to be down. No thanks.

I opened the fridge and moved the milk to the back behind the jug of OJ. "Look," I said to my mom, "we're out of milk. I need to go to Safeway."

She went to her purse for money.

I stepped out into the courtyard and counted the coins, though I knew my mother had given me exact change. I kept my head down until I got close.

"What's up," I said. There were three of them, and I thought they might need an extra player to make teams.

"Hey," they said but continued with their game.

Rob was already six foot. I'd heard him claim he was part-Asian, that his uncle was Bruce Lee. Jim's real name was Jesús—he was Filipino—but to avoid being made fun of, he went by Jim. He was puny. Could've passed for an elementary school kid. Definitely had the squeaky voice of one. 'Dullah wasn't any taller, still in the sixth grade.

Hung over the railing of the staircase landing between the first and second floor was a shopping cart pointed downward. The back side of the cart dangled, and they had a hoop, one short enough to dunk on. I climbed the staircase watching their game as though it was the final play.

"If Dickson plays, we can get a game going," Jim said.

Rob and 'Dullah turned to me for a response.

"I'll be back in ten." I still had to buy the milk we didn't need.

"Hurry up, blood," Rob said, dribbling the mini-basketball between his legs.

I turned the corner on the walkway and sprinted to Safeway and back. I slowed as I returned with the gallon of milk in a plastic bag over my shoulder. I had to stop panting.

"About time," Rob said.

I dropped the milk off at home and told my mom I was about to play basketball in the courtyard.

"Me and you versus Rob and Jim," 'Dullah said with a light stutter.

"Shoot for takeout." Rob shot the basketball, but it clanged off the shopping cart.

I grabbed the ball and inbounded it to 'Dullah. They double-teamed him, and he lobbed it back to me. I dunked the ball through the metal cart, picked it up, and jogged back to the spot that was the top of the key.

I'd learn later the correct etiquette for dunking. Scream after a dunk, preferably in the face of your opponent. Call them a "punk" or a "bitch." Or you could play it nonchalant. Pretend to autograph the ball, then hand it to the dude you dunked on as a charitable souvenir.

We played until dark. 'Dullah's father, Mansur, emerged from their apartment in front of the staircase. He wore a kufi on his shaved head and had a thick moustache. He'd come home dressed in a security guard uniform. My mom had told me he was also a minister. (She didn't have a problem making friends with the neighbors. Whatever social awkwardness I had, I didn't seem to get it from her.) Mansur was the only father of ours who lived with his kids. "*As salaam alaikum*, my brothers," he said.

Rob chuckled out the greeting, "*Wa alaikum salam.*"

'Dullah, without his father saying a word, went home, slipping underneath his father's arm that was propped against the doorway.

"'Dullah's in for the night, my brothers," Mansur said.

"*Sihk faahn!*" My mother called me for dinner.

"Aw, Dickson's got curfew too," Rob said and exchanged daps with Jim. He pulled a wave brush from his back pocket and brushed his hair.

"Come here," Mansur said to us.

"Oh no, here we go," Jim said.

He straightened up and clasped his hands together. "Playing

basketball doesn't develop your most important tool, my brothers. And you know what your most important tool is?"

"My most important tool?" Rob looked at Jim, and they laughed.

"Your mind. That's your biggest asset." Mansur's front door was adorned with bumper stickers. Stuff about pork, Islam, the Devil. The collage of headlines formed a father's manifesto, one I could not grasp.

THE BACK

We'd spit on the tourists below from our walkways. We'd tag in the project stairwells. We'd find elevators in nearby buildings to piss in. Anything worth doing required running away.

We'd play baseball in The Back. A small dirt patch was first base, second was the lamppost, third was a crack in the ground, and the gutter was home plate. I'd been hanging out with the guys on my block for a couple of weeks when we were challenged to a game of baseball by the guys on the other project block. East versus West, they said, though we'd argue over which block was which. Their team outnumbered us two to one. I'd never seen so many dudes in North Beach together, thirty or so. Their side had fans, little kids sitting on the bench that wrapped around the tree, a dugout.

One of the kids looked me up and down. "You weak, huh?" he said, exposing a missing tooth. The row of kids laughed.

"Shut that shit up," Rob said, pointing his aluminum bat at them. The kids were right, though. I struck out often, hit grounders, and couldn't catch a pop fly.

It took us so long to get organized, arguing about batting order, positioning, and which team would get to bat first that we didn't play long before it got dark. No light from the lamppost. The bulb had been knocked out.

In the final at-bat of the game, I was up. We were down by

three, bases loaded, two outs, two strikes. The next pitch came, and I blasted the ball to the other end of the courtyard. If it landed past the grass in the outfield, it was an automatic homerun—we'd win. The outfielder, Moon Rock, whose name either referred to the bumps on his face or the crack rocks he sold, argued that the ball landed on the grass. I heard my teammates disputing this, but I didn't. I ran and ran. I was the winning run. By the time Moon Rock reached the ball, I was on my way to third base. I turned the corner home, and saw Tiger, the catcher, a large Samoan kid, his hands extended, ready for the ball. Behind him, my team was waving me on, fearful faces, worried I wouldn't beat the throw. The ball whizzed by, a couple of feet from me, and Tiger caught it. He leapt at me with the ball in hand. I contorted my body away from him and scored. My teammates piled on me, their hands rubbing my head, arms shaking me, and I couldn't stop jumping, worried that if I did, I'd wake from this dream.

The next week, we were playing baseball again, this time amongst ourselves without the kids from the other project block. I was crouched in a fielding position near the lamppost when I saw Jerome making a beeline toward me. He had a peanut head and was wearing a parka. He was Moon Rock's younger brother.

"What's up," I said. I didn't know Jerome well. We used to have gym the same period, but I hadn't seen him since he'd gotten locked up.

Jerome grinned. "You got a dollar for me?" He patted my pockets.

"Nah." I smiled. I thought he was messing around.

He cocked his fist back and jerked his body. "Motherfucker, I ain't playing with you. Let me see that glove."

I put it behind my back. "It's Rob's."

"I don't give a fuck whose it is. Give it here."

"You gotta ask him." Rob was at home plate, the gutter. He looked in our direction and leaned on his bat as though it were a cane.

Jerome lunged for the glove, but I used my arm to fend him off. Back and forth we went before he finally had a grip on it. We played tug of war.

"Give it, or I'm gonna fuck you up," he said. Jerome wasn't physically imposing. About my size, but he had enough crazy in him to render his size moot. He could've let go and punched me, but giving up the glove wasn't an option. I was just a few weeks into hanging out with these guys, a probationary period. I couldn't give them a reason to kick me out of the crew.

"It's Rob's," I shouted. "It's Rob's!"

I heard the bat drop, the clink of the aluminum.

"That's mine, blood," Rob said.

My grip relaxed. I was ready to step aside to watch the beat down. Rob was a giant next to Jerome.

"It's mine now," Jerome said and snatched the glove.

"'Rome, c'mon man," Rob said. It almost sounded like he was pleading.

Jerome stuck his hand in the glove and with his other hand punched the leathery palm.

"Just give it back," Rob said and made a half-ass attempt at grabbing it.

"Nope. What you gonna do about it?"

Rob reluctantly switched into a fighting stance.

Jerome dropped the glove and did the same.

We encircled them. They bobbed and weaved but neither was throwing any punches. "Hey!" someone yelled. "Y'all quit that. You boys get in this house right now." It was Mansur from his apartment window.

"Yeah, you boys better get on home," Jerome said. He smirked at the glove on the ground and walked away, one hand holding up his sagging jeans, one arm swinging loosely.

We gathered in 'Dullah's apartment, around the kitchen table. His place was dim. They had the shades drawn up for light, but night was falling.

"Sounds like he had the Devil in him," Mansur said. "Next time a boy comes around starting trouble—I'm talking to all you brothers now—you need to give him a good beating. Send him back where he came from."

Mansur didn't play. Once, we were hanging in the courtyard when we heard him scolding Sameerah for not doing her chores. Mansur left the apartment, calmly went into the garden and broke off a switch from a bush. He was from Louisiana, a Southern-style whupping. Sameerah made a valiant attempt to escape the blows. We could hear her pleas as he chased her throughout the house, but all that hollering and running probably made it worse when he caught up to her. 'Dullah might've had it rougher. He'd get his ass beat on New Year's Day for all the shit he *might* do in the New Year—a preemptive whupping. Maybe this was the reason why 'Dullah stayed on the straight and narrow.

Mansur was the first adult to give me the green light to kick someone's ass. This made me feel grown—I had a duty to uphold.

GOH GOH'S ROOM/MY ROOM

My sophomore English teacher, Ms. Porto, frequently had us write in class. Because she spoke to us through a microphone, we called her MC Porto. The room was no lecture hall. It was tiny, half the size of a normal classroom. She'd said she was tired of students always whining, "What did you say?" The mic was the kind you'd clip to your shirt, but she'd still raise it to her mouth.

One day, she wrote on the board: Describe something memorable that occurred at home.

"Don't think about it," MC Porto's nasally voiced boomed from the large speaker in front of her desk. "Just write."

I wrote about the night I woke up and saw Bah Ba and my mother screaming in my room. I was six. They stood on Goh Goh's bed, and my brother, who would've been nine, hid behind my mother, clutching her oversized Mickey Mouse T-shirt at her waist.

There was a satisfaction in seeing my older brother in trouble.

Bah Ba pressed up against my mother. She backed up and told him to get out, her hand extended, fingertips almost touching his chest. She had her hair tied up in a bun with a pink jaw hair clip.

My father knocked my mom's arm away and shook his finger at her face. I couldn't make out what he was saying. His words were barks. I'd heard of Bah Ba hitting my brother, but I'd never witnessed it, or if I had, I was too young to remember. Bah Ba would smack my brother, even in public, if Goh Goh dared to ask our father to buy a toy. Why my father wanted to beat my brother that night, I had no clue. Bah Ba might've just wandered into our room in a drunken stupor and decided to pick on my brother.

My father lunged for Goh Goh, but my mom stepped aside like a matador, keeping my brother tight on her hip. It was the first time I saw Goh Goh shed a tear. I was the crybaby. He'd sock me in the shoulders in front of his friends to make me cry on demand.

I threw off my covers. I'm not sure why. I didn't plan to get up. Bah Ba and my mother turned to me.

"*Bei leih goh jai tai dou,*" my mother said, pointing at me. You've let your son see you like this. She backed herself against the wall with Goh Goh still locked at her hip.

"*Yuhk hoi, diu!*" Bah Ba said. Move, fuck! He reached for Goh Goh.

My mother didn't budge. She spread her arms wide, and Bah Ba slapped her. She fell on the bed, her hand still holding onto Goh Goh. My brother threw his body across hers, his back to Bah Ba. My father made a move toward them.

"Why was I so stupid to marry you?" my mother said. "You don't love your kids. You only love mahjong. Why do you even come home?"

His shoulders slumped. He muttered something to himself and stepped off the bed.

My mother held her cheek, and my brother couldn't stop saying sorry to her. She rose and tucked us into bed.

"*Mouh gong yeh*," she said to us. "*Fun gaau.*" Don't talk. Sleep. She turned the lights off and the room darkened, but she didn't leave. She stood by the doorway, her silhouette still visible.

KITCHEN

I shoved a form at my mother while she was washing dishes. "You have to sign this at the bottom," I said.

"*Yi goh meh yeh?*" she asked.

"This is where I'm going to school." I pointed to the box labeled "First Choice." I'd listed McAteer on the form for my preference of high school. Mac was across town. I knew little about it. I didn't know about its selective arts program, a school within a school. I didn't know that many of its students were coming from neighborhoods at war with each other, that all the dudes in the school claimed something: a turf, a dance crew, a graffiti crew, or that strange cult, ROTC. All I knew, and all I needed to know, was that practically no one from my middle school was going to Mac, which meant no more dealing with kids coming up to me in the hallway telling me how phony I was, reminding me and anyone else around that I had betrayed my best friend.

He was a white kid named Max, skinny, big ears, dark greasy hair, always wore Chucks and baggy sweatpants. His friends became my friends. For every hour spent playing video games, we spent an hour playing sports. Didn't matter which. None of us were particularly good at any, but that wasn't the point. He brought me to my first baseball game. He had an allowance and would break me off some money when we went to the arcades or the comic store. He'd order pay-per-view fights, and his mom would order pizza. He had the latest video game systems, one setup in his room, another in a loft. One night, as I left his house, I snuck one of his game cartridges in my pocket. He phoned later that night and banned me from his house until I confessed.

I can't say for certain that stealing from Max had nothing to do with his racist jokes, how he'd pull the corner of his eyes back, or his cracks about how I was broke because I lived in the projects, how my house was probably cockroach-infested, how I wore the same jeans every day. But none of that feels as honest as what I'd actually told myself: the universe owes you. I had to beg for the few games I had. Max had stacks. Enough that some games went unplayed for months, the cartridges trapped inside a dusty case. I wasn't stealing. I was liberating.

A few weeks later, I caved and came clean, but Max and I were done. He still let me over his house, but he'd tell friends to keep an eye on me, not to leave me alone in any room. His mom wouldn't speak to me, wouldn't even look in my direction. Bye-bye pizza nights. His dog, a dachshund, would bark at me as she followed me to the bathroom.

At school, I tried to switch cliques, but I'd been marked as a thief who couldn't be trusted. Mac was my reset button. New school. New friends. New life. The challenge was my mother.

She leaned into the form and squinted. "I never heard of this school. Why doesn't it say Lowell?" Lowell was the only public high school in San Francisco that afforded her bragging rights, a feeder school to UC Berkeley and where my brother would be entering his senior year. If I were to get in as well, she'd do a victory lap in Chinatown, dragging me around the markets, the newsstand, the bakery, the herbal store, the bank, the takeout place with the fried chicken drumettes. She'd boast to whoever was behind the counter about her second Lowell son. Never mind the long line of grand-mas behind us at the register, eyeing my mother like she was a freak for her long hair that ran down to her knees, for her heavy makeup, for her leopard-skin heels. This was a fish market not a runway! My mom would ignore these looks and chat with the cashier. She'd demonstrate her skills at Praising without Praising. "This son takes school too seriously. Just like his brother. They both go to Lowell. This one can't stop reading. Even takes his books with him to the bathroom. So strange."

"Those are comic books," I'd say, but she wouldn't translate. She'd just pat my head like I was a silly kid.

A splash of water fell on the form. My mother was stuffing plates into the dish rack. "I don't have grades good enough for Lowell," I said. "I've been telling you that for the longest."

"How do you know if you don't apply? Cross that school out. Write Lowell."

"Lowell has a different form. And the deadline was last week."

"*Mouh gong daaih wah.*"

"I'm serious."

"Are you crazy!" She ripped off her dishwashing gloves and tossed them at the cheap wallpaper above the sink. The wallpaper, a grid of yellow and blue lines, functioned as a backsplash.

"You don't understand how Lowell works. I didn't at first either, but the counselor broke it down for me. She showed me a table. No, not a physical table, like a chart. It tells you what kind of grades and test scores you need to get in."

In the beginning of middle school, I'd bring home As and Bs, but my mother would say, "How come not 4.0 like your Goh Goh?" Lowell became a dead-end, but I wasn't brazen enough to blow off school completely.

"I'm like a B student," I said to my mother, "some Cs thrown in, so maybe more of a B-. I wouldn't have had a shot."

"You get As."

"They don't count sixth grade." I decided to not make things more complicated by bringing up extracurricular activities, how I was lacking in this category as well. I played baritone in the school band, but it was hard to be proud of that. I'd started off on the trumpet like my brother but got demoted to the baritone. The music teacher grouped us with our fellow instrument players, arranging us in a row according to skill. She ranked me last among the baritones, fourth out of four. It was a comfortable position. Anything I did was a bonus.

"Tomorrow," my mother said and clapped her hands, "we'll go

down to the district office. Get this straightened out. Sure, sure."

"Mom, it's over." I tried to hand her a pen. "Here. Sign."

She grabbed the cordless phone and stabbed it towards my face, nearly poking my cheek with the plastic antenna. "Call your Bah Ba," she said. "Tell him you want to be a bum."

I placed the phone on the kitchen table. I couldn't take her seriously. She knew I didn't know my father's number, though it wasn't far from me, scribbled on the calendar above the washing machine. On occasion we did speak on the phone. He'd call and I'd play the role of my mother's secretary: Yeah, she's home. Hold on. No, she's not. I'll tell her you called. Did my mother really think my father would lecture me? We all understood Bah Ba was a simple man. Father: make money, send to wife. Mother: kids.

I chalked up Bah Ba's indifferent attitude to genetics, some absent-father gene that plagued Lams. I didn't know his family, but I imagined his brothers, his dad, his uncles, all these men living apart from their families, the Lams—a clan of distant fathers. It wasn't personal that Bah Ba was uninterested in me. He just wasn't capable of it. He was a victim of the Lam gene. I didn't follow my theory to its logical conclusion—I carried the gene myself.

"Lowell is all hype," I said to my mom. "Colleges don't care what high school you went to."

"Lum Goon Saang," she called for my brother.

"What?" Goh Goh was sitting in the easy chair in the living room, next to the doorway.

"Tell your brother how stupid he is."

"I've been trying to tell him his whole life."

"So stupid. Didn't even apply."

"He's not smart enough. He wouldn't have gotten in anyway."

"Ga Jeh didn't apply," I said to my mother. "How come you didn't make a fuss with her?" My sister was a sophomore at Lincoln High School, a distant second-best to Lowell.

"You know your sister is not that smart," my mother said.

"I heard that," Ga Jeh shouted from her room.

"You know what I mean. You never had honor classes."

My sister marched into the kitchen holding a glass with a Hello Kitty straw. Her hair was permed, and it stretched high above her forehead, curling at the ends like a tidal wave ripping over her head. She had that constipated look of hers. That look she'd only have when talking to us. Get her on the phone with a friend, and she'd sound like a cheery customer service rep. "Move," she said to me.

I stepped aside. "Tell her, Ga Jeh. You don't need Lowell to go to college."

My sister opened the fridge and grabbed a jug of OJ. Goh Goh and I were protesting this juice. It was Willie's. My brother always asked our mom when she'd return from Costco, "Did you buy this or did he pay for it?" Anything Willie bought, Goh Goh refused, and I would say the same but would eventually relent. Ga Jeh on the other hand favored my mother's boyfriend, seemingly without reservation. She rode on the back of his motorcycle once, and the next chance I got, I did the same. "Traitors," our brother had called us.

Ga Jeh poured the OJ into her glass. "Mom's only pushing Lowell because you're a boy." My mother didn't have the same aspirations for my sister, never encouraging her to be a doctor or lawyer as she would with me and Goh Goh.

"I don't think like that," my mother said as though the notion were ridiculous.

"Stop lying," Ga Jeh said.

"I'm Mommy. Why would I need to lie?" She waved her hand dismissively.

"I don't care where Dickson goes, as long as it's not my school," Ga Jeh said and left the kitchen, sipping on her juice.

I sat on the cushioned folding chair and set the form on the kitchen table, which was draped with a fruit tablecloth. I took the cap off my pen and slipped a Chinese language magazine under the form for writing support. "It's McAteer or Galileo," I said to my mother. Galileo was my zoned high school.

"Now you want to go to Galileo." She plopped down on the chair next to me. "I ride the bus with those kids. Bad kids. Swearing in Chinese."

"That's why I need you to sign, so I won't go there."

She held the form, inspecting it. "But how come not Lowell?"

"Are you listening? Deadline. Has. Passed. Sign the form, damn."

"*Gong meh yeh*? You love to swear now, huh? Shit. Fuck. Damn. *Gong a. Gong a.*"

"Damn's not a cuss word."

She raised her hand like she was about to slap me, her lips tightening together.

I flinched though she'd never actually slapped me before. She'd only spanked me once, with the lid of a large tin box. My brother had had a friend over while she wasn't home, and apparently we were all responsible.

My mother, though, wasn't against the idea of whuppings. She was raised on them by her grandmother, and when she'd see public service announcements on television about child abuse, she'd scoff at the screen," *Yueh gwo ngoh da leih, ngoh seung leih da dihn wa bei ging chaat. Keuih deih leih, ngoh do da leih. Bei keuih deih laih ngoh. Ngoh do mh gaan a.*" A literal translation fails to capture her attitude. Let me try: I *wish* you would call the cops on me. Let them show up. I'd beat your ass in front of them. I wouldn't give a fuck.

"You don't want to listen to me," my mom said. "You want to do whatever you want, go live with your dad."

The phone was within arm's reach. I hit the "talk" button repeatedly, a steady rhythm of beeps. A red dot sped across the display on the phone, searching for the best channel. Minnesota Dickson would not have to endure lectures. His father would be too tired from work for that. Minnesota Dickson would have his own room. Minnesota Dickson would live in a house. He and his father would watch football together. Minnesota Dickson would become a Vikings fan. Maybe a Twins fan. Minnesota Dickson would make money busing tables at the Chinese restaurant where his father worked. Minnesota Dickson would attend a suburban school, an all-white school. They would know nothing about him except that he was the Asian kid from California. He would make snowmen. Carry snowballs in his pocket. He would ski to school.

"Stop playing with the phone. I sign at the bottom?"

"You really would let me live in Minnesota?"

"If you want to go, go. I don't care."

I handed her the phone. "Can you ask him?"

She looked at the Garfield clock. His striped tail hung and swayed in one direction while his droopy eyes darted in the opposite direction. The clock was my mother's idea, but perhaps Willie had bought it for her. "It's late there," she said. "I'll call tomorrow." She returned the phone to its base.

"Promise?"

"He won't want to take care of you. He has to work."

"I don't need a babysitter."

"Yeah, yeah, you're a big boy now, right? What are you going to do when you get sick?"

"Tylenol?"

"You don't even know how to take pills."

That was true. I had a phobia of swallowing them. My mother would wrap pills for me inside a napkin and hammer them down to powder, then she'd mix the powder with water in a spoon, using a toothpick to stir.

"I'm sure Bah Ba has a hammer."

"Who's going to take you to the doctor?" she said. Our main doctor was an old guy with a cane whose office was a small room in the back of a store. He'd have me rest my hand on a purple pillow, and he'd check my pulse. In three seconds he'd have a diagnosis. To be sure he'd ask me to spit phlegm on a paper towel. He'd examine the color and write an herbal prescription. At home my mother would cook the herbs in a clay pot. The process took over an hour and stunk up the kitchen. You'd think she was boiling a filthy boot.

When I drank the bowl of the dark brown concoction, the foul odor would hit me, and I'd have to pinch my nose just to drink it. It tasted so bitter and nasty, I knew it had to work.

"Are you going to ask him or not?"

"OK, OK. Tomorrow." She signed the form. "Happy? No more talking. I have to finish washing dishes. I have to sweep, mop."

My mother would continue to give me the run around for months. "He hung up so fast," she'd say. "Next time. Next time."

I could've asked Bah Ba myself, but I was too chickenshit. I worried he'd brush me off and tell me to put my mother on the phone. Worse, I was afraid he'd be honest. Tell me he didn't want me around. My hope lay in his duty as a father. We counted on that each month. He was the breadwinner, never failing to mail home the check that paid our bills. Perhaps he could be convinced that it was his fatherly obligation to allow me to move in with him.

One night, the phone rang in the living room and I picked up. It was Bah Ba.

"Jackson?" he said.

"Dickson," I said.

"Get your mom." Bah Ba and I had fallen into a groove. It was understood, no chitchat. Just hand the phone to my mother.

"She's in the bathroom." I lied. My mother was in the kitchen.

"Have her call me when she comes out."

"Hold on. I heard the toilet flush. She'll be out in a sec."

"OK."

"Does Minnesota get hot in the summer?"

"*Gaan haih a*," he said as though it was a dumb question, or maybe I was being sensitive, and his tone only reflected the natural harshness of Cantonese.

"It's not sunny here at all."

"That's better. Never gets too hot or too cold."

"Do you like living alone?"

"*Leih gong mut yeh?*"

"Living in a house by yourself. Isn't that boring?"

"You think I just lay around the house all day?"

"No, that's not what I meant."

"I wake up early. Work. Come home. Sleep. No time to think."

"I'm starting high school."

"So fast?"

"I *am* turning fourteen in a few months."

"Who's on the phone?" my mother asked.

"Bah Ba." I passed her the receiver of the plastic French-style phone.

She held the receiver on her shoulder with her back to me.

I tugged her shirt and pointed at the phone, then myself.

She raised a finger to her lips to shush me.

"Remember to ask," I said.

"Dickson," she said into the phone, "he wants me to ask you something. What? Hold on, I'll find it." She grabbed the base of the phone and carried it to the kitchen. The rotary dial contained a picture of my mom crowned with a lei, and the photo would rotate with the dial of a number.

I couldn't follow their conversation, only hearing my mother sorting through envelopes and shuffling about in her flip-flops.

"*Houh la,*" she said and hung up the phone.

I rushed to the kitchen. "Well, what did he say?"

"What I told you he'd say, 'No time.' See?"

"Call him back. Say I've got no good choices for high school. Say Minnesota's my only shot for college."

"What kind of father do you think you have? How many times has he asked anything about you? About any of you? He doesn't care about his kids."

Maybe a father can see something in his son no one else can, and what my father saw in me repulsed him. Perhaps it was my likeness to him.

My mother handed me the phone to return to the living room. I placed it back on the end table. Hanging above the table was a studio photograph of our family taken in Hong Kong shortly before we immigrated to the States. The five of us sit on the floor of a room, huddled together, as though we want others to believe this is our living room. I'm in the center, a year-and-a-half-old, my body round like a lump of clay, laughing because I do not know any better. My brother and sister sit next to me, one on each side, their legs extended straight out and their backs slouched. My parents lean into each other. My mother's her usual photogenic self, with the same smile she has in all photos. Posed but not fake. She's happiest when being photographed. My dad's rocking bell-bottoms and a burgundy sweater. He looks relaxed, eager for more of whatever this is, as though when the photo is done, he will roll around the carpet with me and raise me high up in the air. But this was all staged. This was not our living room, and the father rendered in this picture was a stranger.

My father was one only on paper, on a form for free lunch, on public housing records, on a family tree assignment. He was a check in the mail. I understood now this was no accident, and it wasn't a shortcoming. It was the way he preferred it, the way he wanted it to remain.

"Don't be so sad," my mother said. "How about I make beef lettuce wraps tonight? Or we can get McDonald's." She went to rub my shoulder, but I brushed past her. I went to my room and grabbed a comic book from the shelf, an issue of the X-Men. I brought the comic to the bathroom, a place where I could steal some privacy. I sat on the lid of the toilet and found myself in the Australian outback.

The X-Men were laying low, building a new headquarters while the world assumed they had died. They were still missing their leader, Professor X. He was probably stuck light years away on a spaceship or some mysterious planet. He'd been MIA since I began following the series a couple of years ago. Perhaps this is what drew me to the X-Men, a band of rejects, each with a particular mutated gene—steel skin, wings, the ability to heal any wound, the ability to turn air into ice—all of them waiting for one man to return. Maybe he never would. Maybe he wasn't stuck. Maybe he was happier in outer space and had no intention of returning to Earth to guide his former pupils. Maybe we'd been suckers for hoping.

On the trip to Minnesota the summer after Javon's death, my father confirmed for me what I had, over the years, come to suspect, that my mother had never relayed my desire to live with him.

"It wouldn't have made a difference," she said when I confronted her. "He still would've said no."

I wish she was wrong, but it's hard to imagine the Bah Ba of my childhood jumping at the chance to raise me. There's little doubt my father would've said no to my proposition, yet my mom still felt the need to fabricate his response. She was a queen of deception, juggling two men, one for romance, one for money—she had three kids to feed and clothe—but more to the point, she reigned as the Queen of Apartment 171, and she wasn't taking chances— her youngest would not flee her queendom.

BATHROOM

My mother was slicing up beef in the kitchen when I came home. Her hair was tied up, and she was wearing Capri corduroys. "*Faan Ke Ngauh Yuhk Faahn*," she said, "your favorite." Beef with tomato over rice.

"I'm going to shower first," I said. "I was playing basketball." Judging from my face, you wouldn't have known I'd just gotten my ass whupped, jumped for my Starter parka by a bunch of FOBs. They'd surrounded me. Someone kicked me in the back. The one rocking a pompadour struck my cheek. I'd punch one of them only to get blasted by blows I couldn't even see coming. It was like fighting a ghost. I fell and rolled around trying to dodge their kicks. It was a cold day, so my jacket was zipped up, and the entire time on the ground, while one hand was shielding my face, the other hand maintained a grip over the slider of the jacket zipper. No way I was giving up my Starter parka. It had cost my mom (dad?) over a hundred bucks. Luckily, a lady from her upstairs window scared away my assailants by saying she'd called the cops. More good luck: I'd only suffer bruises, nothing broken, no wounds. Much easier to take kicks from loafers than say, steel-toe boots. The best news to me: I'd managed to keep my jacket.

When I returned to North Beach, I saw Richie Rich, who lived upstairs, hanging out by the bus shelter, and I told him what happened. Double R sported a Jheri curl and was sipping on a forty. He was in his twenties, just released after serving a stint for robbing some tourists. We saw two Chinese kids getting off the bus across the street. "Think that's one of them?" he asked.

"Probably."

We darted after them, and the Chinese dudes took off. I slowed to a strut, while Richie Rich raced after them in his Nike Cortez's. He stopped to hurl his bottle at them, but it fell short, shattering on the pavement.

My mother now pointed her knife at me. "Any homework?" she asked.

"Already did it," I said.

"Stop lying," Ga Jeh said from the living room. She and my brother joined with my mother to form a three-headed Ghidorah parent. She'd told our mother I was hanging with some shady kids. She'd spotted me once with some graffiti writers. We were easy to identify: ink on our clothes, ink underneath our fingernails, tags written on our backpacks. Goh Goh had snitched to our mom about the stack of hats I had in the closest. Probably stolen, he'd said.

"Mom, don't listen to her," I said. "My school's easy like that."

"Then you should be getting As," my mother said. "How come I never see your report card?"

"I bet he's hiding them," Ga Jeh said. She was wrong. I'd thrown them away. The last report card showed I was failing three courses.

"They probably have the wrong address," I said.

"You're retarded," Ga Jeh said.

"Check with your counselor," my mother said, "or I'll call myself." She always gave me the benefit of the doubt. I'd gotten arrested for graffiti, along with Rob, on Super Bowl Sunday. I told my mother that the marker the cop found on me was for art class. I wasn't even taking that class anymore, but she didn't know that. The weird thing was neither Rob nor I had actually tagged on that bus—the driver was lying. We all had to appear in front of a judge, in his chambers, and our moms mean-mugged the driver, a white woman with gray hair who didn't take off her shades. Even Willie was giving the woman a dirty look. I'd hoped that seeing him in his bus uniform might force her to change her story. Maybe she wouldn't fuck over a family from her own fraternity. But the lady stuck with the bullshit, and we were found guilty. A fine and thirty hours of community service. I appreciated Willie being there, but it changed nothing between us. He was still the secret I had to keep from my father.

I took off my parka and hung it on a hook behind the hallway door. My brother was in our room, lying on his bed, talking on the phone. It had to be a girl on the other end. Goh Goh's voice was gentler, and he was giggling. I didn't understand how this sappy tone could work, but it did. Even back in his middle school days. Once I'd walked in on him and a girl who'd been voted Most Popular fooling around under the sheets.

Every slight shift was now a new wave of pain, felt sharply in my chest and back.

"Why are you moving like that?" Goh Goh said.

I closed our bedroom door. "You gotta promise not to tell Mom."

"Whatever, yeah."

He got off the phone, and I told him what happened. He had said once that if anybody messed with me, he'd gather backup. Though he'd gone to a nerdy high school and had earned high marks, he was not an angel. He'd been arrested for stealing a car.

"So you gonna help?" I asked.

"I'll figure something out."

I grabbed a change of clothes and went to the bathroom. I took off my shirt in front of the mirror. I had clusters of red marks on my chest, promises of blue and purple. I pressed gingerly on the marks. I turned on the shower and slipped out of my jeans.

The door burst open. I was in my underwear. My mother held a wire hanger. She sucked in a breath and started swinging the hanger at my chest. I put my arms out to block her.

"*Gau daam?*" she said. "*Fong sau.*" You dare? Drop your hands. "Think you're so cool, huh? Look at you." She pointed at the marks. "Let people beat you like that. Why do I have such a weak son?" She struck me on my thighs with the hanger.

I dropped to the floor and leaned against the toilet, my arms outstretched to keep her at bay.

"*Fong sau,*" she yelled, or maybe it was more of a cry. "Your brother and sister always say you're up to no good, but I don't listen to them. I say 'Sai Lo's a good boy.'" The hanger whooshed and smacked me on the arm, on my thigh, on my shin. Compared to the earlier beating, none of this hurt, but I began to sob. I tried to say something, but it was hard to form a coherent sentence.

"Talking back?" She threw the hanger at me. Said I'd never leave the house again, then stormed off.

I used my foot to swing the door closed. I rested my head on the toilet. I sat there long enough that the tall mirror I was facing fogged up once again from the shower. I used my fingers to draw my tag, but within seconds the steam covered my name, its outline slowly vanishing.

PARENTS' ROOM/MOM'S ROOM/MY ROOM

Even when Bah Ba was living with us, we never called it my parents' room, just Mom's room. The shag carpet was red. The bed cover was red. Everything on the dresser was hers, a nail polish rack, jewelry boxes, the childhood pictures of us. Hanging on the wall was a framed photo of her in a wedding gown. On top of the radiator sat three Snoopy stuffed animals, each one with one of our initials sewn onto its ear by our mother. All Bah Ba had in the room was a two-drawer nightstand where the boom box sat, and a roll-top desk piled with bills. Inside the desk was a harmonica. I never heard him play it, the box worn and dusty, a holdover from Hong Kong. There was also, above the bed, a black and white picture of Bah Ba and my mother, side by side on their wedding day, my father youthful, my mother without makeup.

Also in this room was my desk, made of particle board, some flimsy shit you had to assemble. There was no accompanying chair. To sit at the desk, I had to sit at the end of the bed, but at least the desk could fit in their room. It didn't fit in mine. Goh Goh already had two there, one made of maple wood, the other a computer desk big enough that included a shelf for his encyclopedia set and a shelf for his printer. His computer was off-limits to me, but when I was younger, I'd cheer for him as he played games, RPGs, *Impossible Mission*, and strip poker. Like Bah Ba, my room wasn't my room.

When Bah Ba moved out, I began to treat Mom's room like it was mine. She'd be in the kitchen the whole day. The only time she used her room was to sleep or when Willie came over. I'd lock the door and get on the phone, using three-way to make prank calls with friends.

My mother began to stay over at Willie's on the weekends. I'd sleep in her room, in her bed. It was better than sleeping in a bed next to my brother. Our two beds were lined against the wall, perpendicular to each other, so that if I snored, his feet didn't have to reach far to kick my head.

Sleeping in my mother's room also meant it was easier to sneak out. I'd pull all-nighters, roaming the streets with a spray can in the kangaroo pocket of my hoodie. By this point, Rob had already quit tagging. If you asked him what he was now, now that he wasn't a writer, he'd say he was a pimp. He broke girls' hearts. I'd listen in on the conversations on three-way, the silent witness.

A few times, I snuck a girl into my mother's room, but that was weird, fooling around in her bed with that wedding photo of her and Bah Ba above it, looking straight at the camera, straight at me. My mother left the photo up, I guess, for future visits from Bah Ba. She didn't want to rock the boat. He was still paying our bills.

Most of the time, I'd just chill in that room and turn on Bah Ba's stereo. I didn't have my own, so it was the only time I could blast my music, Bay Area gangsta rap and East Coast boom bap. Some nights when I had the room to myself, I'd wake up in the middle of the night and peer out the window. The Back would be pitch-dark. Someone was always knocking out the bulbs. The windows across the yard would have their blinds down. Blank faces staring back at me. I'd open the window and smoke a beedi. My elbows on the windowsill, I'd blow smoke through the wire mesh.

LIVING ROOM

The summer after I'd graduated high school, my brother brought home a new girl he was dating. She lay on the floral print couch, her head on his lap. We were watching television together. Or maybe I was the only one watching. I was sitting on the red beanbag in front of them, so for all I knew, they weren't paying any mind to the screen, just goo-goo eyeing each other.

The girl wore dark lipstick and had blonde highlights in her hair. My brother had a blue streak in his hair. That was the thing— Asians coloring their hair. Ga Jeh had dyed hers chestnut. I used to style my hair, gel it, spray it, but now I'd just slap on a hat. It made it so much easier leaving the house. In the morning, I'd wake up with hair that had puffed up overnight, as if it had risen like a sad soufflé. And that's pretty much how my hair was that night. Plus, I was looking bummy in a faded black shirt and sweatpants with a hole at the knee. I didn't know Caroline was coming over. I didn't even know my brother was seeing her.

I used to say hi to Caroline at the bus stop. The first time I noticed her, I was with Rob, and he said, "That's you, dog." He said that every time there was a cute Asian girl. He nudged me to say something, which I refused on principle. Even when he was encouraging, Rob was bossy. He still saw himself as my mentor, and I didn't know how to opt out of that contract.

My brother wasn't doing much with his life. He'd gone to the top high school in the city, had good enough grades for a university but settled for the local community college. He'd said he was saving money. Cheap bastard. We called him the Rebate King. He'd combine rebates so stuff was practically free. A case of Snapple, which he wasn't even a fan of. A printer stand though he didn't have a printer. He was always trying to get over. Goh Goh was a gambler, betting on Sundays. Once, he had to beg my mom for a couple grand. It was that or have his legs broken. I'd thought that was only in movies.

Instead of entering into his fourth year at City, a "two-year college," my brother planned to drop out, or take a break, the answer fluctuating. He was going to work full-time, make more money, his job a stock boy at Toys "R" Us.

"Lum Goon Saang," my mother said. She stood at the doorway of the living room, wearing yellow leggings with black polka dots, pissed as hell.

My brother got up but tried to play it off, like he wasn't about to get chewed out for letting this girl put her feet up on the couch. "Do you want anything to drink?" He turned back to ask Caroline.

"No, I'm fine," she said.

I leaned back in the beanbag like I was reclining in a seat of a car. I stretched my legs out on the red and black zebra-striped commercial carpet. I flipped channels with the remote, still in its original case, cellophane over the buttons. It'd been my mother's idea, but it was my brother who had applied the masking tape that kept the case from falling apart. This was the same guy who had let his Transformers sit on the top shelf of his desk, posed for war, covered by a dusty veil of Saran Wrap. Never once played with them. "One day, they're going to be worth a lot of money," he'd said. He'd let me read his comics but only if I followed his rules. I had to place the comic on a pillow. It prevented creases on the spine, he'd said. To turn the page, I was to only use the tips of my thumb and index finger. He'd stand over me, ready to sock me if I messed up.

My mother and Goh Goh began arguing in the kitchen, so I turned up the television to drown them out.

"What do you got planned for next year?" Caroline asked me. By next year, she meant at the end of the summer.

"City. Maybe a job." Community college was my only choice, my grades too low for a CSU or a UC. When the counselor explained this to me in her office, as we reviewed my transcript together, she was shocked. I'd scored a 1080 on my SAT, close to the national average, but at Galileo, it'd been among the top scores. She wanted me to explain the discrepancy. She hardly knew me. The entire senior class was her caseload, several hundred students. I shrugged, and she let me slip out of her office.

It wasn't a surprise I had few options for college. My mother received a letter in the mail saying I was in danger of not graduating because I was on the verge of failing a required course. I had a C average, a 2.1 GPA, but it was a miracle my GPA was even that high. I'd lucked out on some easy classes.

I had two years of Spanish with the same teacher, a jolly guy, a student favorite. He was a dark-skinned Mexican who'd refer to Spain as the motherland. At the end of each semester, he'd have us put all our work into a folder, write our name on the front of it, and below our name, write what grade we thought we deserved. I'd have just a few completed worksheets to show for the semester. I'd take whatever paper was in my bag, blank, scratch, or even work from another class, and I'd stuff the two pockets of the folder with these sheets, being sure to place a Spanish assignment at the front of each stack. I'd write "A" under my name, and he'd always give me a B. I assumed we had an understanding.

I took a journalism class and in two years had only one article in the school paper to show for it: "Graffiti, Art, or Crime." It made the front page, though apparently from the title, it hadn't been proofread. The journalism teacher, a guy whose face stayed constantly flushed, would often leave us alone in the class. We'd play Connect Four or dominoes. I'd walk to the store to grab some chips. We'd use the phone in the room to page our friends. We'd watch March Madness on a television locked to a cart. "If anyone comes by," the teacher would say, "tell them I'm in the computer lab, and I'll be right back." It wasn't a total lie. He was in the lab, working with students on writing the school paper. We were the *other* students in his journalism class. I was the envy of friends. I got Cs for hanging out in a rec room.

Community college was the only option I could expect. They admitted any idiot who was eighteen. That's where my brother and sister went.

Caroline sat up against a pillow on the armrest. "You should work with your brother."

"It's bad enough I have to live with him." I handed her the remote and left the room. I didn't want to be stuck entertaining my brother's girlfriend. In the kitchen, my mother and brother were arguing, my mom standing tall trying to make herself bigger. Goh Goh had his hairy arms folded.

"It's none of your business," my brother said. "I can talk to whoever I want."

I closed the living room door behind me.

"Listen to how stupid you sound. I'm your mom—everything is my business! First time over and she lies on my couch. And she's younger than Sai Lo."

I went into my mother's room to use the phone. I left the door ajar. I couldn't resist hearing my big brother put in check.

In the next room, my sister had her door closed, but I could hear her techno music. She had her boyfriend over. He was the guy that turned her Civic into a rice rocket. He didn't look like a bad boy, though. Quite the opposite. He wore long sleeve shirts and talked like he'd gone to a private school. My mother liked him. It was only months later when Ga Jeh broke up with him that she realized he was a nut job. Wouldn't stop calling the house. Then he began stalking her. Keyed the Civic. She'd never refer to him by name again, only as the Crazy Guy.

I called Summer. She lived in a suburb south of the city. We'd spoken on the phone for hours but had only met once at a bus stop in front of Wendy's. She was a white girl with gray eyes. When we kissed I felt her peach fuzz moustache. It was the kind of thing you could overlook; she had a chest that made heads turn. The problem was she had a boyfriend, but in my experience, it was just a matter of time before a guy fucked over his girl. She had a soothing voice, like she could've been on the radio.

"You're not even listening to me," Summer said. "Stop eavesdropping on them."

"But it's getting good."

The living room door opened. The only sound in the kitchen was that of shoes being put on. Then the front door shut.

"Let me call you back," I said.

I crossed the kitchen back into the living room. Caroline was gone. I sat in the easy chair, the seat closest to the kitchen.

Two poster-size photos of my mother hung in the living room. One of her drinking a Coke can, tilting her head back, her hair nearly touching the ground. It looked like it could've been an ad. The other picture, on the opposite wall, was my mom near a tree, a rare photo of her with a tentative smile, not posing for the camera, not posing for Willie. He'd taken both pictures, and it'd been his idea to blow them up. The only picture hung in the living room that didn't feature my mother was Jesus.

"This is my house too," Goh Goh said to my mother.

"Are you the one paying the rent?" she said.

"Are *you* the one paying rent?" Say what you want about Bah Ba, but he wasn't a deadbeat dad.

Goh Goh stormed off to our room, his head lowered as if he was preparing to ram it. My mother followed behind waving her arms and shouting.

I closed the door and called Summer back. I heard what sounded like a scuffle in the hallway. "My moms must be smacking my brother pretty good," I told Summer.

"Shouldn't you check on them?" she said.

There was a thud, then a shriek.

"I gotta go." I dropped the phone and opened the door. My mother was on the floor holding her head, her face wincing in pain. My brother loomed over her.

"I told you, I'm too old for that shit."

Leaning against the edge of the doorway for support, my mom rose. Goh Goh stepped toward her, his fists two rocks.

I leapt at him, tackling him onto my bed.

He pushed me aside. I pulled his shirt to drag him back onto the bed, but he shook me off. He walked past our mother and straight out of the house.

Ga Jeh and her boyfriend came out into the hallway, and we took my mother into her room, laying her down on her bed. "Just like his father," she screamed. Her body started twitching, so we had to hold her down. She kept yelling, words not sentences, fragments. I couldn't make sense of what she was saying. She wasn't shouting to us but to God.

"Mom," my sister said, "it's Cindy. Mommy?" She stroked our mother's hand, but my mom only wiggled her head. Her shouts had calmed to mutters, but her eyes remained elsewhere.

"Just give her some space," the boyfriend said. He said it with the authority of a doctor.

"Where's Goh Goh?" Ga Jeh asked.

"I'll go outside to talk to him," I said.

"What are you going to say?"

"I don't know."

"It's probably not a good idea for him to come back," the Crazy Guy said.

Goh Goh was at the bus stop puffing on a cigarette, a hand in his pocket, shivering. It was chilly. He only had on a T-shirt.

"What the fuck do you want?" he said.

"You can't come back tonight."

"Whatever." He chuckled.

"I'm serious," I said. "Mom can't see you. Stay at a friend's or something." I tried to sound like an adult, but I think I came off more like a whining little brother. I didn't wait for Goh Goh's response.

I closed the front door behind me, sliding the top chain lock. The screws of the bottom lock's mount had loosened and fallen off. Mom was still muttering to herself. Ga Jeh and the boyfriend sat with her.

"How'd it go?" Ga Jeh asked.

"We'll see."

I lay on my bed. On the ceiling was a slight crack. This is where water would leak. Upstairs was a Chinese family. Sometimes the grandma would leave the water on in the kitchen and fall asleep. Water would drip, closer to my bed than my brother's. I'd grab a bucket and have my mom call maintenance. The grandma would apologize, then do the same thing the next month.

Goh Goh was trying to get in. He turned the key and unlocked the front door. The chain was yanked. My brother began shoving the door, probably with his shoulder. After a few tries, the screws on the mount gave way. The door flung open, the knob punching the wall.

He came into my room, changed into his pajamas, and lay in his bed. I turned over so I was facing the wall. I had a roll of toilet paper next to my pillow. I had allergies. There was also an empty

Kleenex box, a makeshift garbage can. When I was a child, I used to pick my nose at night and smear my boogers on the wall. They stuck like spitballs. I'd imagined them as my constellation of stars. One night, Goh Goh snitched to our father, and Bah Ba woke me up and made me wipe down the wall. "If I see this again—" he said. He left the ending to my imagination. The toilet paper and garbage can were my mother's solution.

It was clear what had to be done: my brother had to go. I went to the bathroom. I needed a place to think. I locked the door and sat on the lid of the toilet. Next to me hanging on the wall was a phone. It was mainly used by my mother. She'd take calls from Willie when she was doing her makeup or getting out of the shower. I picked up the phone and called the only authority my brother would respect.

Half an hour or so later they came. There were two cops, one Asian, one white. After I explained the situation to them, I told my brother someone was at the door for him.

He sat up on his bed. "Who is it?"

"Mr. Lam. Jackson Lam," one of the cops said from our doorstep. "Please come to the door."

"What the hell did you do?" my brother said, throwing the covers off.

"Better hurry up," I said and followed him to the door.

"You got two options," the Asian cop said, "spend the night in jail or find another place tonight to sleep."

My brother didn't argue. Didn't even shoot me a dirty look. He made a phone call to a friend and packed his stuff. I waited at the front door with the cops. I held the door open as Goh Goh left, his duffle bag slung over his shoulder.

Ga Jeh drove the Crazy Guy home. So for a little while, it was just me and Mom. I knelt next to her bed and examined her head for any bumps. My brother had struck her on the collarbone, she said. As she was knocked down, she'd hit her head on the edge of the doorway.

"Goh Goh's not coming home tonight," I said.

She patted my hand and began to nod off. I fixed her bedcover so that it spread neatly over the sides of the bed and tucked the covers in so she was snug.

GA JEH'S ROOM/MY ROOM

I try and picture her room. I knew it well. I'd snoop around when Ga Jeh wasn't home. I dug through her books and cassette tapes. I'd spend hours in that room bobbing my head to Janet Jackson, Latin Freestyle, and I confess, Debbie Gibson. For all the time I spent in her room, I can't fully picture it.

Some things I can see. Her desk with a cherry finish. An alarm clock sat near its edge. My parents had received the clock as a gift for opening a bank account. Hanging on the wall near the doorway was a caricature portrait of my sister done by a street artist. Her head is gigantic, her neck sprouting from a tiny cable car rolling downhill. The artwork was a birthday present from my father. I don't know if it was Before or After: a gift used to seduce or a gift used to apologize.

What I can see with clarity is the outside of the door. It was decorated with stickers, Scratch-n-Sniff, Snoopy, My Little Pony, but in the middle of the door, Ga Jeh had taped an old birthday card that I'd made for her. It had a peek-a-boo hole that revealed a lopsided cake that I'd drawn. The card remained on her door until she left when she was twenty-one.

She took off as soon as she finished her associate degree at City. She said our place was too noisy, kids always playing in The Back. My sister had the most sensitive hearing of anybody I knew. I'd be in the living room watching TV, not even loud, and she'd pound on her side of the wall, telling me to turn down the volume. She would've made one hell of a librarian.

Ga Jeh's move made her the first of us to be independent. She was done relying on Bah Ba's money. Wouldn't have to see him or answer his calls. When he'd come back for his annual visits, she'd keep her distance from him, staying in her room. Still, she hadn't been a fan of lying to our father for our mother. Tell your own lies, woman, she'd thought.

When my mom discovered Ga Jeh planned to move, she took it as a betrayal. You weren't supposed to leave your parents until you got married.

"We're not in China," Ga Jeh said to my mother.

"We're not from China." My mom slapped her chest. "We're British. We're from Hong Kong."

Ga Jeh moved to a suburb south of San Francisco near her job working at the front desk of the Embassy Suites by the airport. My sister was pretty straight-laced, a square, so I was surprised when she got her first tattoo, a small one on her ankle, the Chinese character for "tiger," her sign. The other tattoos would come later, images of tigers, one on her forearm, the other a large one on her back shoulder, reminders that she was not prey.

Ga Jeh's room became my room. I rearranged the two dressers she left behind and moved in my stuff. The first time I slept in that room, I was jolted awake. A loud motor roared. A leaf blower outside, groundskeepers off to an early start. The noise was right outside the window next to my bed. I'd positioned my bed the same way Ga Jeh had, and I thought I understood why my sister had said that she "had to get the fuck out of there."

Ga Jeh tells me now that it wasn't the noise that drove her out. It was the silence, the things she could not say.

CHAPTER 4

WHAT'S IN A NAME?

林 LÀM

The last name that I share with Bah Ba means forest. In Chinese, it's written as two trees side by side. The origins of the name begin three thousand years ago with the murder of a would-be father.

He was both the uncle of the emperor and his advisor, which would've been fine if the uncle was a yes-man, but he called it like he saw it: the emperor was a fucked-up ruler. Never concerned himself with his subjects. It was more fun to plan orgies. He needed an appropriate setting, something worthy of a true despot.

He had a large pool constructed at his palace, large enough for several canoes, and he filled the entire pool with wine. Perfect for lazy afternoons. He'd lounge in a canoe with his concubines and dip his hands in the pool to get drunk. He had a small island built in the middle of the pool, and hanging from the branches of the trees on the island were skewers of roasted meat. One-stop shop: alcohol, food, sex—all while drifting in a canoe in front of his palace. Top that, future dictators of the world!

To fund his lavish lifestyle, the emperor taxed his people heavily, and the uncle, Mr. Party Pooper, chided him for abusing his power. The uncle knew he was getting on the emperor's last nerve, but he persisted, urging him to repent as though he believed that the emperor, his nephew, his blood, could be redeemed.

The uncle would go down in history as courageous, but I bet his pregnant wife wanted him to keep his mouth shut. His honesty was a death wish.

The emperor sent the royal guards to capture the uncle. They arrested him and, following the orders of the emperor, they ripped open the uncle's chest and cut out his heart. The pregnant wife escaped and hid in a forest. There, alone, she held tight onto two trees as she gave birth to a son.

Years later, a new emperor came to power and restored the mother and son back into the royal family. He granted the son the surname Lam in honor of the forest that had protected them. All Lams descend from this son, but I wonder who the two trees in our name represent.

I could argue that it represents us and a future child, an explicit expectation to continue the royal lineage, to grow the forest. That sounds nice, aligning myself with royalty, but what makes more sense is that the pair of trees represent not What Will Be but What Is, us and our father. Stronger than a desire to multiply was the desire to solidify the father-son bond, for the son to swear his allegiance to his father. The Lam story did not begin with the son. It began with a soon-to-be father.

For the first Lam, the son, his name became a lifelong tribute to his father. He'd tell the Lam story to others to honor his Bah Ba's bravery. For me, Lam has become a lifelong burden. Bah Ba and I do not simply share the same name—he exists inside mine.

狄甥 DIK SAANG

The Chinese name Bah Ba chose for me is not an authentic Chinese name. It's a transliteration of Dickson: Dik Saang. The first character of my name refers to an ancient general, and the second character means "nephew." To a native speaker, these two characters combined results in an awkward phrase. My name sounds like a mistake. Perhaps my father saw no point in giving me a true Chinese name. By the time I was born, my parents had already filed the paperwork to immigrate to the States—I would be a child of America.

There were several choices my father had for the *Dik* character. Other words that make that same sound include the characters for "foe," "oppose," "wash," "cleanse," "enlighten," "guide." Instead my father used the surname of the Song dynasty warrior Dik Ching. Early in Dik's military career, like many common soldiers, he was forced to bear a tattoo on his face, a marker of his poor background, an attempt to keep him in his place. In spite of this, Dik rose up the ranks to become a general and was later promoted to the imperial court as the minister of military. If the story ended here, my Chinese name would serve as a reminder of my father's wish that I become a man of bravery and nobility.

But when Dik Ching served on the Song Court, he discovered that other officials were distrustful of him, fearing the powerful general might one day abuse his military power. They fabricated rumors about the Tattooed Face General, even blaming him for natural disasters. Eventually, they forced him out of office. Demoted, he was sent from the capital to another city. A year later, he died of illness at the age of forty-nine. Perhaps his two sons and wife were at his side. Maybe they had moved with him to his new appointment, but I can't find a record of this. It's possible he spent the last year of his life isolated.

The first half of the Dik story represented the hopes that my father had for me, the second half foretold his own fate: a father scorned.

OUT

Rob gave me my first graffiti tag: OUT. I thought it was a random name, but it probably referred to how often I'd strike out in baseball. I wasn't much better in my first few months as a tagger. I was a toy, incapable of holding a chisel-tip marker correctly, at a forty-five degree angle so the width of each stroke remained consistent. Style was secondary to me. Getting up—that's why I began writing my name for all to see.

Though Rob had introduced me to tagging, trying to pressure me into it, I didn't pick up a marker immediately. It was important that I decide for myself when to begin. I was a child of the "Just Say No" campaign. I'd vowed at a young age never to succumb to peer pressure. That was for weaklings. I'd partake in drugs on my own!

The first day I brought a marker to school, I hid it in the sleeve of my jacket, the barrel of the marker zebra-striped. I grabbed the block of wood that served as the hall pass for Ms. Porto's class and headed to the first floor where there was a stretch of bare white wall, usually reserved for signs made of butcher paper announcing spirit week, bake sales, or some class president candidate. That day the wall was empty. I waited for the hallway to clear, then wrote my name billboard-size, reaching as high as my hand could climb and as low as my knees could bend. My *T* resembled a sai, the ends of the roof dipping down like prongs. But the width of the marker wasn't suited for colossal scale. The proportions were off, my letters appearing as stick figures, sickly.

THE LAM POEM

Dozens of generations ago, my ancestors chose a name for me, embedded in a family poem. Each character in the poem was to be assigned to a specific future generation. Given names contained two characters, one chosen by your parents, the other predetermined by your family poem, by your ancestors. Fathers, knowing the position of their name in the poem, would give their sons names containing the next character. Sons would share this character with their brothers and paternal cousins. Daughters, however, were usually excluded from this practice.

After the end of the poem was reached, when all its characters had been exhausted, what remained was an abridged family tree set to verse. Clan elders could recycle the poem for future generations, or they could compose an entirely new one.

The Lam poem had been passed down through generations, spanning hundreds of years, but in my father's generation, the poem vanished. My mother's family poem was also lost. Though my mother recalls her grandmother showing her their family's poem inked in a notebook, my mom's parents now have no idea where this notebook might be. For all they know, they might have left it in Hong Kong.

It's no accident that generation poems have lost their importance. When Mao came to power, he pushed to rid the country of its Confucian tradition. The sacred bonds of emperor-subject, husband-wife, father-son—all bullshit. These doctrines had produced a submissive nation, a kowtowing species that groveled to foreign empires.

Mao declared a change: "The Chinese people have stood up!" He banned foot-binding. Out went ancestor worship. Women could seek divorce. Genealogy books and generation poems were patriarchal relics. This was to be a new China, though the attack on Confucianism wasn't new.

Thirty years before, on May 4, 1919, thousands of students in Beijing protested the Treaty of Versailles. China, once again, had gotten screwed through a treaty, forced to hand over their land to another imperial nation. The protests sparked unrest across the country. Many were rejecting Confucianism and turning toward Western ideas of science and democracy, but also anarchy and Marxism. They sought solutions for a country in turmoil. China had thrown off the yoke of dynastic rule only to see provincial warlords seize power.

At the time of the student protests, Mao was in his mid-twenties, part of the May Fourth Generation. Inspired by his peers in Beijing, Mao founded the *Xiang River Review*, a local weekly journal. "Oppressors are people," he pens in one essay, "human beings like ourselves." Their tyrannical actions are due to "an infection or hereditary disease passed on to them from the old society and old thought."

Three years later Mao had his first son. Mao's generation name was *Ze*, the fourteenth character in his clan's generation poem. Twenty characters in the poem, twenty generations.

立顯榮朝士　　*Stand tall with honor before noblemen,*
文方運際祥　　*and utilize education to expand fortune.*
祖恩貽澤遠　　*Ancestral favors are handed down through time,*
世代永承昌　　*descendants forever indebted for their prosperity.*

When Mao named his son, he ignored his family's poem, turning his back on his forefathers. He refused to pass on to his newborn the poem's message: Bow Down to Your Ancestors. It was the very Confucian ideas he had railed against.

The characters Mao chose for his first son, An Ying, challenged the Confucian ideals propagated by his family's poem. Individually, the characters *An* and *Ying* respectively meant "the bank of the river" and "hero," but interpreted through the lens of communism, the name became "The Hero Who Reaches the Shore of Socialism." Mao scrapped the generation poem, but he didn't toss out generation names altogether. He would later give three other sons names beginning with the character *An*, but Mao, a critic of patriarchal practices, would not give this generation name to any of his four daughters.

Bah Ba also didn't abandon generation names when he named me and my brother, but like Mao, Bah Ba didn't give his daughter this name. To be fair, Bah Ba couldn't. The character in my Chinese name that I share with Goh Goh is the male identifier, *Saang*. Atypical was Bah Ba's choice to place our generation name as the second character of our given name and not our first. The character rests at the end of my name. Detached from verse. No claims to a clan. No grand instructions to descendants. Only a bond between brothers. The desire of a young father to keep his family whole.

RANK

I leafed through the dictionary for a new graffiti tag, a name I'd choose myself. I began with aardvark and ended with zymurgy. I'd borrowed the idea from Malcolm X. To teach himself how to read and write, he copied the entire dictionary by hand in prison, back when he was still Malcolm Little.

I skipped over any word with more than five letters. Long words were a luxury of time we didn't have. Skipped the definitions too. We prided ourselves as writers, but it wasn't words that we loved. It was letters, how they looked, the way an *S* meandered. The letters of my name, O-U-T, were stiff and uptight, wallflowers. I needed letters that danced and jabbed.

Because of its sharp angles, its final letter punching and kicking, I renamed myself: RANK.

MASK

Dik Ching commanded an army of thirty thousand men and thirty generals. He'd ride into battle wearing a bronze mask. Combined with his long hair, unkempt and billowing in the wind, the bronze mask sent enemy soldiers scurrying. They didn't see a man charging at them, but a demon.

Dik's motivation behind wearing the mask, however, wasn't solely to scare the enemy. It also hid the tattoo on his face, the reminder that he was less than. With the bronze mask, Dik discarded his past and became a deity.

POOR AND BLANK

> "...the outstanding thing about China's 600 million people is
> that they are 'poor and blank.' This may seem a bad thing, but
> in reality it is a good thing. Poverty gives rise to the desire for
> change, the desire for action and the desire for revolution. On a
> blank sheet of paper free from any mark, the freshest and most
> beautiful characters can be written, the freshest and most beau-
> tiful pictures can be painted."
>
> —MAO ZEDONG

MALCOLM

Malcolm Little was his birth name, Little from his father. Detroit
Red was his street name, red for the color of his hair, inherited from
his maternal grandfather, a Scot. "Yes, that raping, red-headed devil
was my *grandfather!*" Malcolm said after he shed his street name.
"If I could drain away *his* blood that pollutes *my* body, and pollutes
my complexion, I'd do it! Because I hate every drop of the rapist's
blood that's in me!"

Malcolm X was his converted name, the *X* replacing the Little,
the unknown erasing the scar. El-Hajj Malik el-Shabazz was the
name he created for himself, the el-Hajj for his pilgrimage to Mecca,
Malik for Malcolm, el-Shabazz as in the Lost Tribe of Shabazz.
His new surname expressed not just his love for his people, the lost
children of Africa, but Shabazz was also a solution to the unknown,
an answer for the variable, a name that could be passed on to his
children and handed down successive generations, an invented
name but a pure one.

MANNY LEE

My mother, like me, was fifteen when she named herself. She chose
Maggie for her English name. When she married my father, she
married into the Lam family, but, as customary, kept her maiden

name. She remained Maggie Lee, but she wasn't thrilled with her name. Maggie, she learned, was all too common.

My mom would later find a nickname, thanks to 'Dullah's baby sister. She'd mispronounce my mom's name as Manny. All the kids on our side of the projects also called my mother this. It was a requirement. She'd tempt them with candy like an evil witch. She'd leave our door open, and in plain sight on the kitchen table was a gumball dispenser.

When a kid stopped at our door, my mom, with her makeup on—she never opened the door without it—would grab a gumball, show it to the kid then hide it behind her back. To get the candy, the kid would have to say my mom's full name: Manny Lee. The kids would sit at our doorstep, and this would be the highlight of my mother's day.

The first time she tried to get my homeboys to call her Manny Lee, I told her, "The name's dumb. Manny Lee is a Dominican shortstop for the Blue Jays."

"Me, I don't care," she said.

邦強 STRONG AS A NATION

My father renamed himself when he married my mother. The second name wouldn't stick, something he tried out, then abandoned.

Chinese folks accumulated names over a lifetime. At birth you were given a nickname, a "milk name." A month or so later you received your given name. When you started school, your teacher gave you a name to be used just in school, a "book name." If you're counting, that's three names by age six. Upon marriage, you took on an "adult name." Later in life, you'd also have a formal nickname. If you were an artist, you'd have an "art name," a pseudonym. And if you were part of the aristocracy, you'd be given another name after death. The posthumous name would reflect your reputation, either a way of praising you or a reminder to all that your life didn't amount to shit.

My father's given name was On Wah. *Wah* had a generic meaning: "relating to China," but *On* meant "peaceful," "safe," "a harbor." Combined, his name could be interpreted as Peaceful China or Peaceful Chinese.

Though the Lam family poem was gone, my Tai Mah remembered bits of it, at least enough to tell my father that the character for his generation was *Bong*, nation. Bah Ba decided to combine this with *Keuhng*, strong, for his "adult name": Bong Keuhng. Literally, it means "strong nation." Applied to a person, the name could be read as "Strong as a Nation." Sounded more kickass than Peaceful Chinese.

Though *Keuhng* means "strong," under its entry in the dictionary, the character that my father had chosen for himself, also has several additional meanings when combined with other characters, including: "bandit," "kidnap," "unyielding," "rape."

PALIMPSESTS

The use of palimpsests was common during the Middle Ages. Parchment, the standard writing material of the time, would be recycled by using milk, oat bran, and pumice to rub and wash away its text. For Christians, this was also an excuse to efface pagan manuscripts, though faint traces of the original writing remained, hidden underneath scriptures.

Centuries later, modern scholars would use ultraviolet light to uncover the lost text, words that had refused to be destroyed.

GRAFF

I never left the house without a marker tucked in the waistband of my jeans. It might've been a marker with an aluminum barrel or one that looked like a super-sized crayon or one that was shaped like a deodorant stick, its tip as wide as a fist.

We'd hop on the city bus and tear off the advertisements that ran above the windows. Blank panels were revealed. We'd tag there, monikers we chose ourselves: LAKE, STEAM, SKY, FUSE, DRUM. Our graffiti names carried a dignity that our birth names, names chosen for us, lacked.

SOUTH BRONX

KRS-One—his emcee name originally his graffiti name—launched his rap career with the song "South Bronx," an attack on MC Shan for his song "The Bridge." Many viewed Shan's song as a claim that his own Queensbridge projects were the birthplace of hip-hop, not the South Bronx, which had been universally credited.

"South Bronx" in many ways resembles Shan's song. The chorus on Shan's song is his neighborhood repeated several times. KRS borrows this idea for his refrain. Shan's second verse describes a park jam from back in the day, naming some of the hip-hop OGs around his way. KRS adopts the same template for his second verse. If you had listened to Shan's song several times before hearing "South Bronx," you'd hear an echo of Shan in KRS's raps. Heard this way, KRS's raps on "South Bronx" are even more vicious, evoking MC Shan only to crush him.

WRITING CREWS

The first tagging crew I joined was PE, Public Enemy, named after the rap group. I'd imagined kids donned in berets and paramilitary uniforms, my generation's Black Panthers, but the leader of PE turned out to be a short white boy. Only a month after I joined, the crew died. Most crews never made it past a year. Not due to infighting or a power struggle. Motherfuckers just got tired of their crew name, bored of having to write the same letters next to their tag.

The leader of PE started another crew, TFB, Taking Frisco Back. It was rebranding. Most of the members in PE wound up in TFB. The ones who didn't had quit writing. It was a revolving-door community. New writers were always being birthed.

Ten months later, TFB faded away, and the core members started KSF, Kings of San Francisco. I was one of the five founding members, though I could only trace our roots back two tagging generations. We were writers who didn't record our past.

PAPER SONS

One in three Chinese Americans are using a falsified last name, though they may not even know it. Their ancestors, during the first half of the twentieth century, came here "illegally," but that term's misleading, suggesting an immoral ethos, when it was the law itself that was immoral. The Chinese Exclusion Act—the name says it all, the first and only time the United States explicitly banned a group based on their race. This law also blocked "legal" emigrants from China from becoming naturalized citizens, yet "illegal" emigrants from Europe were offered a pathway to citizenship. For these white undocumented immigrants, we were willing to grant amnesty, their past transgressions forgotten. Citizenship could be extended or withheld, but this choice had nothing to do with notions of legal or illegal; it had everything to do with affirming whiteness.

Like undocumented immigrants today who can only live and work in the United States by acquiring fake papers, many of the Chinese immigrants who arrived in the first half of the twentieth century also had fraudulent papers. When the 1906 earthquake and fire destroyed city records in San Francisco, Chinese living here capitalized. Many of them lied, claiming they were citizens who had lost their birth certificates in the flames. It couldn't be disproved. Now that they were citizens, they could bring over their children— an exception to the Chinese Exclusion Act—but why stop there? For a large sum, they'd pretend to be the father of someone unrelated to them in China, signing affidavits testifying to this. Paper sons, or in rarer cases, paper daughters, would ditch their family name and adopt the surname of the sponsoring "father." The lie of the paper children would be handed down to their offspring.

The deception, however, didn't guarantee entry into the country for paper children, only arrival at Angel Island, not far from Alcatraz. Known as the "Ellis Island of the West," Angel Island in reality was more of a prison: armed guards, a tall fence with barbwire. Chinese would be detained for days, months, sometimes a couple of years. Their somber stories are told through the poems they carved into the wooden walls of their barracks, rooms crammed with triple-decker bunk beds for a hundred men. One poem reads:

蛟龍失水螻蟻欺   *The dragon out of water is humiliated by ants;*
猛虎遭囚小兒戲   *The fierce tiger who is caged is baited by a child.*
被困安敢與爭雄   *As long as I am imprisoned, how can I dare*
                 strive for supremacy?
得勢復仇定有期   *An advantageous position for revenge will surely*
                 come one day.

To determine if detainees were indeed the children of the supposed father, immigration officials would interrogate them. They'd ask questions about their village, their family, the physical layout of their home, how many steps from their home to the orchard, tricky questions meant to trip up the detainee. Based on their answers, they'd either be allowed to immigrate or they'd be deported. Officials would compare the answers of the detainees with the answers they'd receive from the supposed father—a high stakes father-son version of *The Newlywed Game*. But the game was rigged. The imposter children had secretly been given hundreds of pages describing their supposed family, a book-length cheat sheet.

A small number of detainees were actually the real children of fathers in America, but would their answers to questions about their homeland be the same as their fathers'? Their dads hadn't been back in years, sometimes decades. Things had changed, especially in a country engulfed in war. During the years of Angel Island's operation as an immigration station, the Communists and Nation-alists were waging a civil war, and in the middle of that, the Japa-nese invaded. Poh Poh, my grandmother, had her village thrown into chaos. When she heard the gunshots, she grabbed her younger brother and ducked into the fields. As they hid, she had to keep her hand over her brother's mouth, fearful that the Japanese soldiers could hear the muffled screams.

Too much was at stake. I suspect the real children of fathers were also given a study book to prepare for their interrogation. Answering the official honestly wasn't the goal; answering the same as their father was. Even sons and daughters by blood played a game of pretend, trying to outtrick the trickster. Every Chinese making it through Angel Island was escaping war in their homeland, but for the actual children of fathers in America, entry into the US meant not just escape, but a reunion, an end to the years living without their fathers who they might've been meeting for the first time as adults. They'd uncover what kind of men their fathers actually were.

ROOTS

The Angel Island poem was translated by Genny Lim and Him Mark Lai. Him Mark was known as the father of Chinese Ameri-can history, a self-taught scholar who the FBI kept tabs on during the McCarthy era. His father was a paper son, among the first ship-load of immigrants detained at Angel Island, Lai a paper name, but Him Mark's father also managed to hide the family's true name as the middle name of his children; *Maak* became Mark.

I met Him Mark through my participation in a summer pro-gram he co-founded, In Search of Roots. The program took ten Chinese Americans back to their family's ancestral village. As part of our preparation for the trip, we met as a group on Saturday mornings, and one Saturday Him Mark stopped by and gave each of us a packet containing background info on our villages, research he'd compiled and translated.

When we arrived in the villages, folks would ask what we were doing there. Many of us spoke poor Chinese, so all we could offer was the name tags hanging around our necks. It displayed our Chinese names and our purpose: 尋根, In Search of Roots.

I journeyed to my mother's village in the Pearl River Delta region of Guangdong Province, Bah Ba's village too far for the program. I met my grandfather's older sister, my Goo Poh. I was filming her on a camcorder, but she didn't realize what the device was doing until I flipped the screen so she could see herself. She lived alone in a small house made of bricks. She had one daughter but hadn't seen her in years. The daughter knew she was adopted and no longer felt an obligation to Goo Poh. "Tell my brother to come see me," Goo Poh said. "I'm an old woman."

I paid respects to my mother's grandfather, my Tai Gung. He was kept in a mausoleum. Originally, he'd been buried behind the village, where family members could go and pay respect by burning sheets of paper, ghost money. Tai Gung's body, however, had been excavated to make room for the landscaped garden of a new housing development. The economy, I was told, was booming. On top of where Tai Gung's body had been buried was now a manicured bush.

GHOST YARD

We were the only ones in the Ghost Yard that night. No security guards. Just us and a fleet of dilapidated city buses. I stepped inside one, marker in hand. The scene was apocalyptic: holes in the floor, windows smashed, a seat uprooted lying sideways as if the Hulk had thrown it in a tantrum.

We found lead pipes and swung them at windshields, cracking them. We climbed onto the roofs of buses, hollering at the moon: "Errrrrayyyyyy!"

With only the moonlight, we could barely see what we'd tag, though I could feel the tip of my marker against the surface of the bus, wiping away layers of dirt and dust. All around my tag were faded names, names we didn't bother to read in the dark—our graffiti forebears.

One day, we too would be unread.

ERASED

We introduced ourselves to another writer by asking, "What do you write?" Though we understood our writing had no future, we knew nothing as sweet as mobbing deep, going to work on a bus with the urgency of a pit stop crew, filling the inside of the bus with our tags, as if it were an autograph page of a yearbook—rocking it. The only thing better was seeing the same bus again, our names floating by, more points on the scoreboard. If the bus was stopped at a light, we'd marvel at our work from the sidewalk, sometimes running across the street just to get a peek. A moment had been captured, marking a particular occasion, an opening for a story: Oh, that was when—

How long a bus would run in its current graffitied state was unpredictable. Some tags lasted months. Others half a day. The more we crushed a bus with our tags, the more likely the cleanup crew at the bus yards would take notice and buff away our tags sooner rather than later. Though none of us wanted to see our names erased, we relied on buses to get buffed. Without the removal of prior graffiti, we'd have no space to tag. To write was to accept your own erasure.

LAMSKINO

I retired from graffiti the summer before my senior year of high school. I sensed the ride was nearing the end and began to keep a journal. The first entry: *Aug. 8—Wood got sprayed w/ mace by clown.*

It was a literal clown, makeup and all. He was sitting near the front of the bus. Hollywood had just tagged his name on the window that day, and before I had the chance to do the same, the clown said, "I saw that!" He stomped toward us with a painted grin. Hollywood stood up to confront him, and the guy pulled out a small device, which at first I assumed was some kind of clown gadget, like a squirting flower, until he sprayed Wood in the face with a mist of mace. He pointed the can at me. "You want some, you punk?" Some of the initial shot had somehow reached me. My eyes began to burn. I grabbed Wood, got us off the bus, and we staggered into a sporting goods store. Fortunately, the manager, a Black guy, let us use their employees-only bathroom. We told him the story, and he gave us his card. Said he could get us jobs, but neither of us wound up calling.

The entries in the journal only last for nine days, taking up just a page and a half of a small notebook. I included a crew meeting, a fight at a park, a truce struck on the bus, two all-nighters I pulled, one tagging up a bus yard. My final entry in the journal had nothing to do with writing. It was about school, senior pictures, me in a rented tuxedo. The rest of the book is blank.

Retirement came early for taggers. Seventeen seemed to be the cutoff, a year after you were eligible for a driver's license, a year before you'd be tried as an adult. I knew hundreds of writers, bus-hopping fanatics, but only one over seventeen who was still active.

The next time I'd carry around a marker, they were for dry-erase boards. I was a first-year teacher at a school designed for kids on probation. My new monikers were: Lamborghini, Lambambino, Laminator. My favorite: Lamskino. The student who gave me this name explained from the back row, "Lam is your slave name, Lamskino is your hip-hop name."

A REVERSAL

I'm still a writer, but I labor over words now, not letters, sentences, not tags. Maybe I became a literary writer, a memoirist, for the same reason I became a graffiti writer: to be remembered. A graffiti writer, through their tag, screams to the public, "I will not be forgotten!" A literary writer, though not as pushy about it, says the same through their stories.

As a memoirist, I seek ways to reassemble the past. I composed my own generation poem, combining characters from the names of my relatives. Mine is a reverse generation poem, not constructed to name but from names. It contains blood from both sides of my family, women and men. No hierarchy exists, the characters and generations jumbled. Twenty characters in all, following the form of the Mao family poem, a quatrain comprised of two couplets, each line five characters. I allow myself to cheat once. I don't use the character 甥, *Saang,* from my name, too hard to fit "nephew" into the poem. I break that character in half, only using the radical 生, "to be born." Since it's also pronounced *Saang,* a homonym, read aloud, my character can still be heard in the last syllable of the verse.

玉鳳英能曼　A jade phoenix has superior grace.

燕子瑞安靜　A swallow carries luck and peace.

雪約易培誠　Wipe the contract clean, replace, and foster truth.

明天茵麗生　Tomorrow, radiant flowers will bloom.

* * * * * *

CHAPTER 5

LEFT BEHIND

THE GOALIE

After my father moved to Minnesota, he still thought of himself as part of the family, the head of our household in fact. My mom thought of herself as a single parent, left to raise three kids on her own. If you were to ask my father, he'd scoff at the notion that my mom had been a single parent. "I was the one working six days a week," he might say. "Where do you think the money came from?" According to the forms they'd fill out each year for the San Francisco Housing Authority, Bah Ba was right, my mother was not a single parent, by her own admission. But this was on paper. Day-to-day, she *was* a single parent, thrown into a game where sitting out the next play wasn't an option. Didn't have the luxury of a sub. And forget about double-teaming. She was a lone goalie on a vast field, the last line of defense.

LEFT-BEHIND SYNDROME

One in five children in China has a migrant parent. In a survey of these parents, eighty percent said they sought jobs in the city to improve life for themselves and their children, yet forty percent understood their migration would also negatively impact their children who they'd left in the countryside.

Children of migrant parents were also surveyed. Living in rural villages, a third said they talk to their parents on the phone once a month, and of this number, half of them said their conversations last for less than three minutes. One girl, caught by her grandparents slashing her wrists, wrote in a letter, "if I hurt my hands, my mother will come home." Others have the opposite reaction. An eight-year-old boy claims, "I used to miss my parents, but not anymore." This same village boy also believes he's going to marry his lamb. Another girl writes in her diary: "What's the big deal of having no mother anyway? I can grow up without a mom." These kids suffer from what has been dubbed "left-behind children syndrome," higher rates of psychological issues and criminal behavior.

THIEF

Before I was a graffiti writer, I was a thief. Jim was my mentor. He relied on guile, stereotypes, and insincerity. He'd get to know the workers at stores, their work schedule, what they were studying in college, if they were in a relationship, if they had kids. Jim had these large round eyes that made his bullshit believable. He'd ask them to bring down a jersey that hung on a rack high above, or maybe he'd have them search for a different size in the back room, and then we'd make our move. We'd stuff the hats in our jackets at the same time, on Jim's word.

Sometimes it would be me, Jim, and another couple of guys from our neighborhood, but when Jim wanted to hit a new store, where we didn't know the salesclerks, he'd push for us to ditch the others, for us to be a duo. Store clerks saw me and him, the Asian dudes, as innocent, harmless, and these same clerks would've been on red alert if we had brought our Black homies. It seemed wrong to deceive our friends—we'd make up excuses of where we were going—but I couldn't argue with Jim's logic or the results. I'd wind up stealing over two hundred hats. Kids would place orders with me, what team, what color, the style. It was more efficient than the other way around, stealing them randomly, then acting like a salesman. I went to sleep with a wad of bills in a shoebox underneath my bed. Never had to ask my mom for money anymore.

The day Jim and I got caught at Marshalls, or rather, the day I got caught, the T-shirts we'd stolen weren't for us but 'Dullah's uncle. He hadn't offered us much, ten bucks for three, but he'd taken us to see *Boyz n the Hood,* so we gave him a discount.

We rode the escalator up and left Marshalls with the shirts in our possession, mine tucked in my waistband. I started thinking about the drumsticks at Woolworths across the street. We met the downtown crowd and followed the flow of pedestrians. Jim took out a plastic bag and dumped the two shirts he'd stolen into it. He passed the bag to me. I started to pull out the shirt in my waistband, but someone grabbed my arm. A man with slick black hair. He snatched the bag and examined the tags. "Got one, fellas," he said to a huddle of men.

Jim was gone.

They brought me back to Marshalls and escorted me towards the security room in the back. All these men wore leather jackets and chewed gum. As I passed the workers on the floor, Latino women, they glowered at me, which only made me think they were chumps. You don't own this store, I wanted to say. One of the men tugged me by the arm into the security room.

"Sit down," the man with slick hair said.

I sat and faced a console of small black and white monitors.

"We see everything," he said.

"You can't hide shit from us," a deep voice said from behind me. The owner of the voice was tall and lean. "Show him, Earl."

Earl played with the buttons and joysticks, making the cameras zoom in and out and rotate in every direction. I wasn't impressed. These gadgets hadn't caught me. It was dumb luck. I happened to pull out the shirt in front of them.

I must've made some smart-ass face because Earl took a loud step toward me and said, "All right tough guy, we'll see what your parents think."

He called my mother, getting the number from me by threatening to file charges if I didn't cooperate. I heard my mother on the phone yelling. "I'm glad I'm not you," Earl said.

The guys launched into a lecture, clichéd and rehearsed: See kid, in life you have to be smart. Don't let people manipulate you. It probably wasn't your idea, right? But you're the one paying for it.

I got the sense this was their favorite part of their job. They were talking over each other, fighting over who would get to make which point. Half an hour of this was hard to endure, tuning them out while maintaining a face of thoughtful reflection. There was no guarantee they wouldn't press charges.

My mother finally arrived with Willie. He was dressed in his driver uniform. My mom walked past me, said nothing, and introduced herself to the plainclothes security guards. She wore black boots and a rabbit fur jacket. I hated that thing. I was no animal rights activist; I just knew Willie bought it.

She used a soft-spoken tone with Earl like she was at a funeral reception, then she came back over to me and knocked me upside the head. "*Mouh yuhng a!*" she said, waving her finger at me as if she were casting a spell.

"You've really embarrassed your mother, Dickson," Willie said. I wanted to tell him to mind his own fucking business. He was an extra in the scene. It was unfair that I couldn't hate him more. He made my mother happy, and I was glad someone had that job.

"Mrs. Lam—" Earl said.

"Ms. Lee," my mom said.

"Ms. Lee, you're free to take him home."

"You want to keep him here longer? Yeah. I don't care."

We drove home in Willie's sports car hatchback. I had to squish into the passenger seat with my mother, my face almost pressed against the window. He played some Johnny Mathis and sang to my mom. He reached for her hand, but she pulled back and turned to me.

"Why you steal?"

"I needed money." This wasn't the entire truth. Sometimes I stole just to steal. Anything could be mine. The world became less cruel.

"If you want, just ask."

The next week she made me go to Macy's with her. Had me pick out a new pair of jeans. Said now I'd have no excuse to steal. I grabbed a pair of overalls. I knew my mom felt guilty, blaming our lack of money for my behavior, and I played along. Sometimes I saw my mother as just another adult to manipulate and deceive.

I wore the overalls on the first day back to school with both straps unbuckled. The front flap hung. I let the pants sag. I had no belt, and they were a size or two larger than necessary. There didn't seem to be any other way to wear them.

SQUEEZE

Around the corner from my house lived a guy named Levi. He was a dap-giving fanatic. He couldn't get through a sentence without exchanging pounds. For a few months we were road dogs, in-fuckin-separable. A couple of years later, he'd be out there hustling on the corner, but back then he hadn't started down that path. He was a tagger, a rookie, and I was showing him the ropes. I played the big brother, at least when it came to writing. I vouched for him to join TFB. Plus, he and I also formed our own crew, FMW, the name self-aggrandizing like all crew names: Frisco's Most Wanted. Claiming multiple crews simultaneously, juggling competing loyalties, was a part of the game.

I hooked Levi up with a legit marker, the tip as wide as a base-ball card, not that puny toy shit from Walgreens. I taught him how to hold a marker at the correct angle. His tag name was FBS, Full Blooded Samoan, but his mom was Filipino. I never saw his father.

Once, me and Levi were on a bus, making our way to the rear door, and he said, "Watch this." We were standing over three girls sitting side by side chatting in Chinese. Their hair wasn't styled in any memorable way. No gel or hairspray. I thought Levi might hit his name up before we got off, so I kept my eyes on the driver, but Levi tapped me on the arm. "I said, watch, blood."

He reached down, rammed his hand between the thighs of the middle girl, and squeezed the crotch of her acid-washed jeans. His fingers were a clamp. He jiggled her while she tried to jerk away.

The beep from the rear door signaled our stop. The green light above the exit lit up. Levi bulled past me. "C'mon," he said. I was still staring at the girl's crotch. She had meaty thighs. Her mom probably called her fat. *Feih Mui.* She wore raggedy sneakers.

"Motherfucker, you coming?" Levi was holding the door open for me.

I leapt off the bus, and the rear door swung closed.

I wasn't innocent. I used to grab women's asses and run. I learned from Jim. On crowded buses, he'd brush his hand over a girl's behind, then cup it, right before he ran off the bus. Once, we followed a woman wearing a business skirt up a staircase near a plaza. It was my turn. I squeezed her ass and took off down the stairwell before she could turn around. I felt comfortable enough doing this sort of thing that I once did it on a family trip to Lake Tahoe. At the buffet line of a restaurant, when I saw a woman in a wool dress lean over the buffet table to scoop pasta from a serv-ing tray, I grabbed her butt, and I didn't run. I don't know what I expected to happen, but what she did in response, I hadn't even considered, though it was the obvious reaction: she slapped me. Not my face but my shoulder. Her mouth was agape. Before she could form any words, I fled back to my table carrying an empty plate. I had a cousin get my food, and I spent the rest of the dinner with one hand shielding my face.

Levi watched the girl through the window as the bus pulled off. "You seen her face?" He leaned on my shoulder and laughed. He slapped palms with me, but I didn't slide my fingers to interlock mine with his. They were the same fingers that had clamped the girl.

"You know you wrong for that," I said, but my words weren't firm, chuckles mixed in between. I gave Levi a light shove off the curb, and he continued across the street to our projects, screaming "FMW." It was a two-man crew, just me and him, and we had no intentions of expanding.

GARBAGE

When my mother was out by herself, men constantly approached her. They'd say corny stuff like: "You're the most beautiful woman I've ever seen." I'm sure there were also vulgar comments, but she never repeated them to me. Sometimes a white guy would hand her a business card: "Modeling Agent." Some would follow her around in their cars. Once, my sister had to check a guy that was staring at our mom a little too intently. "You got a fucking staring problem?" she said.

Our mom, decked in red, walked the streets with Guinness-World-Record long hair, which everybody stared at, not just men, but women, kids, old folks. Some women would pay her compliments, ask her how long she'd been growing it out. Others would frown in disapproval, as though my mom was nothing but an attention whore. Either way, people scanning her hair up and down made me feel like these strangers were gawking at my mother naked.

When she'd throw out the garbage at night, after dinner and cleaning up the house, she'd have a homier look. Hair tied up in a bun. No makeup and heels, instead, an oversized T-shirt and flip-flops. Still, the trio of men (fathers?) who'd hang around the bench by the dumpster would catcall her. One night, I heard her getting into it with them, though I couldn't make out the words. If I had had more guts I would've stepped to one of them, made a scene, like knocking the brown paper bag from his hand, but I was fifteen and felt small. That's when I began to throw out the garbage myself.

CREEP

Ga Jeh was no fan of our mother's fashion sense, the leopard-skin leggings, the gold platform shoes. "With those boots," my sister once said, "Mom looks like a hooker." My sister wasn't into jewelry, didn't wear boots or the color red (the red Honda Civic—yep, my mom's choice), and if my sister wore any makeup, it was hardly noticeable. But you didn't need anything flashy to attract the gaze of a man. One time we were at a restaurant, and a Chinese guy at the table next to us kept staring at my sister's breasts like they were the grand prize. The guy was with his whole family. I leaned over to his table and told his son, who was around my age, in his twenties, "Hey, your dad's staring at my sister's breasts. Tell him to stop. It's creepy." I could've told his wife, but forcing his son to shame him promised a special kind of dishonor.

PRAYERS

Girls left behind in China are often targets of sexual violence. In Guangdong Province, home of my mother's ancestral village, ninety percent of sexual assault victims in some regions are girls who have been left behind. "Many of these tragedies might have been prevented had they been living with their parents," an NGO report claims.

For my sister, it was the opposite. Her father was her tragedy. Bah Ba's decision to leave might've been received by Ga Jeh as an answer to her prayers. She was the only one of us still attending church.

You lie in bed dreading that turn of the knob. You know he will enter but not when. When he does, you don't know what he will

do, when he will stop, if he will go further this time. You pretend
to be asleep, like you always do. You don't want to see him this way.
You don't want to see yourself this way. For you to open your eyes,
to face what is happening, would deny you your ability to deny.

Your mother returns the next day bearing a gift: a Disneyland
T-shirt. She shows you a photo taken at night of her and her pal
Mickey Mouse. You go in your room, shut the door, get on your
knees, recite the Lord's Prayer, and beg your Father for an end. One
day, He delivers. Bah Ba must move. Faith is restored.

I'm not religious. I don't believe in miracles. The way I see it, or
the way I'd like to see it, is that my father accepted the job in Minnesota to stop himself from turning that knob, that something was
operating inside Bah Ba, perhaps at a subconscious level, to remove
himself from that apartment. He was a boogeyman who caught a
glimpse of himself in the mirror.

Bah Ba would return every year, but his visits into my sister's
room stopped.

I can't credit my father though. His trips to Cali never coincided with my mother's vacations. She had to stick around for the
meeting with the housing authority—Bah Ba was never left alone
with us again. Whether my father was a changed man or a predator
thwarted by circumstances, I'll never know.

A set of overdue questions: Why do I attempt to reclaim some
small measure of humanity for my father? This was the man who
abused everyone in my family. Why is it, any nugget of informa-
tion, real or speculative, that I can uncover which complicates Bah
Ba, humanizes him, why do these discoveries (imaginations) make
me feel victorious? Why am I obsessed with reminding you that the
Devil was a fallen angel?

TRUST

I was sixteen and on punishment. I'd gotten arrested for having a
backpack full of spray cans on a bus, and just my luck, the next day,

my history teacher called my mother and told her he hadn't seen me in weeks. She showed up to the next class to check on me. I saw her through the little window of the class door. It was a new semester, and she didn't want the same old crap, like the time I stayed out till three in the morning while she had no idea where I was. That was the night I was at the Ghost Yard. While I was running around in the abandoned lot, my mother had gone up to Rob's apartment in search of me, pounding on their door, waking Rob and his mother up. Poor Rob had two moms badger him about my whereabouts, but he honestly had no idea where I was either. He'd retired from writing, was trying to clean up his act, wanted me to do the same, which only made it more difficult for me to put down my marker. I was tired of following in his footsteps.

When I finally got home that night, I went straight to the bathroom. I had ink all over my fingers. My mom was trying to chide me through the door. I told her I'd fallen asleep at a friend's house. I jumped in the shower. I used her shower brush to scrub off the ink from underneath my fingernails. When I turned off the shower, she was still yammering away.

Now, I was supposed to come home straight after school, but on this day, I came home two hours late. She got in my face about it. "Why can't you just trust me?" I said. "I told you I'll do better this semester."

"*Trust* you?" She made "trust" sound like the foulest word in English. She opened the front door. "Like to be outside so much, go out again. Don't have to come back. Get your own place. No rules."

I didn't look up from watching TV. If I said anything, my words would only fuel her anger.

"Maybe you need furniture for your new place," she said. "I'll help." She picked up a chair and hurled it into the courtyard. Rob happened to be walking by.

"You OK, Maggie?" he asked.

She shook her head like a pitcher shaking off the signs of their catcher. "Take my son," she said, waving him inside our house. "Please Robert. Sure. Sure."

It wasn't obvious to Rob that she was being sarcastic, or maybe it wasn't obvious to me that she wasn't. I pointed with my head for Rob to leave.

"You don't want to graduate," she said to me. "Why wait, you can be a bum now." My mom picked up another chair and heaved it outside, knocking against the chain-link fence of the garden.

Rob took a step back. "I think I heard my mom call." He turned and hurried upstairs.

Granny from next door—who my mother called Ms. Johnson—came over. Probably heard the noise. The walls were thin. She lived with her two daughters who also had daughters. "There ain't no need for all this," she said to my mom.

My mom said something to her, and Granny shot me a look. Next thing I knew my mother had her head on Granny's shoulder, and Granny was stroking her back.

THE KEY TO THE COMBINATION

In front of a boarded-up building on Haight and Fillmore, we were huddled in clusters, waiting for the two leaders of 3F to arrive. They were to decide whether or not SHIM would join the tagging crew. He was a goofy dude. He'd smile to himself and make animal noises, the sound perhaps of a dying hyena. It seemed 3F was lowering their standards, and that's why Hollywood had brought me here. "If they letting SHIM join," he'd said, "that loser, they gotta let you in."

Strolling by that night was 4-Tay. His hair, set in finger waves, cascaded down to his shoulders. I recognized him from his album cover. He stopped to give a pound to a couple of us, though I doubted they knew him personally. It felt too hit-and-run for that. Probably just a Fillmore show of love.

The smell of weed lingered in the air. Night had snuck up on us. The neon sign of a pizza shop had lit up. Headlights cruised by. None of the guys had said anything about me showing up unexpectedly with Hollywood to this meeting for 3F, Fresh Fillmoe Funk. If anybody was Fillmoe it was Hollywood. He tagged "Fillmoe" almost as often as his graffiti name, which actually wasn't Hollywood. That was his nickname. How he got that, or what his real name was, I didn't know. We'd only begun hanging out that summer. His graffiti name was SYMER, but no one called him by that. What the hell was a symer? Granted, plenty of guys chose tags for themselves that ended in "-er," many of which sounded nonsensical—SIZER, KRYMER, VESTER, but at least these were based on actual words. It was hard to take Wood seriously as a writer. His style was unrefined, the loop in his *R* always too low. But he was down to fight, and I don't mean if he was backed in a corner. The dude hunted for fools from rival turfs, though he was no bigger than me. He flaunted his set by wearing a custom-designed baseball hat, the kind hardcore cats from the Moe were rocking at the time—name and your turf airbrushed in bubble letters dotted with rhinestones.

My pager vibrated in my jean pocket. It was my mom. Probably wanted to complain about how I'd missed dinner. Or maybe she wanted to tell me she was staying at Willie's for the weekend and had left some pasta in the fridge. Staying at his house was a new thing, a compromise, her response to his cheating. His defense had been that he'd left his wife years ago for her, but she had yet to divorce my father. He needed more of a commitment. I told my mom not to fall for his crap. "Shifting the blame is the oldest trick in the book," I'd said. "I use it all the time."

I thought she'd really leave him. She'd tell us to pick up the phone for her, and if it was Willie, to say she was out. I was used to doing that with my father, so I had no problem lying to another guy who had hurt my mom. But eventually, my mother gave in, and it was back to only lying to one man for her.

A bus approached. I stuffed my pager back in my pocket.

All of us rushed to the curb, pushing each other aside for a better view. Wood's tag sailed by on the window of the bus. Black
smoke belched from the exhaust. "I stay running," Wood shouted,
as though he scored a goal. He had beady eyes and a rough-looking
face, wrinkles you wouldn't think a sixteen-year-old would have.

"Why *you* here?" TYMER, the co-leader of 3F, said to me. His
annoyance was so exaggerated I assumed he was playing around. I
hadn't noticed when he arrived, though he was one of the tallest in
our bunch. He wore a Rasta beanie and army fatigues.

"It's about time my boy RANK get in 3F," Hollywood said and
slapped my chest. I rocked back, the blow harder than was probably intended.

"That right?" TYMER said to me.

"Sure, why not?" I said.

"Motherfucker, do you want in or not?" TYMER said.

"Yeah, I'll hit up 3F."

TYMER pulled aside the other leader, SIKE, who twisted his
short dreads and nodded along. I thought I was in. Joining a crew
had always been this easy. No hoops or hurdles. We weren't gangs
on some blood-in-blood-out shit. If you were cool with the leader,
you were a shoo-in. And I didn't just know the leaders of 3F, I knew
all the members gathered this night.

LC, Lil' Cut, was like a little cousin. He was the youngest, a
scrawny twelve-year-old who was all business. He'd plan out the
buses he'd hit at the start of a day: the 43 to the 6 to the 7 to
the 71 to the N to the K back to the 43 for another lap. ROME
would show me his sketch book during history class. I studied his
tags. His letters had depth, vigor. The legs of his *M* slanted inward,
and sprouting upward from the foot of his *E* was a curved line, a
whip in motion. There was CLUE. We called him Black-C. The
first time I met him we were supposed to fight. He'd been crossing
my name out, so when I saw him at a bus stop, I stepped to him,
though if it weren't for all the damn people watching, I would've
ducked away. He was six foot and wore a puffy trench coat. Luckily,

he offered a truce. Said he'd just wanted to test me. See what I would do. From then on we were cool as shit.

These were the guys in my tagging circle. We'd bus-hop around the city, take a break at a hilly park, trudge up to a bench with a view of the city, and puff puff pass on a honey-coated blunt. We'd coordinate what we stole at Safeway. One person would get the bread, another the meat, another the cheese, another the sodas. We'd have a picnic at the bus stop. We were always in the same crews: PE, TFB, KSF, but 3F had seemed off-limits.

I didn't reside in the Fillmore, so how could I claim Fresh Fillmoe Funk? I couldn't even pronounce the neighborhood correctly, which is to say the way they did: Fillmoe. When I would try to say it, it came out "Fillmore," as if I had an English teacher stuck in my head. I'd resort to the monosyllabic version, the Moe. But more than living in the wrong neighborhood—I lived in North Beach, the housing project near our high school, which had to count for something—what made me most uncomfortable with asking to join 3F and simultaneously what made me most want to join, was that everyone I knew in it was Black.

I had a confusing relationship with Blackness. It nurtured me, and to a degree, raised me. The parents of my homies in North Beach were my second mothers and fathers. It wasn't uncommon for friends to say, "Dickson's Black." I'd hear this enough that at times I'd forget it wasn't true.

I'd refuse watermelon because I didn't want to play out a stereotype.

I existed in-between. A homeboy, in reference to other Chinese, would use the word "Chinamen" but immediately afterwards, say to me, "No offense, my nigga."

I'd never heard anyone state that 3F was intentionally or exclusively a Black tagging crew, but it sure seemed like it in a city where the majority of writers were white or Latino. If there was one thing I wanted to respect, it was Black unity. It was a year after the Rodney King verdict, and in the aftermath of the riots, I sought answers.

I tuned in to daytime talk shows. An audience member on *Oprah* called for revolution. Said we shouldn't fear the word. All it meant was change. Others clapped in support.

Flipping channels, I stopped on a Black-owned public access channel when I heard the word revolution again. It was Malcolm X giving a speech, a reenactment. Malcolm argued that Black folks were using the word revolution too loosely, that if they understood what it really meant, they'd think twice about using the word. Revolutions, he said, are bloody, based on land, not loving your enemy. He cited an article in *Life* magazine that he had read in prison. A nine-year-old girl in China is pictured aiming a gun at a man on his hands and knees, an Uncle Tom to the revolution—her father.

I became a Malcolm groupie, but I was an undercover groupie. I didn't wear an *X* hat or a shirt with an image of Malcolm. The only Malcolm X paraphernalia I had was a book cover. On the front of it was a quote from Malcolm arguing that history was the most important subject to study. I'd skip class after lunch to plow through history books at the main library, books that illuminated a neglected past, George G. M. James's *Stolen Legacy*.

Malcolm simplified my life. He gave me dos and don'ts. When a white girl showed interest, I'd ask myself, WWMD? I told my mother no more Spam. No more cans of Vienna sausage. No more steamed spare ribs. The pig was part rat, part cat, part dog. *Chi seen*, she decried. What kind of Chinese person doesn't eat pork? Who's telling you this garbage?

What Malcolm said that stuck with me the most was that my father was not my father. "Just 'cause you made them, that don't mean you're a father," he said. "Anybody can make a baby, but anybody can't take care of them."

Malcolm believed Black folks needed their own space, and I agreed. I had never pushed to join 3F. More than anything, I didn't want to come off like a wannabe or worse, be rejected as one. Honorary status was bestowed, not begged for.

In 1966, a year after Malcolm was assassinated, the Black Panthers were formed. One of the original members was Asian, a Japanese American, Richard Aoki, who supplied them with their first guns. You can find black-and-white photos of him from that era, dressed in shades and a beret. In one picture, a cop wearing a riot helmet has a baton in one hand and grips Richard's arm with the other, the guy much larger than Richard, who stood only five-six, but Richard isn't scared. He doesn't even look mad. He looks tough, seasoned. Though he's facing the cop, Richard's eyes are off to the side, perhaps focused on the other officer closing in or maybe something else at the protest. The cop is tugging him, and as a result Richard's legs are crossed, but somehow Richard maintains his balance and appears graceful, as though dancing with the cop. Perhaps the most striking image of Richard is him strutting around Sproul Plaza, hair slicked back, shades and a leather jacket, and in his hand, at his side, a two-by-four.

I was in college when I discovered Richard Aoki, thirty years after he joined the Panthers. An Asian American magazine featured a story on him. On the cover of that issue, one of the headlines read: "Black Panthers and Yellow Power." I tracked him down for an interview. I told Richard I was writing a research paper about him, and I was, but the paper was just an excuse to meet a Yellow Panther. He chose a donut shop for the interview. He wore cowboy boots and pronounced police "PO-lice." He said he was down with the Panthers from the jump. He'd grown up in West Oakland with Huey P. Newton and Bobby Seale, and they grew closer at Merritt College. They'd chop it up about politics over drinks. The year after Malcolm was assassinated, the three of them "sat down one night with a fifth of Scotch and hammered out the Ten-Point Program," the Panther manifesto.

In an interview on public radio, Richard recalls it was at the Panthers' first formal meeting that Huey asked him to join, to which Richard replied, "I know you two guys are crazy 'cause you got this program together, but are you blind as well? I'm not Black."

"That's not the issue, Richard," Huey says. "The struggle for freedom, justice, and equality transcends racial and ethnic barriers. As far as I'm concerned, you Black."

"Grab your .357," Bobby says, "we got work to do."

"To the park," TYMER announced. He lighted up a beedi and crossed in the middle of the block with SIKE.

"Come on, RANK." Hollywood nudged me.

SHIM flicked CLUE's ear and ran across the street, unconcerned that we hadn't received an answer.

Flattened cigarette butts were strewn about the sidewalk. A girl and two boys, all of them wearing spiked collars and leather jackets with an inordinate number of zippers, were smoking on the stoop of a house. We passed a bar, a tattoo parlor, and a small boutique. I called these Places for White People. That's probably why Lower Haight became our stomping grounds—neutral territory bordering Fillmore. Though Fillmore was one neighborhood, it was more accurate to call it a coalition. Members of 3F repped different turfs, usually tied to a housing complex: Banneker Homes, Thomas Paine, Freedom West. Claiming one Fillmore turf didn't gr ant you a pass to hang on the block of another Fillmore turf; the bond was tenuous.

We rounded the corner toward a cul-de-sac of Victorian homes. The entrance to Duboce Park sat at the end, wide steps breaking up a stone retaining wall. Past the steps an open patch of grass met us under a blue-black sky. The park was empty, as though it had been reserved for us.

"Time to slap box," SIKE said, ambling around the grass.

"If y'all want to get in the Tray," TYMER said, "you gotta know how to chucks 'em."

For 3F, writing took a backseat to throwing down. In an article about graffiti in San Francisco, dated the year of that summer, the author, a freelance journalist, who would later become an editor with *Wired* magazine, concludes, "3F is one of the most notorious tagging crews in the city, known by almost every graffiti writer as disrespectful of the art and violent." The article begins with an anecdote about four graffiti artists painting a mural inside a tunnel. They're confronted by three teenagers, who they believe might be from 3F. "How about you give us your paint," one of the teenagers demands. No fight ensues, but the graffiti artists leave, their mural incomplete. The anecdote sets up the main subject of the article—the tension between taggers and graffiti artists. The graff artists interviewed don't deride us for our lack of artistic talent. They don't call our tags scribbles. They saw us as part of their graffiti family, one with an established hierarchy based on artistic skill. Their beef: we didn't respect them. They'd spend hours, sometimes days, painting on a wall intricately designed figures, words with three dimensions, only to discover when they'd return that their work had been defaced by tags. "These kids have lost their roots," an OG graff artist says. Maybe we had. Not because we sullied their fresh murals. That was a minority of taggers. The rest of us were in awe of them. Graff artists were the better-looking sibling, the one with more talent. They made their way into galleries, books, forever photographed. The darlings of the family. We were the runaways. Several hundred strong. Duking it out for supremacy on the city bus, our home—a mobile battlefield. Most of us had never heard of the older graffiti artists mentioned in the article. We didn't write to connect to a past. We wrote to break from it.

"Let's get this shit over with," SIKE said, as though slap boxing would be a formality.

SHIM was up first. He and his opponent feinted and dodged each other's swipes, their match resembling the first round of a boxing fight. Though SHIM was silly, he played on the school basketball team, was athletic—rare for a tagger—but he wasn't landing any of his strikes. We booed, and I knew the same boos awaited me. The last time I slap boxed, I'd gotten smacked left and right. Wood had to call time-out to remind me to guard my face. In the distance, overlooking us on a hill was a three-prong antenna tower, layered red and white, its aircraft warning lights blinking, as if communicating with some celestial entity.

"Next!" TYMER said.

"Me and you, RANK," Hollywood said. He took off his rhine-stone-encrusted hat, which he had on sideways, and set it gently on a nearby bench.

I took off my hoodie and threw it across the same bench. I rubbed my hands for warmth. I emptied my pockets: keys, pager, and bus pass. On the back of the pass, I'd scribbled a bunch of numbers. Half belonged to 3F members. One belonged to a girl I'd spent hours talking to but had yet to meet. I also had Willie's number on there, unlabeled, the only number written in blue ink. I used it as little as possible.

I pulled out my marker from the waistband of my drawers. It was the size of a small remote control. I'd wrapped it in black electrical tape for a better grip. It was comforting how it pressed against my belly throughout the day, a constant reminder of who I was. At the bottom of its base, there was a recess exactly the length of two pennies. I'd fitted two snugly side by side, one minted in my birth year, the other, the current year.

Someone slapped me lightly on the crown of my head. "Keep your hands up, boy," Hollywood said. He stood in a southpaw stance and bobbed and weaved. The rest converged around us.

I went on the offensive, swinging away. I imagined his head was a basketball. I had quick hands on the court. Blocking shots and stripping the ball came easily. I landed a blow across Wood's cheek. He smiled, surprised, and backpedaled. I pressed forward, throwing jabs and crosses, scared he'd get closer.

CLUE jumped in front of Wood, handed someone his coat and pulled up his pants, but CLUE had no belt. His jeans dropped below his waist. He had a slim frame. His fists were up, elbows out.

I couldn't connect. He used his longer reach to keep me at bay, circling around me and snapping out jabs, but then he stumbled on the grass, and I was all over him.

"Oooh! Fucked him up," someone said.

"Let's see you do that shit against me," SIKE said.

"You gonna tae kwon do my ass," I said. I'd heard he won a martial arts tournament. I wanted to quit while I was ahead. I folded my hands on top of my head and tried to catch my breath.

TYMER and SIKE conferred again together. TYMER counted to three with his fingers, slow, as though to accentuate each number.

"We've been letting too many motherfuckers in," TYMER addressed the group, pacing back and forth with deliberate strides. "From now on, this is how you get in 3F: Pull a lick. Pull a runner. Fade on a blunt."

"Start with pulling a lick," SIKE said to me and SHIM.

The dramatic tension was reversed, the toughest task first. The other two would be easy. Pulling a runner was amateurish. Any idiot could grab something and bolt out of a store, and forking over cash to buy weed was no test, but the first challenge, robbing someone, wasn't my kind of thing. I didn't aspire to bully. I'd been on the receiving end enough to know better. That's what I told myself when I wanted to feel self-righteous, but this masked my fear of fighting. It wasn't the physical pain I feared the most. Bruises heal. It was the public nature of it, the potential of being humiliated, branded as a joke.

"All right," I said, "but me and SHIM get to pick the mark."

"This ain't a negotiation," TYMER said.

"Bus!" someone shouted. A streetcar had emerged from the Duboce Tunnel.

We raced across the park to the bus stop. SHIM broke ahead of the pack, and I hustled to catch up. The streetcar pulled alongside us and slowed to a stop. Its back door glided open. We jumped on and held the door, waving in the rest of the crew. They had one hand at the waistband of their jeans, holding up their sagging pants, as graceful as competitors in a three-legged race.

Hercules completed twelve tasks as penance. His sin—slaughtering his wife and kids, a result of his evil stepmother casting a spell of madness on him. When he snapped out of it, he became distraught, suicidal. The only path toward redemption, the oracle at Delphi advised him, was to serve his archenemy, King Eurytheus, who was also his cousin.

Many of the twelve labors Hercules was given sound heroic: capture the Erymanthian Boar, the Cretan Bull, the Golden Hind of Artemis. Slay the Nemean Lion, the Stymphalian Birds, the Lernaean Hydra. Other labors reduce the son of Zeus to a glorified thief: steal the Mares of Diomedes, the girdle of Hippolyta, the cattle of Geryon, the apples of Hesperides. The most humiliating labor: clean the Augean stables, shoveling the shit of over a thousand cattle, immortal cattle, their dung gigantic. His final and most difficult labor: enter the underworld and kidnap Cerberus.

I wrote about this in sixth grade, a report on Hercules, part of a packet of makeup work I had to complete. I'd caught the flu weeks into the start of middle school, staying home for an entire month. I'd lie on the couch during the day with a stuffy nose, rereading the story of Hercules during commercials of sitcom reruns, *Good Times, What's Happening!!, Diff'rent Strokes,* the protagonists of these shows, sons without their fathers. J.J. lost his in a car accident. Roger's dad was MIA so long that when he returned for a visit, he mistook Rerun for his son. Arnold lived with a father, but Mr. D didn't count to me. Not because he was white but because he was a replacement, the original elsewhere.

My mother brought me from doctor to doctor, herbalist to herbalist, all Chinese men. Their medicine had little effect on me, a kid whose father had just moved halfway across the country.

Hercules spent his mortal life apart from his father. His demise occurred when he was tricked into wearing a poisonous cloak. The poison ate through his skin to his bones. Before Hercules died, he built a funeral pyre and lay across it. He lit the flame and his body burned. Watching from Mount Olympus, Zeus, king of the gods, intervened. Thunder ripped the air, as if the sky itself were cracking open. A cloud formed below Hercules and carried him upwards to his father. His mortal half had perished, and he entered Olympus as a god, joining the ranks of the other immortals, the son and father finally united but only upon the son's death.

A flock of pigeons dawdled on Market Street, chests puffed out as if patrolling their grounds. They didn't scatter when we approached till SHIM charged at them. I could hear skateboards, their wheels rolling on the ground.

"If the white boy says anything stupid," Hollywood said, "bust his shit with the quickness." He threw a haymaker in the air.

Skateboarders lounged on the concrete steps that rimmed the brick plaza of the Embarcadero. They took baggy pants to another level—the potato-sack look. They wore their hats perfectly backwards, not the least off-centered, as though for aerodynamic reasons. One leapt off a platform, his board flipped underneath him, rider and board reuniting on the landing. No adult in sight. This was before the Giants ballpark was built by the waterfront, before tracks were laid behind the plaza for vintage trolleys, before the ferry building across the street with its clock tower received a facelift, the former baggage area transforming into an upscale marketplace, chic restaurants calling the renovated building home. Before all of that, the immediate vicinity around the Embarcadero Plaza would be abandoned at night, and the plaza belonged to skaters, an unintentional gift, their lair, their jungle gym.

"Which one?" SIKE asked.

"Don't give them one of the little ones," CLUE said.

"Nah," TYMER said, "can't make it that easy."

On the far side was a fountain, a monstrous sculpture, a family of cubic tentacles that bent and twisted around each other. Water would pour from the faces of the tentacles, square holes, but this night they were dry, the basin an empty pool.

Two skaters coasted towards us on their boards. The one with dreadlocks greeted TYMER. They knew one another. At first the guy tried to dissuade us, but when that didn't work he asked us not to pick on his friends. Instead, he offered up a group of skaters he said nobody gave a shit about.

"I bet one of them got some bread," Hollywood said. "RANK, SHIM—showtime."

We mobbed across the plaza. Skating ceased. I tightened my fists and recalled a scene from *Malcolm X* where a fellow inmate explains to Malcolm that the white man is the Devil. Malcolm flashes back to the white men he has known. All seem evil. My best friend in middle school, a white kid, would pull his eyes back to slant them at me. "Go back to your own neighborhood," a white cop had said. "Do that stuff there." A white bus driver had testified she saw me tagging on her bus. The red marker she swore she saw me passing to Rob was actually red Play-Doh. I hadn't written a thing and showed the judge photos of the bus. None of the graffiti was red, yet the white judge found me guilty. He'd made my mom pay a $271 fine and sentenced me to scrub buses.

I needed more fuel. I thought historically: slavery, genocide, rape.

"That one in the middle," TYMER said.

The skater he referred to sat slouched, smoking a cigarette, his board at his feet. He didn't appear to be the sharpest tool in the shed—the only skater in his group not to notice us marching toward them—but he was bigger than me, a little on the chubby side, someone it wouldn't be wise for me to wrestle. He didn't look up until SHIM and I stood over him. His friends inched away.

"What's up, man," he said innocently.

SHIM looked at me as though it were my turn to go. Everything I thought of saying sounded like something from *Menace II Society*.

SHIM patted the pockets of the skater's cargo pants, and I followed his lead.

"Hey, what are you doing?" The skater dropped his cigarette

and pushed my hand away, but not with much force, as though not wanting to antagonize me.

SHIM dug his hand deep into one of the pockets. I reached into another pocket and pulled out some change. I opened my palm: a nickel and a few pennies.

"That's all I got," he said. He took out his keys and a bus transfer and turned his pockets inside out. We fingered the lining of each pocket, but there was nothing, not even lint.

I tried to hand the coins to TYMER.

"Fuck I'm going to do with that?"

"He's got to have more," SHIM said. He patted down the skater's socks.

The guy apologized profusely.

I kicked his board to the side.

"This don't count," CLUE said, laughing. He shook his hand in the air, as though waving the whole thing off.

"Bust his shit, RANK," Wood said.

I had seconds to make a move. The window would close and boom—RANK's a sucka. Told you. But what if my swing missed? Or if it landed but weakly? Or if he fought back? My first punch had to be a knockout. I had to swing with anger, rage, revenge. Go bonkers.

I thought I smelled my father, but it was just the skater's cigarette burning on the ground. My father's story might've been complicated, but my version was simple. He'd abandoned us; he was an asshole. He'd slapped my mother to the floor, her hair tied up in a bun coming undone.

SHIM threw the first punch, his only punch, a cross that snapped the skater's head back. His pasty neck was exposed. I pounced on him. A barrage of punches to the head. His torso fell back onto the platform, and he rolled his head side to side to dodge my blows. He tried to kick me away, but it only made me pummel him harder. When he'd lift his head up, I'd hammer it back onto the platform, his head knocking on concrete. I couldn't let him leave. I wanted to draw blood, proof. I wanted my knuckles to scrap his soft tissue, his nose, his cheeks, his eye sockets, but he shielded his face with his forearms and then turned over face down. I pounded the back of his buzz-cut head. He was saying something, begging perhaps. He curled his body almost in a fetal position, still guarding his face with his arms. My fists couldn't penetrate, so I began striking his ear. His legs weren't flailing anymore; they jerked feebly.

I was pulled off, swallowed in a parade. Bodies heaped upon me. I was grabbed, shaken by the shoulder. I heard my name as a growl.

"That's my dog!" Wood said.

"Fucked that white boy up," TYMER slapped my hand.

"Good shit," SIKE smiled.

"I ain't never seen a Chinese dude that quick," CLUE said and swung viciously at the air. "You should see that dude's face," SHIM said.

One of the skater's friends checked on him. The skaters in the plaza were all standing, eyeing me, as though waiting for my next move.

"Time to bounce," I said. I kept my fists balled up as we swaggered across the plaza. I was so amped, it was hard to imagine the adrenaline leaving my body, where it would go.

I teach my students how to attack the king. I co-teach a course called Peaceful Warriors. We play chess. We box. We kick. We grapple. We roll. We write. We chase each other with paper knives in the school gym. "This is a real-world application," the guest instructor says. I say, "Everything is related." We bring in other guest instructors. One is nicknamed the Flying Lion. Another the Rhino. He trains us at a gym owned by The Pitbulls. We have the students the whole day for three weeks. We're an obstacle, their last hurdle before summer break.

I use a projector to show my high school students the "Opera Game," a chess match played by Paul Morphy in 1858 at an opera house in Paris. Morphy, a twenty-one-year-old sensation, hailing from New Orleans, had embarked to Europe to challenge their top players, to claim the title of world champion. Perhaps the opera was a break from his quest. His opponents, two aristocrats teaming up against him, the Duke of Brunswick and Count Isouard, were only casual players, albeit strong ones.

I push a button on my laptop, and the narrator of the chess program begins. He has John Madden-like enthusiasm. If a pawn promotes, he shouts "Touchdown!" If a king flees check, he yells, "Avoiding the sack!" The students laugh at the metaphors. They say it's silly, but they pay attention. I show them the CD case for the program. On the cover the narrator is dressed in a white shirt and tie, his sleeves rolled up.

"This guy's the first Black grandmaster," I say.

"What that mean?" a boy with cornrows named Junior asks.

"There's only a thousand grandmasters in the world."

"Only? Sounds like a lot."

"Can we play now?" the other students ask. One student's eyes fix on the crate crammed with rolled-up chessboards and zipped bags stuffed with plastic armies.

"Watch how Morphy develops his pieces," I say, "how they work together to ensnare the king." I fast forward the game to a position we reach shortly after Morphy sacrifices his knight in exchange for something intangible, momentum. I ask the students what move Morphy should make next. They're all wrong. Morphy castles queenside. His rook now covers the file adjacent to the enemy king. The Duke and Count line their rook up with Morphy's. A flurry of exchanges ensues.

"White to move," I say. "Morphy has mate in two."

The winning move is White sacrificing its queen, but the students miss this. They hoard what they have. Their minds won't consider a variation that begins with losing their strongest piece. But Morphy's sacrifice involves no risk. I show them that the checking queen cuts Black's king off in every direction. Black is forced to capture the queen with his knight, and White's rook, on the next move, barrels down the file to mate the king. This two-move combination might be classified as an amateur-level puzzle, but my students have difficulty seeing even one move ahead.

We attempt to make connections between chess and life. Develop a plan. Follow through. Persevere. Get back up. Survive. We don't discuss the dangers of devoting your life to attacking the king. Players have gone nuts. It's rare but an undeniable phenomenon. Bobby Fischer's the poster child. The biggest star in the history of chess, so big that to call him a star actually diminishes his impact. The Jewish kid from Brooklyn conquered Russia single-handedly, a tale from scripture. That's when he quit. Holed himself up somewhere, studying conspiracy theories. Next time we hear from him, he's got the beard of a bedraggled Santa and quotes *Mein Kampf.*

Vladimir Nabokov dedicated a novel to the mad-chess-player phenomenon, he himself a composer of chess problems, including ones requiring retrograde analysis, where the solver must work backwards to find how the present position was reached. In Nabokov's *The Defense*, Aleksandr Ivanovich Luzhin, based on an actual player, begins as a child prodigy and rises to become a contender for world champion, only to suffer a mental breakdown, eventually going insane. He enters a room and sees chess moves "in every corner." A champagne bottle is "a bucket with a gold-necked Pawn sticking out of it," a drummer is a chess knight, his head "arched, thick-maned." Luzhin lives in a chess puzzle and realizes that mating the king is impossible. A metaphor cannot be contained. He does believe, however, that he's found the solution, the "key to the combination." He leaps from his bathroom window and perishes.

Morphy's life has a similar arc, though less dramatic. When he returned to New Orleans, he quit chess, at least professionally, and became a recluse. He believed someone was trying to poison him and would only eat food prepared by his mother. He'd roam the streets having conversations with himself. After one of these walks, he suffered a stroke and was found dead in his bathtub, forty-seven years old. We remember his "Opera Game," the speed at which he attacks and crushes his opponent off the board, but most of Morphy's games weren't as thrilling. They're slow, methodical. Attacking the king is one side of the coin. Defending it is the other.

It can just as easily be the pressure to protect that drove Morphy, Fischer, and Luzhin mad—Nabokov's title pointing us in that direction—the paranoia cultivated by hours over the board imagining the ways your adversary might attempt to destroy your kingdom, the stress of escaping from the blitzkrieg of a foe, and then the endgame, where the major pieces have fallen, and your king is out in the open, exposed, the piece you had been shielding from action, now expected to lead the charge in the phase of the game where checks are fired at you at every turn, sending you scrambling for shelter behind a pawn.

When Luzhin entered the room with the bucket and drummer, he saw a knight and a pawn but no king. His majesty was elsewhere, tormenting Luzhin from afar.

They decided to waive the last task on the list, fading on a blunt. It was getting late, and there was only so long you can keep that many of us together, but I still had to pull a runner, a bottle of malt liquor the objective. Sharing a forty would end the night.

SHIM and I went into the liquor store alone. An Arab guy with a light beard sat behind a high counter. The store was small and cramped like we were inside this guy's trailer home. We opened the fridge and each grabbed a bottle of St. Ides. We slithered down the narrow aisle, and the cashier glared at us.

"Put that back!" He slammed his hand on the counter.

We darted out the door and down the block, past a crowd of dope fiends who cheered us on. The Arab guy was giving chase. He was big, a bear. "You son of a bitch!" he said. I ducked into an alley, forcing him to commit to one thief. He stayed on my tail, close enough I could hear him panting. I tucked the perspiring bottle of malt liquor under my arm like a football, and the bear began to recede in the dark, but his roar didn't fade. A cry sharp and desperate, it boomed through the alley, an echo I couldn't outrun.

FAKE IT TILL YOU MAKE IT

I'd just started at City, turned eighteen, when I learned Bah Ba's name was dropped from our lease. He'd still send checks, but it was official—he was no longer part of our household. Wouldn't have to fly back for those meetings with the housing authority, and he'd be spared from having to see us, and from us having to see him. It was a joint decision between him and my mother, perhaps mutually beneficial, though it wasn't clear who came up with the idea. Four years would pass before I'd see him again.

Ga Jeh was still going to City as well, finishing up her associate degree in the Hotel and Restaurant program. I'd stop over at the cafeteria, and she'd come out from the kitchen in her chef outfit and hook me up with lunch. I didn't know what she had planned after graduation, whether she'd be a cook or work in a hotel. All that seemed certain was that community college would be the end of her education. She was ready for a full-time job, enough money for her own place.

I had to get used to rolling solo bolo. Rob and most of my friends were a year younger, still trying to graduate high school. The friends I knew at City, we'd see each other around and stop to chat, but hanging out at a community college wasn't like high school. Nobody posted up in the hallways. People were in and out. They had jobs. I had two. One at a video store, the first time someone ever called me "Sir." The other was tutoring two elementary school kids. We'd read together at the library, easy money. Sometimes their grandpa—their moms and pops were out of the picture—had to work late, so I'd take the kids for pizza. Other times he'd work so late I'd take the two of them back home to Oakland on the BART, walking them to their house in the Fruitvale, past taquerias and prostitutes.

I got the tutoring job on the strength of my first report card at City, four As and a B. Maybe my turnaround had something to do with the collegiate atmosphere. Teachers weren't interested in controlling you. Didn't ask you to take off your hat, force you to spit out your gum, and no more senseless worksheets. Best of all, you didn't need permission to take a piss. And if you thought a teacher was lame, you could drop the class with no hassle. Not like in high school, where you had to persuade a counselor who'd give you some BS, talking about how in life you couldn't change your boss.

After that first report card, transferring to a big-time college was possible. Universities wouldn't factor my high school grades into admission, an offer to expunge the past.

My brother had quit City, and now he'd quit his job stocking shelves at Toys "R" Us. His new goal: become a millionaire. His path to riches—peddling water filters. Boxes of them sat neatly stacked in our room. The blue gadgets were also installed under our kitchen and bathroom sinks. They stood a foot tall, shaped like a torpedo head.

"Equinox is nothing like a pyramid scheme," my brother said. He didn't sound defensive about my accusation. Far from it, he acted like I'd lobbed him an alley-oop, an excuse to yap on about his company, how they made $200 million in revenue, how his friends were raking in six-digits, how I had to get in on the action. Quit college. It wasn't like I went to a real one anyhow. Quit working at a video store. Make some real dough.

We were in his beat-up Celica, driving back from San Jose, from a seminar starring his company's founder, Bill Gouldd. The guy had given himself an extra *d* based on the advice of a spiritual guru who had deemed his name to be "out of balance."

When this Bill character had appeared on the stage of the auditorium, the crowd went apeshit, hollering and hooting. Gave him a standing ovation before he even said a word. I might've been the only one not on their feet. Double D's face looked meaty, like he could've been a baseball catcher. He began pointing at audience members as if he was at a school rally. He wore two Rolexes, one on each wrist.

I tried not to listen too carefully to what the guy was saying, scared he was some sort of hypnotist. "Who believes they deserve to be happier?" he asked the crowd, and these fools shot their hands up with the quickness, practically leapt out of their seats with the enthusiasm of kindergarteners. Double D had them trained, Pavlovian-style. My brother was sitting on the edge of his seat ready for the next dumbass question.

I'd been suckered here, at least that's what I wanted my brother to think. He'd offered to pick me up from my girlfriend's apartment if I came with him to the Equinox meeting. She lived in the Tenderloin, overrun with addicts, and that night Goh Goh might've thought I was trying to avoid TL's pissy sidewalks, but that's not why I took him up on his offer. I wanted to see his operation, wanted him to attempt to recruit me. I was the type to open the door for Jehovah Witnesses. I liked the attention.

"You can be a manager," Goh Goh said on the way back home.

"Get your friends on board. Everybody needs water."

"When you start actually getting paid, I'll think about it."

My brother had spent weeks working for Equinox but had yet to turn a profit, though he was flying around the country for seminars that charged fees in the hundreds. He subscribed to magazines for the first time: *Men's Journal, Esquire, GQ.* When I asked him what was the point if he never bothered to read them, he explained, "It's not about reading them. It's about believing you are the kind of guy who would read them." During the seminar, I heard this attitude summed up in the Equinox expression: "Fake it till you make it."

My brother had an office, but he had to rent it from the company. Had to pay for the landline too. And to attain the title of manager, he had to fork over five grand. In return, he received a cut of the commissions earned by his recruits, kind of like a pimp. But in that sense, Goh Goh, who had himself been recruited, was also a hoe. The one at the top pimping them all was Double D.

Besides a smart aleck remark now and then, I didn't push my pyramid scheme theory on my brother. I told my sister, though. We'd scoff at our brother in private, but we were reluctant to discourage him. Our asshole brother was now Mr. Enthusiastic. He dressed in suits and ties, carried around a leather clipboard, smiling all the damn time, even when he was talking about the poisons in tap water. How could I be mad at my brother for smiling? The dude believed he was on the brink of a fortune. He promised he'd buy our mom her own house. That kind of positivity couldn't be all bad.

Boxes of products began to pile up in the hallway. Not just water filters, but other Equinox goodies including various bottles of pills, the labels of which all featured an image of Da Vinci's Vitruvian Man. Some pills were for sleeping. Others were diet pills. Then there were a few that seemed to have the same purpose: "Stress," "Balance," "Serenity." One box was filled with bottles of an herbal tonic, and the picture on the bottle was a goofy-looking dragon, the first cross-eyed one I'd ever seen. The name of the tonic, printed in chop-suey font: Emperor's Chi. I was surprised they didn't slap on the label some Chinese guy in a rice hat for the full Oriental effect.

Goh Goh had someone lined up to buy a bulk of these products, perhaps one of his recruits, but when the woman balked at the purchase, and he was unable to dump the products on anyone else, my brother finally accepted defeat and put down the clipboard. He tried to sleep away the ensuing months. Moped around in his pj's twenty-four seven.

I couldn't stop clowning my brother about his failure. The junk in the hallway made it impossible to forget. My mom was the only one to use anything from the boxes. She'd drink the Emperor's

Chi. Said we all should. She and my brother had in their own way patched things up, which is to say they (we) pretended like nothing had ever happened between them, that I had not called the cops on my brother for punching my mother. I saw the changes, though, at least in my mother. She didn't put her hands on Goh Goh anymore, not even for a hug.

The only time I remember Goh Goh leaving the house during that time was for me. I'd started taking kung fu classes way out in the avenues, not far from Ocean Beach, and since my brother wasn't doing shit, my mom would make him pick me up at night.

Martial arts wasn't something I would've done in high school. Neither was track, but my first semester at City, I tried out for it. Only lasted a few practices. The stair workouts on the bleachers kicked my ass. The sports I did play in high school were team sports, park and rec basketball teams. I was a benchwarmer, but I didn't care. It was good to be part of a winning team. Maybe that's why I'd never tried individual sports—I couldn't hide.

Kung fu was part of the makeover I was giving myself. I'd set goals: a black belt and a bachelor degree, things nobody in my immediate family had. I'd seen Bruce Lee movies, but that never made me want to learn kung fu. Probably the opposite. I didn't want to fit someone's stereotype.

It took the Wu-Tang Clan to turn me on to kung fu. The rap crew was from Staten Island but claimed Shaolin. I didn't get the metaphor, but it sounded like some deep shit. They'd sample kung fu flicks, Chinese guys getting philosophical: "The game of chess is like a sword fight. You must think first before you move." I'd dwell on these sampled lines like they were proverbs from my forefathers. I didn't consider that the original lines had been dubbed over in English by voice actors, most likely white guys, channeling their inner Confucius.

The sifu of my kung fu school didn't teach beginners, only his most trusted pupils. I'd have to put in years of training to be able to learn directly from him or fork over a hundred bucks for one of his special seminars. Everybody had a hustle.

Goh Goh would wait for me outside the kung fu studio with the Celica running. I'd jump in the car, slamming the door behind me. "Roll down the window," he'd say. "You stink." In the cup holder of his car, there'd be a plastic bottle filled with cigarette butts floating in dark liquid, a mixture of water and leftover coffee, his ashtray.

We'd head through the Presidio, a former military base that had been converted into a huge park. Empty roads, winding and dark. Goh Goh would put on his high beams. No oncoming cars, only trees lit up in front of us, a white light that tempted us to believe everything could be made visible.

BOSS

The crumbling of my brother's water filter empire coincided with my father opening up his own restaurant. Bah Ba had convinced his youngest brother to partner with him. All his brothers were businessmen, groomed by their father, my Yeh Yeh. One brother owned a motel in Montreal, one a restaurant in Toronto, another had run Yeh Yeh's shops in Hong Kong.

If Bah Ba hadn't succeeded like his brothers, he also hadn't succeeded like his sisters. Though they were told the family business could not be theirs—daughters were temporary Lams who'd one day marry into another family—Bah Ba's sisters were encouraged to pursue studies abroad. One in London, the others in Canada. My father, the oldest son of ten siblings, a year shy of fifty, had no college degree and owned no business, the only son who wasn't his own boss.

I learned about Bah Ba's siblings through constructing a family tree, with the help of my mother, an assignment for a cultural anthropology course. I used a pencil to draw circles and triangles, women and men who shared my blood, a ruler to make lines that connected one generation to the next.

Bah Ba bragged to my mom that "two thousand people" had applied for employment at his buffet-style restaurant, that a line of applicants stretched from his office to the parking lot, men and women awaiting my father's word.

To lure customers to his grand opening, Bah Ba devised a raffle. Every customer would automatically be entered. My father didn't play it safe with the prize. He gave away a brand new car, a Camry. Loyalty could be bought.

BOYS

My father's restaurant did not arrive as good news. It'd be awhile before he'd turn a profit. No more checks home. My mom circled job listings in the Chinese newspaper, one for a jewelry store in Chinatown, but Willie talked her out of it, worried she'd get harassed coming home at night. So with my sister living on her own, and my brother locking himself in his room, rent fell on me.

I had a new job, my first full-time gig. I bused tables at a fancy restaurant on the top floor of the downtown Nordstrom. My uniform was a pinstripe shirt, black khakis, a black apron, and a clip-on bowtie. My girlfriend hooked me up with the job. M worked at the same Nordstrom, in a department specializing in clothes for middle-age women. M and my sister were alike in that they were both naturals when it came to customer service. I didn't see how you could get so happy making small talk with strangers. Being a buser suited me. I'd pour customers water, place a plate of focaccia bread on their table, clean up after they were gone, and besides saying "You're welcome," I never had to say shit. Trying to connect with diners, that was the waiter's job. Busers were to remain silent. We were the help. It was my kind of job.

I was nineteen at the time, M was twenty-two and she also had a three-year-old daughter, A. We'd sleep together with her daughter between us. I'd hold A's hand as we trucked up the hill to their apartment. I'd play a game with her where I'd squat and walk around pretending my hands were tied behind my back, and only she could liberate me. A would wave her hand and proclaim, "You're free!" I'd rise in disbelief that my shackles had vanished. I'd pick her up, dig my face in her belly, and blow a raspberry.

When I first began talking to M, she had a boyfriend, but it was obvious their relationship was falling apart. If it wasn't, the weak game I spit at her wouldn't have worked, some version of what's-a-girl-like-you-doing-in-a-place-like-this. We were at Mickey D's. M had high cheekbones, and I threw in that she looked like Spinder-ella from Salt-n-Pepa. She wrote down her number but told me she had a boyfriend. I found out what kind of guy he was weeks later when she asked me, "If a boyfriend forces himself on his girlfriend, is that still rape?"

M had moved to Cali from DC looking for a new start. She left behind A's father who was now in prison, another case of Good Girl Falls for Bad Boy. M was a square bear. Didn't drink or smoke. Wouldn't even cuss. I liked that she was a grown woman. She wore business suits and had her own place, my sugar mamma. Paid for our meals. Broke me off when she cashed her checks. But what made me stay was how she made me feel. She'd tell me about her absent father, past asshole exes, how her grandfather had molested her. When I'd hear about the failings of men—this seemed an ines-capable part of life—somehow I'd feel responsible, as if I shared in the blame, as if these men were me. By listening to M and comfort-ing her, it was like I had found a way to redeem myself.

I began to consider the possibility that I might raise A as my own daughter, if things kept going the way they were. I was getting used to the provider role within my family. On top of the buser job, I was also a tutor at City. I was working fifty, sometimes sixty hours a week to pay the rent, also giving my mom money for our groceries. I was the man of the house, but I wasn't good at playing daddy. I'd weasel out of doing anything with A that a dad might do. Never took her to the park or pushed her on a swing. Wouldn't even take her to the movies. I was full of excuses: I had a paper to write. I was behind in my readings. My homie's going through a bad breakup. Next week.

I'd stall until A went back to DC. She'd stay there for months at a time, cared for by M's mom, some arrangement they had. M would get on me about my lack of interest in doing anything public with her daughter. Maybe it had to do with her skin color.

A was several shades lighter than M, and when people would see the three of us together, some would think, at least at first glance, that A might be my daughter. Women would smile at me as if I'd done something noble for racial harmony. Or maybe it was the rare sight of a teenage dad handling his business. The thought of this made me feel like a fraud. I wasn't up for fatherhood. My biggest fear in life was turning out like my old man, a cold-hearted and unloved father. The only sure way to avoid that—don't become a dad.

Yet, I kept getting M pregnant. Abortion. Miscarriage. Abortion.

She told me about the first abortion at Wendy's. I was in the middle of eating a cheeseburger. "I wasn't planning on telling you," she said, "but now that it's done, I thought you should know."

I put the burger down. I had ketchup on my fingers. We were sitting in a nook, empty except for us. "You don't keep something like that secret."

"That's why I'm telling you."

"I should've had a say."

"I knew what you would've said."

"That's not the point."

"I was trying to be discreet."

"Then you should've kept it to yourself."

The next time she did. I visited her in the ER. She made up some excuse for why she was there. I wouldn't discover for another year that she'd had a miscarriage. I acted mad that she'd hidden another pregnancy, but truth be told, I was relieved I'd dodged another bullet.

The third pregnancy, she was upfront, asked me what I wanted to do. I was getting As at City, setting myself up to transfer to a university. I wasn't trying to tie myself down. Plus, what the hell did I know about commitment? I was cheating on M every chance I got.

On the weekends, me and Rob—himself a recent father—would roam the malls for girls. My favorite way to get numbers was to approach a girl at work. They were required to talk to you. Hooking up with other women always sounded better than spending time with M. All she'd want to talk about was what should happen with our unborn child.

"Whatever you decide," I'd say, "I'll support you." It was another way of saying, "You figure it out."

Sometimes, I'd put the phone down while she was talking. When I'd come back to the phone she'd still be yapping to herself. Then finally, I'd have a call on the other line. I'd tell M I had to go, it was for my mom, but it was really another chick, a girl who sang me love songs.

M entered her second trimester, still undecided.

On a visit to DC to get A, M had the abortion. I wasn't sure why there instead of here. Maybe she knew having it done here was doubling down on the hurt. I'd worm my way out of taking her to the clinic.

We would manage to stay together for another year until we broke up a month after I received my acceptance letter from UC Berkeley.

The night of the operation, M called me and told me we would've had twins, a pair of boys.

If M had kept the twins, they would've been two years old when I graduated Berkeley. I might've carried them across the stage as I received my diploma.

They would've been six when I became a founding teacher at June Jordan School for Equity.

They would've been eight when I visited my father in Minnesota after Javon's death. I might've brought them to see Bah Ba, their grandfather. This is the way I'd remember the twins, each year another birthday lost.

LOST GENERATION

The act that Mao is perhaps most vilified for is the Cultural Revolution. If we were to only examine his life up until the first few years of his rule, when Mao was in his fifties, most scholars would accept Mao as a savior of China. He unified a nation that had been engulfed in a civil war. He fended off the invasion of the Japanese by combining forces with his rivals, the Nationalists. His early reforms transformed China from a semi-feudal society to a modern nation, a country to be reckoned with, practically overnight. But characters in history are judged by the totality of their deeds.

Mao launched the Cultural Revolution to target the very party that he'd helped birth. He'd been a founding delegate at the first official meeting of the Chinese Communist Party. Now, at seventy-two, he was no longer the top dog, forced to relinquish his position as the chairman of the country, but he wasn't ready to pass on his revolutionary torch. Not to these dudes. "These days," Mao said, "a Party branch secretary can be bribed with a few packs of cigarettes." Party officials had taken the place of landlords as the country's new ruling class, but Mao stopped short of calling for a complete overthrow of the Party. Ninety-five percent of cadres, he said, could be redeemed. This revolution post-revolution was not going to be based on land or economics, but it would be a war of ideas, a cultural revolution that Mao said would "touch men's very souls." To wage this new revolution, he pinned his hopes on the youth.

Mao directed students at universities and high schools to "bombard the headquarters" of the Party. Students had been waiting for this their whole lives, an opportunity to be revolutionaries, too young to have participated in the communist revolution. Now it was their turn to save the nation. Teenagers dressed in green paramilitary outfits with a wide leather belt. The faded uniforms had belonged to their parents. They'd dusted them off and added a red armband inscribed with the characters: Red Guard.

It's easy to see these kids simply as victims of Mao. Dictator brainwashes youth. They carried around *Quotations from Chairman Mao Tse-Tung*, a small red book you could fit in a breast pocket. Parroting his words, they'd try to out-Mao each other. They wore badges displaying his image pinned right above their heart. Posters depicted Mao as the Red Sun. The cult of personality was in full effect, no doubt, but this tempting narrative masks the complexity of the Red Guards. These teenagers weren't mindless pawns. The resulting violence was largely spontaneous, unpredictable, and layered.

The Red Guards may have all quoted Mao's words like scriptures, but competing factions arose from the outset with fundamentally different interpretations, all claiming to be the true disciples of Mao. The most radical of the Red Guards were, ironically, the children of former landlords. They were stigmatized and discriminated against by the class backgrounds of their parents. A couplet that was often recited: "If the father is a hero, the son is a brave man; if the father is a reactionary, the son is a rotten egg." These radical Red Guards responded to the Cultural Revolution by calling for an attack on the Party. The political system had to be reconstituted to pave the way for yet another new China, where you wouldn't be judged by the deeds of your parents.

On the other end of the spectrum were the conservative Red Guards, children of Party cadres. They went to elite schools, ones that the children of landlords were banned from. These privileged kids weren't about to attack a system that benefitted them. Instead, their spin on Mao Zedong Thought was that the traitors to the revolution weren't Party cadres like their parents but members of the former ruling class—landlords, intellectuals, the bourgeoisie— plotting to recapture power. The conservative Red Guards attacked remnants of bourgeoisie culture, burning books and smashing art.

They ransacked homes searching for Confucian texts and record-
ings of Beethoven. They'd chase anyone down with long hair.
They'd pinned them to the ground, serve them with an ass kicking
and a haircut at the same time.

The two factions of Red Guards, known later as the Lost Generation, duked it out in city streets. The question that divided
them: Were we destined to repeat the mistakes of our parents, or
was it possible to transcend the failings of our forebears?

REACH!

My first week at Cal, I was reeled into a student organization,
REACH! Our organization's primary activities were of the typical
do-gooder variety, visits to high schools to encourage youth to apply
to college. We'd present info on higher education in the form of a
jeopardy game, tossing lychee candy at kids when they answered
correctly. They'd leave with Cal folders and pencils. The university
claimed us as their ambassadors, but we were also activists. We
marched, rallied, and camped out on Sproul Plaza. We participated
in civil disobedience, disrupting a speech by the Chancellor, a sit-in
outside the office of the mayor of Oakland.

We were the Asian Pacific Islander Recruitment and Retention
Center, known simply as REACH! The name was an acronym,
standing for something convoluted, really just an excuse to capital-
ize all of our letters, a "backronym." As if all caps weren't enough,
we insisted on an exclamation mark at the end of our name. We
feared being ignored. Asians were already the largest racial group
at Cal, but those weren't the kind of Asians we'd recruit, the ones
from affluent suburbs with mommies and daddies with professional backgrounds. We targeted underrepresented Asians, basically, Asians in the ghetto, mostly Southeast Asians: Cambodians,
Vietnamese, Hmong, Mien, and Lao, their families arriving in the
country as refugees. We'd ask counselors to send us kids from these
backgrounds who weren't even on track to graduate high school,

the fuckups, like me.

The heart and soul of REACH! was a pair of charismatic and dynamic sisters, Jidan and Danfeng. Although American-born, they'd only been given Chinese names, names couched in Maoist revolutionary ideals. The three of us would talk politics nonstop. I thought people like them only existed in history books. Jidan and Danfeng were both brilliant leaders but each in their own way. Jidan was process-orientated. Had the vibe of a counselor, warm and nurturing. Danfeng was the executive director, the one who made sure we got shit done, the general. Neither let me get away with any male bullshit.

When we were brainstorming how to get members out to a rally for affirmative action, I said, with all sincerity, "We gotta tell 'em, if y'all don't come, y'all some straight bitches."

Jidan pulled me aside. "Think of the b-word like the n-word."

Jidan and Danfeng's parents had also gone to UC Berkeley, student activists in the '60s. Inspired by the Black Power movement, the shift from "Negro" to "Black," their parents and their friends rejected "Oriental" and its exotic connotations. Fuck being a foreigner in your own country. They proclaimed they were Asian American. In fact, the term can be traced back to the Berkeley student group that Jidan and Danfeng's parents were members of, along with Richard Aoki, the Asian American Political Alliance (AAPA), the first organization to ever call itself "Asian American."

They united with the Afro-American Student Union, the Mexican-American Student Confederation, and the Native American Student Union to form the Third World Liberation Front, a coalition that demanded a radical multicultural education, and to that end, organized one of the longest student strikes in US history. The administration at Cal called in the police, the Alameda County Sheriff's Deputies, and the California Highway Patrol. Mace and tear gas were shot at students. More than a hundred and fifty were arrested. Ronald Reagan, the governor then, ordered the National Guard to squash the protests, but the heavy-handed approach backfired. The faculty union joined the strike, and two days later, the university conceded. The Ethnic Studies department was established. Thirty years later, I majored in Ethnic Studies.

Jidan and Danfeng's parents had raised them to fight for social justice. As kids, they didn't play Cowboys and Indians; they played Oppressors and Freedom Fighters. While I was watching Saturday morning cartoons, they were fighting apartheid, marching down Telegraph Avenue, trying to pressure the UC Regents to divest from South Africa.

These two sisters envisioned REACH! as our generation's AAPA. Claiming REACH! made me an heir to the struggle.

I had Bah Ba to thank for having time to volunteer with REACH! He was able to send checks again. I didn't have to work. I'd received enough in grants to cover tuition and spending money, and now Goh Goh was paying for the groceries at home. He'd finally come out of his funk and started working again, picking up a job as a delivery boy for a Chinese restaurant. I'd try to talk to Goh Goh about going back to school, but he'd just grunt in response, as though what I was saying was taboo, his little bro giving him life advice.

I'd volunteer with other student groups, including one that visited a group home, the youth referred there by their probation officers. We didn't try to mentor or teach the kids, at least in any traditional sense. More than anything we just listened, why they were there, what they regretted, what they didn't, the kind of men they wanted to be. The youth, Black and brown, looked more like the guys I'd hung with as a teenager than the kids REACH! served, but REACH! was the group I'd drop everything for.

It was a new feeling working with kids who saw themselves in me, who'd say, "Dang, you look like my cousin." It was a moment of recognition I couldn't turn away from.

BANDAGED FIGURES

I saw my father through the peephole. It had been four years since I last saw him. I knew he was coming, but none of us understood why. His name had been dropped from the lease. The trip wasn't required.

"Hey," I said, opening the door.

"Hi," Bah Ba said, almost inaudible. He looked smaller, or maybe it was that I'd grown. My father's hair, though still thick, had grayed, and his face had begun to sag unkindly. He grunted as he lugged his suitcase across the kitchen. It was the same suitcase he'd always had, hard-shell with clasps and a handle, an oversized briefcase. I could've given him a hand, but I didn't want to send mixed messages. Neither did my mom or brother. They barely acknowledged him as he walked by. It wasn't like in the past when we'd roll out the red carpet, but my brother and I would at least offer a half-assed hug. Now, even that gesture seemed juvenile, like leaving milk and cookies out for Santa.

Bah Ba came home as I was watching television in the kitchen, highlights from preseason football games. He grabbed a Budweiser from the fridge and sat down.

"49ers, *haih meih gum yaht waan?*" he asked.

"Yeah, they already showed them," I said. "Vikings are coming up though."

Bah Ba went into the living room—where there was a perfectly fine television, a larger one at that—but he left his beer can on the kitchen table. He'd been relegated to the pullout sofa. My mom kept her door locked, so there wouldn't be any funny business.

He returned with a nail clipper and a waste basket. His shoulders were slumped forward, body deflated. It was the first time I realized I could kick my dad's ass. Not that I had the urge to. His life had already done that for me. The restaurant he opened had flopped, and now he was back doing what he'd done damn near my whole life, sitting on a stool for hours, hunched over a table making dim sum, shrimp dumplings perhaps, using his fingers to join together edges of dough. The literal meaning of "dim sum": "touch the heart."

"That's my favorite quarterback," I said. Randall Cunningham was competing for a starting job with the Minnesota Vikings. In his twenties, he had thrilled Eagles fans with his scrambling ability, nicknamed Gumby for the way he'd contort his body to elude opponents. He'd take off near the end zone, leaping over defenders, soaring for a score. The acrobatic feats ended after he tore his ACL. Now Cunningham had come out of retirement and was attempting to reinvent himself as a pocket passer. That was the story told by the anchor delivering the highlights, but if you had asked Cunningham himself, he would've said his biggest transformation was off the field. During his time away from football, he'd been baptized.

"I hope they start him," Bah Ba said in Cantonese. He let out a belch and began to clip his toenails, eyes stuck on the TV. Next to him on the edge of the kitchen table was a large sculpture. Carved from soapstone, it was an abstract family of four, faceless figures connected to one another through their limbs. I'd traded my Jordan XII's for it. I'd spent the summer in Zimbabwe through a study abroad program, and I'd see folks everywhere hawking sculptures of families, but I wanted one that represented my family, a family of four that included just one parent. I was ready to give up my search when I finally found one. I threw in an extra thirty bucks to the sculptor to sweeten the deal. But I was dumb enough to pack it in my luggage instead of as a carry-on. It broke apart en route. I duct-taped it back together though, thinking the black tape would blend in with the dark stone color, but I wasn't fooling anyone. It was an eyesore, bandaged figures.

I thought about how awkward the conversation would be if Bah Ba were to ask what the story was behind the sculpture, how

I'd have to explain that I'd been in Africa through a summer program at school, that I was a student now at UC Berkeley, entering my senior year. He might act stunned, maybe he'd say something complimentary. Worse, I'd feel obligated to ask about his life.

I sat with him until the end of the football highlights. As I got up to leave, I slid him the plastic-wrapped remote.

The last night my father was in town, I waited up for him in the living room. It was a little past midnight. His flight was at dawn, and I thought someone should at least say bye. For all we knew, this could be his final visit. We'd acted like we wanted it to be, leaving the room when he'd enter.

Jerry Springer was on. A woman was in a soundproof room, waiting to reveal a secret to her boyfriend who was on stage. The guy was professing his love for his longtime girlfriend to the audience, cheesing so much you knew this was going to end badly.

I was lying on the sofa when Bah Ba came home. It was the same sofa he'd owned in Minnesota, a twill sectional. He'd shipped it to us when he sold his house.

"Dickson," Bah Ba said, "*meih fun gaau?*" He seemed overly concerned, as though I had a bedtime. It reminded me of his last visit. I was pouring boiling water into a bowl of Cup Noodles, and he said, "*Siu sum.*" Be careful? I was eighteen. Maybe he had difficulty grasping that my childhood was gone.

"I'm going to stay up for this show," I said.

The girlfriend had come onto the stage and was sitting next to her boyfriend, holding his hand.

Bah Ba sank into the bean bag. He wore a polo shirt tucked in, a pack of cigarettes in the breast pocket. The shirt fit loosely on his skinny frame.

"You ever watch this?" I asked.

"I have to wake up early for work," he said.

"Right."

The girlfriend confessed she had been born a man. The boyfriend shoved her away, almost knocking her off the chair. Then he stood up like he was going to sock her. The audience started cheering as the security guard leapt up to the stage, "Steve! Steve! Steve!"

"So stupid." Bah Ba pointed with his chin at the boyfriend duped by his lover. "How could he not know?" My father laughed.

I cringed at the irony. On top of one of the stereo floor speakers was a glass bottle in the shape of the Eiffel Tower. It was filled with slanted layers of sugar, each layer a different color, a souvenir from my mom's trip to Paris with Willie.

I didn't want to have to tell Bah Ba the truth. That was my mother's responsibility. The fact that my father still didn't know about Willie made him more pathetic, an aging man continuing to be deceived. I'd thought he deserved it, but the man on the bean bag was not the same man I knew. He was harmless.

I was a college student yapping about change. I'd tell kids how I'd gone from Ds in high school to UC Berkeley, how anything was possible for them—I was living proof—but when it came to my father, I could only conceive of him as a fucked-up dad.

"It's not too late," I said.

Bah Ba turned to me, and he somehow knew what I was trying to say. There was an openness in his expression, almost like that of a child.

"You haven't always been there," I said, "but you can still be our Bah Ba."

He placed his hand on my shoulder, his touch gentle. He nodded. "Yes, OK." His eyes glistened.

"I forgive you," I said and hugged him. We pulled away without looking at one another.

"*Fun gaau*," he said. "It's late."

"*Houh la*," I said. OK.

At the time, I thought this was my Hollywood ending. That's not to say my relationship with Bah Ba didn't change at all. He called when he returned to Minnesota. Asked specifically for me.

My mother wondered what the hell was going on. The day I graduated Berkeley, I phoned Bah Ba, wanted to share that moment with my father, and a week later, I received a card from him saying congratulations. He also included a check for a hundred bucks. But that was more or less the extent of our relationship for the next three years, until the birth of my brother's son. I knew how to complain about a relationship, but I didn't have a clue how to build one.

STAND-IN PARENTS

"Sharing the Blue Sky" was a national campaign in China launched to support left-behind children in four sectors:

1) daily care
2) education
3) safety
4) psychological and personal development

Volunteers, known as "stand-in parents," were recruited to aid in the campaign. Many of the stand-in parents were teachers who came from the same villages as the left-behind children.

WARDS

My first teaching job was back in San Francisco, at a school in Hunter's Point, on Third and Newcomb. It was a neighborhood on the other side of the city from where I'd grown up, but I wasn't unfamiliar with it. As a teenager, right up the street from that school, once, I was at my boy's girlfriend's house along with several others. We were playing cards and dominoes listening to Tony! Toni! Toné! but then the girl's mom came home. She wasn't supposed to have guys over. We ran upstairs to her bedroom as her mom was opening the door. The girl went to stall her mom, but before she left the room, she told us, "My mom don't play, y'all need to jump." We peeked out the bedroom window. We were on the second floor, and below us, there was nothing but concrete. I was going to hide in the closet, but one of us squeezed through the window and dangled from the ledge. He let go and landed awkwardly, stumbling onto the ground, but he was still in one piece, so when we heard the mom coming up the staircase, the rest of us jumped too. Besides having to crawl around my house, unable to walk for the next day, I was fine.

The grandfather of the two elementary kids that I'd tutored managed an apartment building also in the Point, deep in the Point, at the end of a road, and during one summer, I'd catch the bus out there to tutor. The grandfather worried about my safety, but I didn't have the heart yet to say bye to those two kids, a sister and a brother.

Paul Robeson and Diego Rivera Academy was the name of our school in the Point, two names for one school, which was reflective of the amount of services we crammed into that place. Founded only two years before I joined, Robeson Rivera was an intense program launched collaboratively between several agencies, created to serve youth specifically who were wards of the juvenile justice system. They were mostly violent offenders, a dream team of fuckups, each kicked out of their previous school.

To attend Robeson Rivera, students didn't just need to be on probation, they had to be experiencing severe issues in three of four areas:

1) family
2) school
3) delinquent behavior
4) substance abuse

We'd have less than ten kids each day in the entire school. My classroom may have looked like any other classroom, thirty desks, but I'd have a class of only three kids, three spread out amongst a sea of empty chairs, a reminder that others had moved on without them. They'd gotten so used to being further than arm's distance from the next kid that when I'd attempt to bring them closer to each other, to set the empty chairs aside, they'd freak out and invariably get into a scuffle with each another.

With so few students, we were given only a wing of a floor, in a building that we shared with a preschool. A nonprofit ran our school and worked to incorporate arts into the curriculum. Some dope stuff: dance, poetry, playwriting, deejaying. Down the hallway from my classroom were two mental health counselors. They'd have sessions with students individually and with their families, mostly comprised of single-parent households. The school was designed as a one-stop shop for students and their parents. Educators, counselors, a probation officer, and social worker pitching together to meet the needs of struggling youth. Sounded good in theory, which was why I was there, but isolating the students away from their peers at regular schools probably backfired. Our students saw the school as a prison. I'm not speaking metaphorically. At the entrance to the school, they had to swap their clothes for the school uniform, burgundy polos, and then they were patted down daily by their probation officer as part of a "check-in." Their PO had an office across the hallway from my classroom. He'd pee test them occasionally as required. If they violated their probation, he could take them straight to juvie. Placement at our school was part of their probation. Hard to have school spirit about a school like that.

We were lucky to get through a week without a student cussing us out. Our response: Take a time-out. There was a Time-out Room with nothing but pillows, a fluffy solitary confinement.

We were taught "nonviolent crisis intervention." We were given a workbook that included self-defense techniques, sketches of a teacher escaping the hold of a student: The One Hand Wrist Grab Release, The Two Hand Wrist Grab Release, The Hair Pull Release, The Front Choke Release, the Back Choke Release. And who could forget, The Bite Release: Staff should lean into the bite and use their fingers to create a vibrating motion above the upper lip of the student to get their jaw to open. The vibrating motion causes a parasympathetic response. Staff should use the minimum amount of force necessary to effect the release. Avoid pulling away from the bite. Move out of the way.

One student had stolen a teacher's car from the school parking lot and took it on a joy ride through the Sunnydale housing projects. During gym class, two students threw rubber balls at the PE teacher's head. It probably wasn't the first time, but on this particular day, the teacher snapped. Put each of the students into a choke hold, putting them to sleep. I'd thought of the teacher as a gentle guy, the kind of guy you'd peg as a vegan or a Buddhist. It was the same guy who, when I'd first started at the school, taught me about resiliency.

The teacher I'd replaced had left a vine plant in my classroom. It hadn't been watered over the summer, its vines yellowed, its soil dry. I put the plant on the top shelf of a lateral file cabinet and hid it behind a stack of books. One day, the gym teacher took a look at the plant and assured me it could be revived. "Plants are resilient," he said, "like humans." In a couple of weeks, the vine plant started growing again, its vines stretching along the cabinet.

I'm not sure I'd use the word resilient to describe my year at Robeson Rivera. That sounds self-flattering. The only thing I know is that I endured. I'd have nightmares about students, kicking my then-girlfriend in my sleep. I lost my usual appetite and fifteen pounds, not a good look for someone already thin like me.

I was in over my head. I'd done my student teaching at Urban Academy, a small alternative school in New York City where students of color graduated at high rates and went on to universities. Kids could leave their backpacks in the hallway unattended without fear of theft. Each class period was filled with heated discussions, the students engaging each other thoughtfully and with respect. The only classroom management I needed was writing down who raised their hand. I taught a class on hip-hop. I brought in guest speakers, Fable of the legendary Rock Steady Crew. He declared hip-hop was dead. The original culture had been bastardized. My teenage students thought he was acting like an old fogey, too stubborn to change with the times.

In my class on gentrification, we took field trips around the city. We met with an owner of the fourteen-story building in Harlem that Bill Clinton was set to move into. We stood in the space that would become Clinton's personal office. The Mountain Dew can that the former president had drunk from during a prior tour had been left untouched on the window sill. One of my students, a Harlem resident, charged the owner of the building, who had also grown up in Harlem, with being a sellout. Starbucks and Old Navy had just arrived on 125th Street, and rent was skyrocketing. Nothing would remain the same.

I'd thought I could bring the skills I'd learned at Urban back to the Bay, helping to create a school that not only engaged students in lively debates but would also send students of color to college in high numbers. The problem was I wasn't equipped with the right set of skills, at least for the students at Robeson Rivera.

At RR, I was just trying to get respect. My loose teaching style resulted in kids spending most of the class cracking jokes at each other and at me. One wrote a dis rap: "Goddamn, Mr. Lam / Breath smells like ham." This was Craig, the same student who had refused to participate in our class project where students were to read to the preschoolers in our building. As part of that project, I had students write letters to the preschoolers, introducing themselves. "I got no business acting like those kids should be listening to me," Craig said. "I know better than that. *You* should know better than that." A year later, after we both had left Robeson Rivera, Craig called me in the middle of the night. He might've been high. Sounded paranoid, like something in the room was about to pounce on him. Several years later, I'd bump into one of the mental health counselors from Robeson Rivera. He told me Craig was locked up. For what, I didn't ask. The counselor also updated me on another former student. He just had a baby, and he'd named the counselor the godfather.

That year at Robeson Rivera, I threw out my student-centered playbook and became a busy-work teacher, a worksheet for everything. Mindless activities worked like a charm. Nothing like asking a student to write down definitions to shut them up. It's what they were used to. But once I figured that out, I turned the worksheets into the baby steps of an essay, a thesis, topic sentences, and so on. When they combined the series of worksheets together, boom—they'd written an essay. It was the only way I could get them to do work, by tricking them.

In the spring, I heard of a teaching opportunity for the following school year in Oakland, at Dewey Academy, a second-chance school. They were cleaning house. A new principal and half the staff would be new. The one overseeing the hiring was the Director of Alternative Education, and not only had she been a principal in New York at a school similar to Urban, but she had in fact student-taught at Urban. Her vision of education reform sounded like mine.

I'd taken her job offer, but I wasn't psyched about informing the students at Robeson Rivera that I was leaving, quitting on them. Fortunately for me, unfortunately for the school, the board of the nonprofit decided to pull out in its capacity as administrator of the young school. The collaborative fell apart, the school set to be closed down. Students would have to be sent to a traditional school where there'd be much less support. I feigned disappointment at the news. I rushed home afterwards to celebrate, juiced about a new start with new students.

A PERFECT FAMILY

For my nephew's one-month old Red Egg and Ginger Party, my brother invited family, friends, and co-workers, everyone but Bah Ba. My father didn't even know he was a grandfather, didn't know my brother had been married for the last year. It was another thing

I was expected to keep from my father. "He's a stranger," Goh Goh had said. "Why should I invite him?" I didn't think it was my place to break the silence.

That's not what my aunt thought. My mom's younger sister, Sai Yi, took it upon herself to tell Bah Ba he had a grandson. I'm surprised she didn't also spill the beans about Willie while she was at it.

After Bah Ba found out, he called my brother, and in no time, they were chummy, two fathers bonding over fatherhood. Bah Ba would be coming to the Red Egg and Ginger Party after all. They'd always had a connection I couldn't compete with. Both were first sons. My brother, the first son of a first son, now had begot a first son. (Whoop-de-fucking-doo. My sister was the first daughter of a first daughter, but nobody gave a shit about that. Patriarchy rules!)

My brother had married a woman that he'd only been dating for a month or so. He'd met her through work, a cousin of a waitress. She was from Macau, and her green card was about to expire, so they took off and got married in Reno.

"That girl is using you," my mother had said.

"Playing you like a sucka," I said.

"This is real," Goh Goh said. "I love her." He said it was such heartfelt emotion that my mom and I couldn't help it, we busted up laughing.

My brother had chosen an Asian buffet downtown to hold the party. His friend worked there and had gotten him a discount. Goh Goh needed it. Though he'd quit the take-out job and landed a gig behind a desk at a small shipping company, my brother was living check to check with three mouths to feed. He wasn't even paying his own rent. Bah Ba was, but unbeknownst to my dad, my mother was no longer living in that apartment in North Beach. Sure, she still had her room there, but she was sleeping in Willie's bed every night. I'd moved out as well, so the money Bah Ba was sending home, not a substantial amount, in effect went to Goh Goh via my mother. The leftover money from Bah Ba's checks went to paying for his life insurance. I guess my mother figured, you just never know.

On the far side of the restaurant, a band wearing Hawaiian shirts was playing an Elvis song. The walls were a tacky violet. Light gleamed from the metallic "Happy Birthday" banner hanging above the registration table.

My mother spotted me and waved me over. Bah Ba and Ga Jeh were also sitting at that table. Our section for the party was separated by a wooden partition. My mom ran up to embrace me as if she hadn't seen me in years. "My baby," she said, louder than she needed to.

"Stop saying that," I said.

She smiled. "Even if you are 100 years old—"

"New jokes, please."

"I'm not joking."

My sister came over and hugged me. "I'm so glad you're here," she whispered. "Mom won't shut up."

"The trick is to ignore her," I said. "Let her talk to herself."

"I'll try that," she chuckled. Ga Jeh wore a dark blouse, probably was going for a formal look, but it came across as somber. I was wearing a dress shirt that my brother had given me. All the buttoned-up shirts in my closet were short sleeve plaid shirts.

Bah Ba rose from the table, dressed in a suit and tie. The only time I'd seen him in a suit was in old photos, the wedding picture that still hung over my mother's bed. I gave him a quick hug, the way men do. I asked the typical questions, "How are you doing?" "How's work?" and got the expected one-word responses, "Fine." "OK."

We sat around the table according to age as though we'd planned it—Bah Ba, Mom, Ga Jeh, and me. A balloon hovered over each of our heads, the ribbons tied to our bright colored chairs. My mother kept fidgeting in her seat. She cuffed her hair over her ear, revealing a gold hoop earring. She placed a shimmering clutch bag, also gold, on the seat next to her, between herself and Bah Ba. Willie wasn't coming now—she'd had to disinvite him—so my mother wasn't saving the seat, just preventing Bah Ba from sliding over.

My father muttered something to me, but I couldn't hear over the noise of the restaurant, the chairs scraping against the floor as people left for and returned from the buffet. Bah Ba stared at me, waiting for a response.

"I don't know." I shrugged. Seemed like a safe response.

Busboys swarmed around an empty table nearby, grabbing plates of leftovers. I was hungry but decided to wait for the crowd around the buffet to thin. My mother curled her lips when she saw Sai Yi at another table, along with Gung Gung and Poh Poh. Sai Yi had her hair parted in the middle, revealing a generous forehead. She worked as a clerk at Walgreens.

"My family likes him more than me," my mother whispered loudly to me and my sister. According to her family, a father or husband could do no wrong. "He's still your dad," they'd loved to remind me.

Bah Ba slid the small basket of red-dyed hard-boiled eggs my way. He gestured with his palm. "*Sihk.*"

I grabbed an egg and peeled the shell. Red-dyed eggs and a plate of sushi ginger on each table, that was about all there was to a Red Egg and Ginger Party, a baby shower post-birth, minus the silly games. I didn't know if I had to eat a red egg for good luck, or if the mere appearance of the eggs had already granted us good luck. Maybe the whole red-egg-good-luck thing wasn't for us at all but only for my nephew, Jordan.

Bah Ba gestured for Ga Jeh to grab an egg. My mother used one hand to shield her face from Bah Ba, turning toward my sister. My mom scrunched up her face to Ga Jeh, as if to secretly impart: the eggs are poisoned! My mother was recruiting for Operation Ostracize Bah Ba.

"Is something wrong with your face?" my sister asked.

Not registering Ga Jeh's annoyance, my mother smiled at my

sister as though for a camera. My mom picked up the small dish of
sushi ginger and held it out for me and my sister, grinning with one
finger on her cheek. "It's good for you." She angled her finger so that
the two diamond rings on the finger faced us. Her wedding ring was
in a safety deposit box. My mother pushed the dish of ginger toward
us, her gold bracelets clinking against one another like Slinkies.

She knew I never ate pickled ginger, so I shot her a confused
look.

"How come like that?" she pointed at me.

"Dickson doesn't want any," Ga Jeh said. "Eat it yourself."

My mother pointed at my father when she thought he wasn't
looking. "He shouldn't be here."

"Bah Ba can hear you," I said.

"So, I don't care."

Bah Ba stared at her, but my mother continued, though in a
whisper.

"Now he comes along, gives your brother some money, and
the past goes away? When I was pregnant with you," my mother
pointed at me, "Ga Jeh was only two. She had a 102-degree fever.
I begged him to stay, but—"

"We know," I said. I was a teenager when she began telling me
these stories. My mother and I would sit at the kitchen table, and
she'd share with me all her guy problems, past and present. I was
her therapist.

"Your Bah Ba," my mother began again, "once he was drunk
and tried to pull me to the bedroom. I wouldn't go, so he pushed
me to the ground, and then—"

"You're screaming in my ear." Ga Jeh tapped me on the arm
and rolled her eyes.

My mother banged her plate on the table. "You think Bah Ba
would've given your brother money if he didn't have a baby? He
used to hit Goh Goh, and now your brother wants to be his best
friend!"

Bah Ba turned toward Mom. "*Leih gong meh yeh?*" What are

you talking about?

"*Mouh yeh!*"

An older woman came to our table, my sister-in-law's aunt. We all stood to greet her, shaking her hand. I wondered if Bah Ba knew who she was and vice versa. "*Tai hah leih,*" she said to my mother, "*gum leng.*"

My mom raised her arms in the air, forming a *V* shape to show off her slim waist. Her red blouse sparkled with beads arranged in columns. She ran to the aunt and whispered, loud enough for us to hear, "I've had this blouse for thirty years." My mother cupped her hand over her mouth and giggled. "This is my youngest son," she said. "He's so smart. A math teacher."

"I teach history and English."

She laughed, leaning on the aunt. "This is my daughter," my mom said and pulled Ga Jeh close. My mother did her Vanna White impersonation, waving her hand over my sister as though she expected Ga Jeh to strike some pose.

"She looks more like your sister than your mother," the aunt said to Ga Jeh.

"You're going to make her feel old," my mother said, cocking her head as if surprised.

Ga Jeh pulled away from our mother and sat down. If she were a son, our mother would've introduced her by saying that she had a degree in Hotel and Restaurant Management. Probably would've lied and said that she went to some famous culinary school.

"You two are so lucky to have a mother so pretty," the aunt said. She inspected my mom's long hair as though she were looking at a piece of art.

Bah Ba sat down. None of us had bothered to introduce him. He straightened up when he saw Jordan nearby, dressed in a white bodysuit with a white beanie, held by his mother.

"Do you have to work when you go back to Minnesota?" Ga Jeh asked.

"I get back in the morning," Bah Ba said, "then straight to work."

"You'll need some rest," I said.

"Money." Bah Ba rubbed his fingertips together.

My mother returned to her seat. "Why don't you sit here next to Mommy," she said to me. "Later, I'll help you crack crab." She patted the seat between her and Bah Ba.

I shook my head and rubbed my forehead. She always referred to herself as Mommy, so much so that I'd called her that much longer than I should have.

"I can crack my own crab," I said.

She smiled at Ga Jeh and patted the seat next to her again.

"Don't even think about it, woman," Ga Jeh said.

"Bah Ba," I said, "do you want to get some food?"

Bah Ba pointed at his mouth. Said he had a hard time chewing.

My mother sucked her teeth at me and left the table.

"*Leih go* Ma *sau a,*" Bah Ba said. Your mom is crazy.

"I know," I said and sipped my tea. "I know."

Ga Jeh nudged my shoulder, getting up from the table.

I followed her to the buffet. A member of the Hawaiian-shirt band crooned a Frank Sinatra song about a love that got away. We passed up the salad bar, the Chinese dishes, and went straight for the seafood. Mounds of crab legs, oysters, and shrimp sat on a bed of ice.

"Total drama queen," Ga Jeh said. "She needs to get smacked. If she's going to disrespect him, don't do it in front of us. I don't want any part of it." My sister spoke to our mother everyday on the phone, even though many of these conversations left my sister frustrated enough that she'd have to vent to me.

"Divorce him already," I said. I used a tong to grab a couple of crab legs and put them on my sister's plate, then put a bunch on my plate, extra for my father.

A hand gripped my shoulder. "How's Bah Ba doing?" Goh Goh asked. His hair was slicked back, and he was wearing a suede suit that he'd bought just for this occasion.

"All right, I guess."

"Watching Mom act around him is so freaking annoying," Ga

Jeh said.

"Mom came back to the apartment," Goh Goh said, "just so she could lock her door to keep Bah Ba from sleeping in her bed. He asked me, 'Why does she act like this?' I'm sick of lying to him."

"Mom isn't going to change," Ga Jeh said. "She's always talking about the past. Get over it, already."

"I got to get back to the front," Goh Goh said, "but we should talk about this later."

We'd said that before. We each wanted our parents to divorce and had each expressed this to our mother, but she would only say, "I'll tell him everything. Soon." Our conversations about our parents never went much farther than discussing our need to discuss.

Two days later, Bah Ba would return to Minnesota, and for the next few months, he'd continue to send money home. I didn't think much about him. All my energy went to the kids I taught. The gym teacher, who'd already been reprimanded, though not fired, for choking two students, got into another altercation with a pair of students, two brothers, and this time was canned. The younger brother had thrown something at the gym teacher's head, maybe a chalkboard eraser, and the teacher snapped. Put the student in a headlock. That's when the older brother jumped on top of the teacher. My goal was to not get fired, to not snap like the gym teacher. I was determined to live stress-free outside of work. Plopped down with my dinner in front of the TV, let my girlfriend win every argument, then slept. It was a recipe for survival.

Bah Ba would call the North Beach apartment, looking for my mother, and each time, my brother covered for our mom, like always. Through these phone calls, some brief, some much longer, Goh Goh and my father grew closer.

Five months after the Red Egg and Ginger Party, our father wrote us an email asking us to explain our mother's, his wife's, behavior.

Why? I want to know!

For so many years, I have been working out of state. That's not what I want. Just imagine how sweet to close to home. But I was forced to part from the family according to some of the bad situations with my work. I felt I was betrayed at that time. I had the chance to come to Minnesota as head dim sum cook to show everybody I was a valued worker. So I thought why not, I could make twice as much for my family. Let them had a better life, as all of you were growing older. All expense in the family were growing too!

For so many years, I am the only one to support the family. Mom takes care of the family while I am not home, so I am glad both are doing our parts to support the family. This is a perfect family, everyone admires.

Gained one thing, but lost one thing!

For the first few years, everything was fine, everything were in the track. But the relationship with Mom changed slowly. At first I did not realize, after several times when I came home, I felt I was up set time after time. I came home with happiness, but I left with sadness. After my restaurant closes, we lost a lot of money for the attempt, we had to pay the debts, but I could not return to SF with empty hands. I tried to work seven days and more hours in order to make more money, still I failed. I sent money back less by less. I wrote if Mom could work to help my burden, to help support the family with me together. All I heard were nothing?!!!

Now, everything is clear, I need to save money when I retire; I need to plan for my future.

Don't blame me, just compare!

Now I need to say something, as all of you are grown up, judge by yourself whose wrong, whose not, what to do next. Please don't put hate in your mind, as we are one family.

I confess I did not communicate well with you, many things I don't want to speak about, focus for the future, that's not a good idea to talk about the past, after all, past was past!

If you blame me not to communicate well, I want to know how many messages, family news, cards and calls I received from you including Mom for so many years? How many minutes she talked with me when I called home? As a member of the family, why I had to sleep in the sofa when I came home? Why she didn't talk with me before she bought Honda for Cindy? Why didn't she tell me about Jackson's marriage? Why she always talks about the past in Hong Kong? I know I was wrong, but what can I do now? Kill myself to pay back? All I know is working hard, hope all of you have a better life.

Me, member of the family, you, members of the family, try to solve the problems between everybody, let me know any idea, if you have conclusion.

Dad

* * * * * *

I was floored. My dad had personality, a range of emotions he'd been holding back, at least from me. His words in the email, his writing, created a new father for me, a complex man that I wanted to understand. The way he saw it, he was the one who'd been left behind.

He'd handled his responsibilities the way a husband and father should. Yet his wife had pushed him away for years. His children had never recognized the sacrifices he'd made for them. They'd been playing for the wrong team, siding with a mother who'd turned her back on a good man.

None of us responded to our father's email. We also didn't write to each other. We acted as if that bomb of an email would defuse itself. We ran from it.

The following week, Bah Ba called home and Goh Goh was tired of running. He finally confessed: Mom had a boyfriend.

My parents would exchange a couple of letters filled with gripes. My mother filed the paperwork for divorce; I paid for the lawyer. I wanted to be the one who freed my parents from their doomed bond.

* * * * *

PART III

CHAPTER 6

HOPE YOU SOLVE

PATTERN RECOGNITION

I picked up chess in my late twenties. I had thought of chess books as a foreign language, the mystifying notation, but I discovered some with detailed explanations, grandmasters expounding on strategy and tactics. I got hooked. Before long, I had shelves of chess books. Grandmasters were mentors I could hold in my hand or keep on my shelf.

Some chess books have no words. They're just pages of puzzles. To solve, you have to find checkmate or a winning combination. Occasionally, the best move is something subtle like retreating a piece. I've been advised not to spend too long on each puzzle. If you don't see the answer after a few minutes, take a guess, check the solution in the back of the book, and go on to the next position.

You're not seeking an answer so much as you are seeking to understand patterns. Tactical themes and motifs repeat. The more puzzles you attempt, the more patterns will emerge. To test your knowledge, after you finish the book, return to the beginning. See if you do better this time around.

I'm a low-ranking chess tournament player, but when I have time, I train by using this method, cycling through positions. Even when I don't solve as many as I would like, I have faith that the patterns will become ingrained in my memory, so that when I play a live game, the traps I stumble upon won't be unfamiliar.

VISIT

The summer after we lost Javon, I met Bah Ba at six in the morning in the lobby of his apartment building in a suburb just east of Minneapolis. The building suffered from peeling paint, and the hallways were dingy.

I took my shoes off as I entered his apartment, placing them on a yellowed newspaper, next to his black sneakers, speckled with flour. Stale smoke hung in the air. We walked through the small kitchen. The plastic dish rack was a faded red, filled with mildew. On the counter was a hair dryer, the same bulky orange one my father had when he lived with us. As a child, I'd use it on my action figures, imagining the hair dryer was a flamethrower that roared in my hand.

Bah Ba cleared the coffee table, sliding the ashtray to the side and picking up the red cups, the empty beer bottles, and a bottle of E&J, nestling them against his chest.

E&J had also been my liquor of choice in high school. I shared a locker with Rob and a few other guys, our designated hangout spot. In the locker, we'd keep a bottle of Coke mixed with Erk and Jerk. The first time I drank from the bottle, I gulped it down like I was in a drinking contest. Afterwards, on a whim, I jumped a flight of stairs. I landed on both feet but lost my balance and fell on my ass.

I toned down the drinking after I went over to a girl's house drunk. Her parents were away. She had curly hair, was Black and white but looked Mexican. I was seventeen, she was fourteen. It didn't seem like a big deal. We lay together in bed, my naked body next to hers. She was giving me a hickey on my neck when I knocked out, snoring away my opportunity.

Bah Ba took swigs from two cups before tossing them into the garbage. The beer bottles clinked as they landed. "*Choh a.*" He motioned for me to sit on the purple couch. It had cigarette holes, and when I sat, I could feel the couch springs. I shifted my weight and leaned on the neatly folded blanket and pillow, presumably meant for me.

He turned on the TV and handed me the remote. The buttons were sticky. I rubbed my fingers. "*Leih choh.*" I motioned him to sit.

"I have got to work." He stammered as he pronounced each of those one-syllable words, his eyes blinking. His English was worse than I remembered.

"You have Internet?" I pointed to the computer on the kitchen table, the keyboard submerged under stacks of paper.

"It works, but ignore the woman pictures. Things pop up." He opened the sliding door and turned on the AC, and it began humming. The smell of cigarette smoke was entrenched. It reminded me of a class at Dewey. Half the students would come in after lunch reeking of weed. The scent would cling to my clothes. Days later, I'd grab my jacket from the closest, and I could still smell the marijuana.

"Come to the restaurant for lunch," Bah Ba said. "No food here. I forgot to ask Joe take me to grocery." My father had no car, so Joe would help him run errands. He was Bah Ba's former neighbor, back when my father had a house. He couldn't keep up the payments. The name of that town: New Hope.

Bah Ba went in his room to change, and I fell asleep, tired from the red-eye flight. When I awoke an hour later, he was gone. I tried turning on the TV but the remote didn't work. The batteries were dead.

At lunchtime, there were only three tables occupied at Bah Ba's restaurant, all single diners. Not a complete hole-in-the-wall—they used linen tablecloth—but the tablecloths were stained. Brightening up the dull white walls was colored paper listing the specials. The waiter sat me at the largest table, a round table with a clear rotating tray.

"*Leih houh chih leih goh* Bah Ba," he said.

I used to get that a lot, people saying that I looked like my dad. Less so since I'd shaved my head. We had the same eyes, the same thick lips, the same round head. Once as a teenager, I woke my mother up, and she pulled away from me like she was waking from a nightmare. She'd thought my father had returned.

Bah Ba came out of the kitchen wearing a white apron. "Are you hungry?" he asked.

"Starving," I said.

He poured me tea out of the metal teapot. "Vivian's coming too."

I hadn't noticed the third plate setting. Vivian was Bah Ba's goddaughter. What that meant, I wasn't exactly sure. I didn't know anything about her, other than she existed. She was the one who'd contacted us when Bah Ba was kept in the hospital overnight. He'd passed out on the street a couple of days after my brother broke the news to him about Willie. Vivian called my brother to explain the situation and that had been the first time I'd heard of her. My dad had his own secrets.

I wondered if "goddaughter" was a Chinese euphemism for "young lover." That I could handle. It would make him and my mother even. It would also absolve me of any wrongdoing, for the lies I'd told him. I couldn't fathom a goddaughter in the usual sense, that my father had been playing daddy for someone else's kid instead of us.

"She used to work here, a waitress," Bah Ba said. "She came from China for school, by herself. I look out for her."

"That's nice of you," I said.

He looked over my shoulder. It was Vivian. She was in her early twenties, not unattractive. She gave my father a hug and shook my hand. "So happy to meet you," she said. She wouldn't stop smiling. I thought something was wrong with her face.

The waiter dropped off a couple of dishes on our table, shrimp dumplings and rice noodle rolls.

"Start eating," my father said. "I have to get back to kitchen."

Vivian sat next to me. The rest of our round table was empty, the vacant chairs staring back at us.

"Your Bah Ba was so excited when he heard you were coming," she said.

"How long have you known him?"

"Oh, a few years now. He thinks he takes care of me, but it's the other way around. I bring him groceries, make sure he's OK."

"Does he always drink in the morning?"

Vivian laughed off my question. "He's made some mistakes, I know, but he talks about you guys all the time. He's really a sweet man." She used her chopsticks to cut a noodle roll in half and placed it on my plate. "Eat before it gets cold. Try the *ha gau*." She tapped her chopsticks on the metal rim of the bamboo steamer.

During my weeklong visit, Vivian would bring me out with two of her school friends, a couple. We went to a late-night bowling alley that served cocktails. Another day, we drove out to Great Adventure. I wore a throwback Warriors jersey and got sunburn from waiting in the long lines. Before I left, Vivian gave me a parting gift, a wallet.

She had a fiancée in California, and as far as I could tell, everything between her and my father was on the up and up. They filled a need for each other. She hadn't seen her parents in years, so my dad became her father figure. For Bah Ba, having a goddaughter meant starting over, forming a new family, a chance to redeem himself with another daughter.

On Bah Ba's day off, he took me to the Mall of America.

We were on the fourth floor overlooking Camp Snoopy, an amusement park in the center of the mall. Trees and log cabins surrounded the rides. Kids posed for pictures with costumed characters.

That was my mother's sort of thing. She had a framed picture of herself and Pinocchio hung in the hallway of her home. In the photo, she has her arm and leg extended out to the side, as though she's been waiting her whole life for this moment.

A rollercoaster zipped by with screaming passengers, circling the indoor park. "Do you want to go?" Bah Ba pointed below at the inflated Snoopy, two stories tall, holding up his paw as though he was waiting to be called on.

"Ga Jeh would love this," I said. "Snoopy's her favorite."

Bah Ba's eyes tracked the roller coaster as it zipped around the track. "I've worked thirty years in a restaurant," he said and began to stare at his palms, as though angry at them. "I'm done. No more."

"You're retiring?"

"A father should be with his kids. And now there's Jordan."

"Better to be close to your children," I said.

"I could live with your brother and take care of my grandson. No more drinking. No more smoking. I'm going to be the best grandpa."

"It would save them money. Babysitters are expensive." I leaned over the railing. Kids were playing tag below.

Bah Ba tilted his head up to the skylight. "My Bah Ba is gone," he said. "My Ma too. And my Ga Jeh. I don't want to die from my family. When my dad got old, we moved him from Hong Kong. Why should he die alone? We must forgive. That's what Jesus says."

Earlier that day, Bah Ba had brought me along to his church picnic. He'd become a church-going man since his older sister had passed away. Most of the members were senior citizens. We'd gathered in a circle to say grace. The woman leading the prayer thanked God for sending me here, a son returning to his father. The story sat especially well with this crowd—aging parents afraid of being abandoned by their kids.

Bah Ba's breathing grew heavy. "I have to retire. Live my life. My boss complains and complains. For any machine that goes wrong, we pay the cost." He shook his head like a boxer pumping himself up before a fight.

"Retire." I gripped his shoulder. "*Faan ah.*" Return.

We strolled around the mall, passing two GAPs and two Victoria's Secrets. When we saw Hooters, Bah Ba nodded toward the sign and began chuckling. We only explored one shop, a massive outdoors store. We had no intention of buying anything, but we sifted through racks of lumberjack clothes, picked up lanterns, testing their weight, their portability. We ducked inside a family-sized tent.

"Where should we put the TV?" I asked, imagining that we were decorating our new house.

"This is for sleeping."

"I'm just pretending."

"Oh, over there." He pointed at nothing in particular.

We were to meet Vivian for dinner. I searched online for directions to the restaurant, though Bah Ba had argued that we didn't need directions. It was hard to understand exactly what he was saying. He'd been drinking and was slurring and laughing like a child.

In the car, Bah Ba slumped low in the passenger seat. He was mumbling something to himself. We couldn't have been on the freeway for more than two miles before he shouted for me to get off at the next exit.

"That's not what the directions say," I said.

"I go there all the time. What do you know?" His head rolled around like he was doing neck stretches. He stuck his head out the window as we passed the next exit, the wind blowing his graying hair around. He turned back and shot me a puzzled look.

"Not yet, Bah Ba. We're still a few exits away."

He dropped back into his seat and drifted off. I couldn't imagine him taking care of my three-year-old nephew. My dad was clearly an alcoholic. (I had yet to accept he was also a pedophile.) Maybe we'd let him think he was needed to babysit, but really, the setup would allow us to keep an eye on him, similar to his relationship with Vivian.

"That's the exit," Bah Ba said.

"Go back to sleep. That's what you said last time."

"What are you talking about? This is the exit, right here. I'm telling you, this is it. You're passing it. What are you crazy? Great, my son is going to get me lost."

"Oops, I'll get off at the next one."

"Good, good."

"Just relax. Lie back."

He fell asleep with the seat belt running across his neck. His head dangled over it. I reached across and tilted his head away from the strap. Soon, he began to snore.

The day I left, while Bah Ba was working, I replaced his nasty dish rack with a new stainless steel dish rack, the most expensive one they had at the store. I wondered how long it would take for mildew to grow on this gift, the first I'd ever bought for my father.

A REEVALUATION

MC Shan had been unable to repair his damaged rep as the loser of the battle with KRS-One. Queensbridge rappers in general also took a hit. Nearly a decade would pass before someone from QB— the largest housing projects in America—would make a notable rap album, but when that rapper did, he dropped the most critically acclaimed hip-hop album of his generation: *Illmatic*. Nas, in an interview, cites MC Shan as a major influence coming up. "His rap style," he says, "it helped me craft my rap style." Shan's legacy deserved a reevaluation.

Nas would later collaborate with Shan to record "Da Bridge 2001." The track also features other Queensbridge rappers, but the younger emcees allowed Shan, the QB elder, to lead off the song, the beat, a version of the original, sampling the original. Spitting the first verse, Shan's voice hasn't aged, just as fresh. His opening line, the same as in his classic: *You love to hear the story again and again.*

In hip-hop, anything could be recovered.

A SQUARE LEFT BEHIND

In chess, everything has a cost. A move is a loss. Moving one piece means not moving another. And moving any piece, whether it's swinging the bishop across the board or just taking one step with your old king, will always involve leaving something behind, a square undefended or less protected.

THE LAST EXCHANGE

Dad,

I'm having a hard time accepting your "plan" for retirement. It's very hard for me to discuss what I'm feeling especially since I sent you an email four years ago and you never responded. It was during the divorce and you were busy trying to get that straightened out. My problem just ended up being deleted from your memory. I am still feeling a lot of pain. You might not have noticed when you've seen me. We were in Toronto for sad reasons so I had to hide how I felt to be strong for you and the family. Deep down inside, it still hurts and haunts me. With your plan to move back, it is very hard for me to accept. If you feel that moving back to SF is what you would like to do, that's fine with me. It might be good cuz the family is here, however, I will not be able to live here. I will move somewhere far.

Cindy

* * * * *

Hi Cindy,

Sorry to respond so late, I am so misery of my job, sometimes the owner want you to do this, and they change their mind because of the whether and than the taste of the customers, so I don't know what I am doing, it look like I am pulling by something, it has so much stress for my job, I don't know when I can stand it, as thinking about my grandma, she died at 93, my father at over 80, my mother 70 something, than my sister at 60, these give me a signal, my family's age might go lower and lower, that's why I am thinking about retire, I have not see the world yet, I don't won't to work until I die like my sister, recently, a school bus driver at 78 crashed in the traffic accidence, he died when he worked, my friends in MN many of them have heart attack or died when they were working, which give me a signal should I retire or keep working? But I know my health, I am not that good, I feel I am getting slower and slower when I work, I don't know who I can keep up until 62, every week I have to run with the clock in order to complete my work which make me so tire, like this week I work 14 hours on Sat and 12 hours on Sun, the life of my job you will never taste.

It's tough for you and it's tough for me too, you have so much bad memory, I have nothing in my mind, my mind is blank, I don't have anything which I can recall, I don't know, where, I don't know, when, I know something did happen, because I trust my children, you never lie to me, so I know I had did something wrong which I still can't recall.

Dad

* * * * * *

Dickson,

I think all the alcohol has killed his brain cells!

Cindy

ERASURE

sweet

home

I

betrayed

family

Gained   lost

retire ██████████ my future.

██████████ past

██████████ hard █ hope █

█ you

█ solve

RETURN

Our school year began two weeks before the students arrived, with staff development days to reflect on the prior year, what had to be changed. A mural had been painted of Javon in front of the school. Next to his face was an angel, wings, and a crown above a cloud.

It was after lunch, and we were meeting in a classroom, the student desks arranged in a circle. Leading the session was Toni Gill. She'd refer to other staff as Brotha and Sista, as in Brotha Lam. Her son also attended the school, and some students would call her Mama Gill. Toni was facilitating a discussion on ways to prevent sexual harassment among students. I tried to ignore her as best I could without looking obvious. This was just a few days after Ga Jeh had revealed her true feelings to me about our father, how it gave her suicidal thoughts.

Now when I thought of my father, all I could think about was the image of him in my sister's room. "He used to touch me," my sister had said. I asked nothing about the details, what exactly happened. Like Ga Jeh, I also wanted to keep my eyes closed. But my mind ran wild with the possibilities. They'd play out in my head, and I couldn't say, "No, that didn't happen"; it all happened.

My father was everywhere. I'd pass a Chinese restaurant—Bah Ba. I'd see an old Chinese man—Bah Ba. I'd see a father—Bah Ba. I'd look in the mirror—Bah Ba. The guy was in my fucking blood. He was a Lam; I'm a Lam; my children will be Lams. They will call me Bah Ba.

Walking around the empty school hallways, I'd tap my fist against the wall, lightly at first then with more power until I reached a point where any stronger, I'd break my hand. In my classroom, I'd be on my laptop, then for no reason, I'd slap the desk as hard as I could. Pain soothed me.

I brought my lunch to the meeting on sexual harassment. I hadn't had the chance to eat yet. I'd picked up Hawaiian takeout from a spot on Mission Street, loco moco in a small Styrofoam box. As Toni continued with how prevalent sexual assault was at our school, boys grabbing girls' butts, I broke the fried egg, the yoke spilling over the burger patty. I cut the meat into slices. I picked up a slice and ate it with a spoonful of rice. I reviewed my to-do list on my clipboard.

"We're blind," Toni said. "You wouldn't believe some of the things I hear from the girls."

My sister was trapped in her room with our father again—I had to leave.

I walked out of the room, turned the corner, walked down the hallway past my classroom, and past the front office. I left the building. I went to the courtyard and sat on a bench. There was no shade. The sun was warm, arrogantly so. The rims of the basketball courts had been tampered with, the front ends slanting toward the ground, from kids hanging on them. Next to me was a garden enclosed by a chain-link fence.

I imagined my sister at school, a preteen Ga Jeh hanging out with friends at lunch, gossiping about boys, pretending the night before was just a bad dream. When she'd arrive home, later that night, she'd see the boogeyman again, this time with the lights on.

I was eight or nine when it started. My room was directly across the hallway from my sister's, a footstep separating her door from mine. I wanted to empower that young Dickson, give him a weapon. I'd been old enough to pick up a knife but had chased the wrong tormenter.

I dropped to the ground and did knuckle push-ups on the concrete. My knuckles reddened and were dirty. I banged my fist against the edge of the bench until I cut my knuckles, the blood mixing with dirt.

It was a few weeks into the start of the semester, and I'd thrown myself deeper into work. As a teacher at June Jordan, we already had plenty to do, had the advisor role on top of teaching, but I'd volunteered for more: volunteered for the School Culture Committee, the Academic Equity Committee, the Hiring Committee, chaired our Humanities Department, signed up to lead a yearlong professional development program for the staff, and agreed to mentor a student teacher. The shit was exhausting.

I'd come home and still have papers to grade, lessons to plan, and parents to call, the mothers and fathers of advisees who'd gotten kicked out of class. The conversations could turn lengthy. Parents often vented to me, but I had enough family drama of my own.

One day, I was running a discussion in class on abortion. A student was making a case that it was murder. I jotted down his points, as I did during all class discussions, but the student, Peter, began to ramble, veering off on tangents. He had a disability that made him walk with a limp and drag his foot. On top of that, he had a speech impediment. Words came out nasally. He'd tested out of special education, but he wasn't trying to merely fit in. He wanted to be the most popular kid on campus. During lunch, Peter would jump into freestyle rap cyphers—and win. When we brought Challenge Day to the school, and they led us through a set of cross-the-line questions, Peter, a Chinese kid, crossed the line to identify not only as Asian but also Latino and African American. He claimed he had friends of all stripes; thus, he identified with (as) them. "It doesn't work like that," I'd tried to explain, but Peter wouldn't be swayed.

I quit writing Peter's repetitive points. Murder, we got it. Usually, I'd refocus him or move on to the next student, but I found myself doodling. An outline of a face, its mouth opened wide as though gasping for air. I began to fantasize about killing my father. It'd been a recurring daydream.

Bah Ba was asleep in his bed; my hands hovering over his neck. He awakens and tries to squirm away, but I throw him to the floor. I pounce on his back, press my weight on him, and sink my hips low to the ground. I had a piece of string in my hand that'd been snipped from my mother's spool of string. Ga Jeh and I would cut string from this spool to play Cat's Cradle. I loop the cotton string around Bah Ba's neck and pull. The string turns into wire, a garrote. It cuts into his skin. He tries to shake his head free. His panting eventually trails off, and this pleases me. I pull harder.

"You don't know what the hell you're talking about," a student screamed at Peter. It was Roxanne, who shouted all her sentences. She could make, "Can I borrow a piece of paper?" sound violent—she would've been a natural Cantonese speaker—but when she'd realize she was too loud, she'd flash an innocent smile and apologize earnestly. This wasn't that sort of shout.

"It's still a life, Roxy," Peter snapped back.

"If it is, then you might as well say condoms are killing life!" Roxanne stood up from her desk. "You gonna say birth control should be against the law too? No, didn't think so!"

An "oooh" erupted in the class.

I checked the clock. "Roxanne had the last word," I said to the class. "It's time to go. Make sure you grab a handout." I placed a stack of papers on the table in the middle of the room, which all the desks faced.

"Wait," Peter said. "I get to respond. She asked me a question."

"Didn't you hear Lam?" Roxanne said. "Time's up!"

"All you who think it's OK—" Peter stood up and shouted like he was a preacher on a corner downtown. He accidently knocked over his two-liter bottle on the floor. The kid drank a lot of soda.

"It's over." I glared at him, but he wasn't looking. He was trying to pick up his bottle. I couldn't find my stapler. It was my go-to method for getting their attention or shutting them up. I'd tap the stapler three times against the edge of the table. The teacher next door used a Zen meditation chime.

"What if your parents had aborted you?" Peter said to the class, saliva spewing from his mouth.

"Peter, stop." I grabbed an empty metal chair and banged its rear feet three times against the floor.

"You guys are all murderers," he said and pointed at the class. He launched further into his diatribe.

I gripped the chair by its wooden backrest. I raised it high in the air. For a long second, I was fully conscious of what I was about to do. Breathe, I told myself. Put. The chair. Down. I weighed my options. Big mistake. Once I considered the violent act, the urge became irresistible. I needed the release.

I slammed the chair to the floor as hard as I could, twisting my torso, pivoting on the ball of my rear foot. The chair fell to the side, one of its metal legs bent at a sharp angle.

Peter sat in his chair silent, hugging his two-liter soda bottle, fingering the cap. The students wouldn't look at me. I knew I should say something, an explanation, an apology, but I couldn't take their faces. They looked petrified.

"Y'all can go," I said.

They cleared out in record time, not saying a word. I hadn't checked their notebooks to ensure they'd written down the homework, and none of them mentioned the slip in routine.

I sat the chair up. It was wobbly because of the broken leg, wrecked. No one would sit in the chair again, but I never tossed it out. I'd keep it in the middle of the room, at the table, front and center, a reminder, of what, I wasn't sure.

CHURCH

Hi Dickson,

How are you? Are you enjoying your Thanksgiving break? Last night, we drove your dad to my sister's place for Thanksgiving. The last couple of times we had our monthly church meetings, your dad seemed very tired and down because he said he didn't sleep well, and he wasn't very sober. I told him he needs to go see the doctor and check things out, but he said that if the doctor told him to rest, he couldn't afford to take time off. Do you call him on the phone often? He said he hasn't heard from you since you visited. Please send him your love!

Sarah

PUBLIC SHAMING

Compared to other landlords, my great-grandmother had gotten off light during land reform. Tortured but not killed. Over a million landlords were executed under Mao's sweeping land reform. Some condemn him for the bloodshed. He initiated the campaign, but to suggest he orchestrated the results underestimates the rage of the peasants. They ran the tribunals and decided the sentencing, not the communists. For the first time in China's history, peasants confronted their oppressors without fear of retribution.

Given free rein, it's not shocking that many peasants, particularly those most mistreated, were bloodthirsty. What surprises me is that the overwhelming majority of landlords were spared from execution. In a nation as populous as China, a million landlords accounted for a small percentage of the entire landlord population, seven to ten percent, according to one study. I cite this not to argue that a million deaths is insignificant—that would be insane—but to point out just how many peasants were not in favor of revenge killings. Public shaming was a preferred form of justice. Villagers could mock and attack the ones they held responsible for their bleak lives. Even kids picked up rocks and hurled them. It wasn't solely about inflicting pain or even humiliation. Some villagers weren't seeking revenge so much as a confession.

TRUTH AND RECONCILIATION

The Mao unit was the last unit of our yearlong course on world history. The first unit examined apartheid in South Africa. We'd watched the documentary *Long Night's Journey into Day*, a film about South Africa's Truth and Reconciliation Commission. To help the nation recover from a legacy of apartheid violence, the commission had been authorized to offer amnesty to perpetuators of "gross human rights violations." Perpetuators had to confess their wretched acts in a public forum, not only in front of television cameras, but also in front of an audience that often included their victims or the families of their victims, a voluntary public shaming. The intention was not retributive but restorative. "This process is not about pillorying anybody," Archbishop Desmond Tutu says. "It's not about prosecuting anybody. It's ultimately about getting the truth, so that we can help to heal and also so that we may know what to avoid in the future." To be granted amnesty, perpetuators had to meet several criteria including satisfying the commission's requirement for "full disclosure." Honesty was a prerequisite for forgiveness.

In the last segment of the documentary, Rian Bellingan, a white officer, applies for amnesty for his involvement in the killing of seven young activists, but during his testimony, Bellingan does not admit any wrongdoing. Self-defense, he claims.

Thapelo Mbelo, a Black police officer, Bellingan's colleague, also applies for amnesty for his participation in the same case. In Mbelo's testimony, a starkly different account from Bellingan's, he admits that he shot one of the activists in the head, even though the activist had approached the officers with his arms up in surrender.

Later, in an interview, Mbelo discusses how he dealt with betraying his own people, "The only time when you think something is going to bother you, the nearest place or the nearest thing to do was take booze. Then you stay drunk, you remember nothing." As he speaks, his left eye constantly twitches.

Mbelo requests to meet the mothers of the seven slain men, including the mother of the son he killed. He meets the mothers in a private room and asks for forgiveness.

One mother tells him she'll never forgive him. Her son died for freedom, while Mbelo sold out to the Boers. The camera jumps from the face of one mother to the next. Cynthia Ngewu, the mother of the man Mbelo shot, has taken off her sunglasses, eyes glistening, like the rest of the mothers. Some time passes because when Ngewu speaks again, she has her glasses on, lightly tinted. You can still see her eyes. Something clicks in her. She remembers the meaning of Mbelo's first name, Thapelo: "prayer." She thinks about how he and her son are the same age. "God will be the judge," she says and adds, "we want to get rid of this burden we are carrying inside, so that we too can feel at peace. So for my part, I forgive you, my child."

This is the kind of end I want for this book. My father expresses remorse; my sister forgives him; I can forgive him. But Bah Ba's testimony is one of denial, the opposite of Mbelo's testimony, but it's also a different form of denial from Bellingan's. Bellingan disputes the facts. My father claims not to remember them: Maybe I did, maybe I didn't.

Full disclosure was not made. Amnesty will not be granted to my father. No contrition, no redemption.

UNCOVER

Javon's killer remains at large, though footage exists of him, taken from the surveillance camera on the bus from that fateful afternoon. In the video, a teenage boy fires shots through the window. The boy was later identified with the help of this footage, charged with felony gun possession but not with Javon's murder. Because this shooter's gun was never recovered by authorities, there was no forensic evidence tying him to the bullets that hit Javon. It's possible Waga was killed by another kid on that bus. Three other boys, filmed but not identified, ran off the bus to get a better shot. A decade has passed, and the case hasn't been solved, but there's more to the story than who did the crime.

Every April, to commemorate Waga's death, Javon's folks organize a peace march of hundreds, a family-friendly event with inflatable jumpers, face painting, and a marching band. They turned Waga into W.A.G.A., War Against Gun Activity, a family tragedy morphing into a community movement.

Once at a subway station, I ran into Javon's younger sister. I was exiting the turnstile, she was entering. "You're Mr. Lam, right?" She was soft-spoken and wore glasses. I didn't recognize her at first. Several years had passed since I'd last seen her at the memorial for Javon.

I asked her about her family, how her mom was doing. The conversation was brief. I didn't know what else to say. I still felt responsible in some way for her brother's death. I hadn't admitted this to anyone. I wasn't looking to be comforted or pitied or even forgiven. I wanted to forget.

I sought the same defense used by my father.

But to be a writer, a memoirist, I must uncover what I wish to hide.

MOTHER AND DAUGHTER

My sister was at our mom's house, surfing the net in Willie's office. Willie was in his bedroom across the hallway singing karaoke, Frank Sinatra's "My Way," Clarence Henry's "You Always Hurt the One You Love." Willie sang these songs over and over, as though he was in a recording studio and the producer was telling him, "Again, this time, more feeling, more emotion."

My mom was at the doorway of the office, talking to my sister about Bah Ba, but Ga Jeh didn't turn around, her eyes stuck to the computer screen. "Why do you have to move just because he's coming back?" my mom asked in Cantonese.

"I can't stand him." My sister had secured a transfer to another resort down in San Diego. No way in hell she was sticking around with my father set to return.

"You went to Toronto to see him, and now you want to get away from him. I don't understand you." My mom didn't want my sister to leave, but she wouldn't say it explicitly. She never wanted to appear as if she needed anyone.

As Ga Jeh clicked the keyboard to jump to another website, my mother came up beside her, put her hand on the backrest of my sister's chair. Before my mom had a chance to continue, my sister told her, "Just leave it alone, woman."

"I thought you guys love your Bah Ba," my mom said. "Ever since we divorced, you guys keep seeing him."

"For funerals."

"Jackson talks to him on the phone all the time. Dickson thinks he lonely, goes to see him. Maybe you should let him move in with you."

"I'd rather be dead!"

"Don't say that, it's bad luck."

"That's how I feel."

"That's crazy. A daughter doesn't need to run from her father."

"You're crazy. You're the reason why." Once she started, she couldn't stop. "Every time you used to go away with Willie, Bah Ba would come in my room—he'd touch me."

My mom pulled back. She wasn't sure what she heard, so Ga Jeh said it again. Slower this time. "He'd. Touch. Me. And only when *you* were gone."

"*Leih goh sei leuih baau a!*" My mom said, a Chinese version of "good for nothing daughter," but our version is worse, the central part of the expression, two characters, "die" then "daughter." My mom started to lunge at my sister, as if she thought she could beat back what my sister said, what my father did, but she stopped herself. "Why didn't you tell me?" she asked. Her tone accusatory.

Ga Jeh pushed past her to leave.

"OK, OK," my mom said. "*Mouh haam, mouh haam.*" Don't cry, don't cry.

My sister put on her shoes. She ignored what my mom was saying. She grabbed her purse and stormed down the stairs into the garage. She squeezed past Willie's Camry, careful not to bump against his tools hanging from the wall: wrenches, screwdrivers, hammers, saws. She hit the button to open the garage. She heard the sound of the motor and ducked under the rising door.

Ga Jeh didn't call my mom that night, or the next, though they usually spoke every day. But in a week, they were on speaking terms again. That's how it was in our family. We concealed our pain and mistook it for Being Strong.

The next time my sister stopped over at my mom's house, my mother told her that she had written a letter to Bah Ba calling him every name in the book. This was my mom's version of an apology. She wanted Ga Jeh to know that she was on her side. She kept talking about my father and what a despicable person he was, but it didn't make my sister feel any better. Sometimes, Ga Jeh felt angrier at my mother than my father.

She'd think about our mom as it happened. Wished that she'd come in to save the day. Each time it wasn't just her father betraying her, but her mother abandoning her as well, off pursuing an affair while the forsaken husband snuck into her room, into her bed.

"Time for dinner," my mom said. She went to the fridge and took out a bowl of marinated chicken. "This will be fast."

My sister cleared the kitchen table while my mom tossed the chicken in a wok. Soon you'll be in San Diego, Ga Jeh said to herself, a job near the beach. No friends, no family, the life of an unknown. Perhaps you should've moved further, to another state. How many miles does it take to escape your family?

THE BOARD

The chessboard contains 64 squares. Each square has a name, a coordinate, e4, d5. Columns are called files. Rows are ranks.

A city is a board. Its streets, files and ranks.

My sister thought she was leaving the board, but cities are also squares, the state a larger board. Highways are files and ranks.

A state is also a square, the country a board.

A country is also a square, the planet a board.

A planet is also a square, the solar system a board.

Everything is a square, everything a board. You can flee a square but not The Board.

Reverse it. Work backwards to the micro-level. A neighborhood is a square within the city, but a neighborhood is also a board, comprised of blocks, squares.

An apartment complex is a board, each unit a square. Inside each apartment unit, rooms are squares, the hallway a file, a rank.

Any square can be revisited, but not all squares are equal. The ones at the center of the board are most valued. Place your pieces here, and they'll wield the most influence, controlling the most squares, but the center squares are also the most contested, the riskiest place for your pieces, exposed and vulnerable.

NORTH BEACH PLACE

I had a parent conference to attend, a home visit. The family of my advisee lived in my old neighborhood, North Beach. I wasn't sure if you could still call them projects. The city had torn down the old North Beach and replaced it with a townhouse complex. Slapped a cute name on the property: North Beach Place. At least you could still claim NBP. Each unit now had a washer and dryer, an upstairs and a downstairs, a balcony or a patio.

The new NBP was a "mixed income, mixed-use complex." Forget cracking down on hustling. In the new North Beach, a gated complex of townhouses, you couldn't even dribble a basketball—too loud. Space was tight. From the balconies across from each other, you could hold a conversation without having to shout.

On the ground level facing the street, there were storefronts: Trader Joe's, Starbucks, Edible Arrangements, a bike rental shop, a ballet school for kids—somebody was getting paid. Most of the original tenants hadn't returned. Though the city had offered units in the new North Beach to all prior tenants, five years had passed since the first tenants had been asked to leave—kicked out, really. You had to settle elsewhere. It wasn't a choice. The wrecking ball was on its way. Residents could've either rented an apartment in the city using the Section 8 voucher they were given, like my brother, or they could've moved into another housing project. Some said screw the city and left for the East Bay where rent was cheaper. By the time North Beach was rebuilt several years later, most prior tenants weren't about to pack up and start over again. Rob was living in the new Army Street housing projects, also remade into townhouses, with his wife, a teacher at a private elementary school. They'd had a city hall wedding, and I'd been the lone witness. 'Dullah lived in a housing project in Hunter's Point, but his folks had moved to West Oakland. Mansur, I'd heard, was regulating on the young cats on his block. None of that dope dealing here, son!

My brother returned to the new North Beach with his wife and his son, and now they had two additions to the household, a new baby girl, Alana, and Bah Ba. I'd stopped visiting after Bah Ba moved in. Wouldn't even drive past North Beach. If I wanted to hang out with Jordan, I'd have to have my brother drop him off. My father would walk Jordan to kindergarten and back each day. Goh Goh, unlike me, could separate Bah Ba the grandfather from the Bah Ba that haunted my sister. She didn't give him grief over this, so I didn't either. Part of me felt relieved that my dad lived with family. If he had retired alone, I might feel sorry. I wanted to be free to dismiss him, not chained by pity.

Goh Goh's apartment, fortunately, was not on the same block as the apartment of my advisee. My brother's block was our old block. I called him as I approached North Beach to find out if Bah Ba was home. "He smokes on Francisco," my brother said. "Just park on Bay."

Doing a house visit for my advisee wasn't my preference, but Lakida's mother, due to work, couldn't make it to June Jordan in the evening. And skipping a parent-teacher conference wasn't an option. We'd made an agreement that we'd meet with all of our advisees' families.

Lakida's mom, Tanya, had invited me to eat dinner with them. I sat on the leather couch while music videos played on the television.

Tanya handed me a strawberry margarita. She wore a velour track-suit, and she couldn't have been much older than me.

"Cheers," I said.

We clinked glasses. At another advisee's house—we did all our parent-conferences during the same week—I'd gotten tipsy off vodka and juice. That mom kept pouring, and I kept drinking.

"Is this going to be bad?" Tanya asked.

"Not all."

"Lakida!" Tanya called her down for dinner.

"Do you want help setting up?" I asked. I could smell the bar-beque sauce. I got up but bumped into the folding tray, knocking over my margarita. The glass broke on the linoleum floor.

"Don't worry," Tanya said. She poured me another glass.

I fingered the rim of salt and licked it off my fingers. "Sorry, I'm a klutz. Let me clean up."

"It's nothing." She took out a broom and swept the broken glass into a dustpan.

Lakida came downstairs wearing a hoodie and sweatpants. She was one of the shortest kids in school, but she'd call some of her friends, "daughter," as in "How come you didn't come to school yesterday, daughter?"

"Oh my God, Mr. Lam, what are you breaking in my house?" Lakida asked.

"'Kida stop playing. Check on your cake," Tanya said. She leaned in towards me and said, "She's making carrot cake for you."

"Either she's real sweet," I said, "or she knows she's in trouble."

"Don't play me like that, Lam," 'Kida said.

"Go ahead and sit down Mr. Lam. 'Kida will bring your plate over."

The living rooms of these new units were smaller, the ceiling also lower. The kitchen was a kitchenette, no room for a table. I pic-tured my father eating with my brother's family. They'd sit around the couch, the same one Bah Ba had shipped from Minnesota years ago.

I took a gulp of the margarita. Lakida brought over my plate: barbeque chicken, corn, and potato salad on the side. They sat down with theirs.

The conference would go as expected. I showed them Lakida's grades. I recycled comments from previous conferences, "Do these grades reflect your best?" "What's stopping you from achieving the way you know that you can?" We ended with an action plan, what each of us would do differently to help Lakida succeed. I took notes and promised copies.

This was a breeze compared to two other parent-teacher conferences I'd had that week. One was another house visit with Eric, a Chinese kid with a single mom. It was always the missing Chinese fathers that made my own father loom over the parent-teacher meetings, never the Chinese dads who showed up to the conferences. That wasn't the kind of dad I had.

Eric had crummy grades. He'd come late to school all the time. His mother didn't know what to do. She had to leave for work early in the mornings, so she couldn't get him out of bed herself. She suggested that if her son arrived tardy, I should go old school on him, reach for a ruler or just slap him upside the head. I explained why I couldn't do that, but I couldn't think of the Chinese word for "illegal." I just kept saying "I can't do that." She thought I was a softie.

The other parent conference was held in my classroom. I thought it was going to be a normal meeting. Student wasn't doing great—action plan. Boom, go home. But we almost didn't get to her grades. The father had come back from El Salvador, and his wife and his daughter Jenna, my advisee, had discovered that he had been cheating with a woman in El Salvador. No wonder Jenna's grades had taken a dive. The parent-teacher conference would be the first time they'd have a real conversation since the news of the father's affair. At home, there'd been a thick silence. I'd learned all this just minutes before the meeting began when Jenna confided in me in the hallway.

We didn't get far in the parent-teacher conference before the father said something about Jenna needing to be honest. He meant about her skipping classes, but she interrupted him before he could finish. "You're full of shit," she said to him. "You talk about *me* being honest. Look at you." She had dark eye shadow and lipstick. I was secretly cheering her on—Tell him! Tell him!—proud she was calling out her old man.

"Don't talk to you father that way," the mother said.

"No," the father said, eyes tearing up, "I deserve it."

The conflict resolution strategies I knew, I-statements or paraphrasing, seemed absurd for this. Couldn't imagine saying to the father: "Can you please paraphrase what your daughter just said about you?"

Jenna left and skedaddled down the hallway. The mother went after her, so it was just me and the dad. He was slightly shorter than me, but his meaty hands and broad shoulders gave him a rugged look. I liked him, liked his parenting style, firm but compassionate, but this didn't make it any easier for me to sit with him, a father who betrayed his family.

The walls of my classroom were mostly bare. A lifeless teal dominated. Decorating was at the bottom of my to-do list. The most ornamental thing in the room was two table runners hanging vertically, orange and red-striped. On the chalk tray rested Mao's "Little Red Book," thank-you letters from students, and a laminated picture of Javon that was made for his memorial at the school.

"I don't know what to do, Mr. Lam," Jenna's father said. "She won't talk to me."

I had to get him Kleenex from my desk. I probably needed a tissue myself, but I was trying to hold it together. "Give her time," I said.

"I don't see her changing."

"I know you're a good father," I said. It was like I was talking to my own father. I didn't want to continue, but I forced out some lines. "Don't give up on her," I said, "even though she's got nothing but mean things to say. You'll have to take it for a while. Prove to her you're truly sorry."

We managed to reconvene and actually talk about Jenna's grades. I'd convinced her to come back in, give her dad a second chance. I was a hypocrite, I know, but Jenna wasn't me, and she wasn't in my situation. She was mad, but I could tell she didn't want to write her dad off forever. I ain't gonna lie though, I was tempted to advise her, "Once a cheater, always a cheater." I wanted Jenna to join my club: Children Who Had Disowned Their Fathers. I had to remember, this wasn't about me and my issues; it was about my advisee. That's when I knew I couldn't keep doing that job.

Ga Jeh was visiting from San Diego. She wanted to spend the day with Jordan and Alana. The movies then the park. And of course the ice cream truck by the sandlot, even though she knew Goh Goh didn't want his kids eating sweets. The thing was, she had to drop them off in North Beach, and only Bah Ba would be home. Goh Goh was out of town, and his wife was working. My sister hesitated when Goh Goh told her this, but he assured her that it'd be fine. The plan was simple. Jordan and Alana would ring their apartment, and Bah Ba would buzz them in. Ga Jeh wouldn't have to see or talk to our father.

It had been months since she saw the kids. Jordan was seven, his cheeks less chubby. Alana was three, and Ga Jeh worried that it might take them a bit before they'd warm to her. She was Yi Goo Jeh, Second Aunt. I was Saam Sook, Third Uncle. It doesn't translate well. There weren't two aunts or three uncles. The numbers signaled our birth order. My sister loved being an aunt, loved to hear them say, Yi Goo Jeh, so I started calling her that too, and she'd call me Saam Sook.

She'd phone my mom on weekends because our nephew and niece would spend the night. She'd ask our nephew, "What does Yi Goo Jeh like?"

"Good boy," he'd reply. Even though this was an old routine that they had, Ga Jeh would celebrate his answer like he was a prodigy.

It was an overcast day, and my sister thought how odd it was that she'd already forgotten how summer in San Francisco wasn't summer at all. She parked her SUV near the entrance at the gate, a few parking spots away rather than the parking spot directly in front, a precaution. Didn't want to be in plain sight if Bah Ba came out.

She kept the engine running as she looked over her shoulder, waiting for Jordan and Alana to be buzzed in at the gate. Goh Goh had told Bah Ba that a friend would drop off the kids. Ga Jeh hadn't seen our father in a few years, and she wanted to keep the streak alive. She kept busy with a new job, a promotion, more responsibilities, people to supervise, a new relationship with a guy who wasn't a jerk—a first. After work, she'd walk across the beach. The way her toes sunk into the sand put her at ease. She'd close her eyes and hear the waves, a cleansing.

Once, when Bah Ba was out of town, I hung out at Goh Goh's apartment. I saw a Father's Day card pinned on Bah Ba's room. On the front of the card, a large balloon contained the words "World's Best Grandpa." Jordan flipped the card to the next page, and he pointed at his own name on the bottom, the letters unaligned.

I could've opened Bah Ba's bedroom door, saw his new life, what it smelled like, the pictures he might've had up, but I didn't touch the door. The less you know, the easier it is to forget.

The card on the door was Goh Goh's idea. It was weird seeing our brother in this role, a father teaching his son to be thoughtful, sweet. For Christmas, my brother stayed up until five in the morning wrapping gifts for his kids. He tried to do Santa's work. He assembled a Big Wheel and a kitchen play set, which took forever because of the stickers. He couldn't figure out where they went. Harder than it sounds, he'd told me.

This is the way I'd like to think I'd be as a dad. My brother was the one who spent time with the kids. My sister-in-law, Dai So, worked a graveyard shift, supervising at a mahjong parlor, though

it wasn't always clear when she was working and when she was playing herself. She wasn't home often. Anything to do with school,
anything recreational with the kids, taking them to the park or
a movie, getting them into extracurricular activities, martial arts,
ballet, or just sitting at home with them, that was all on Goh Goh.
Dai So was like our father in that way—unavailable. But at least
she'd handle dinner. It was as though, to her, this was her sole duty
as a mother, anything else optional. As soon as dinner was over,
she'd be out the door with the quickness.

Goh Goh and Dai So used to argue about this, her always out,
but now they fought less. They'd settled into the routine. "I've
failed as a father," Goh Goh once told me. He wanted more for
his kids than *he* had, but he was struggling to pay the rent, having
to borrow money occasionally from one of us. He was raising his
family on the same block that he'd grown up on, a new version of
his old housing complex that didn't feel new enough, the dynamics
in his own family too similar to the one that had raised him.

There was no answer at the gate of the complex. The kids
turned back to my sister confused. She lowered her rear window
and reversed so they could hop back in the car. Take them to their
mom's job, she thought.

"I think Yeh Yeh is asleep," Jordan said. When Jordan calls Bah
Ba, Yeh Yeh, my sister's body shudders like mine. Our father has a
new identity, untainted.

Ga Jeh unlocked the car door. Through the thick bars of the
gate, she saw a figure approaching. "Yeh Yeh," Alana hollered. They
didn't understand that we didn't speak to our father, their grandfather. I wondered what we would tell them when they got older,
how honest we'd be.

My sister reached behind the passenger seat, past the Snoopy
tissue box that hung over the seat and pushed the rear door open.
"Get in, Jordan." Ga Jeh came around the car and picked up Alana,
brought her to the other side and stuck her in the car seat, fastening
the buckle.

"But it's Yeh Yeh," Jordan said. My father was at the gate.

"I said now, Jordan," Ga Jeh screamed. "Get in!"

My nephew climbed in and closed the door.

"Jordan!" Bah Ba waved his hand like he was flagging a taxi. Ga Jeh screeched off. My father didn't know my sister drove an SUV.

The kids were silent in the car, scared of how angry my sister had gotten. Ga Jeh neared downtown and saw Alana's face in the rearview mirror. She looked as if she was bracing herself to be hit. My sister pulled over.

"I'm sorry I yelled," my sister said.

"How come you don't like Yeh Yeh?" Jordan asked.

Ga Jeh leaned toward the backseat. "He's a very bad man," she said to both of them, her voice cracking. "Don't forget that."

My father lived with my brother for several years before Goh Goh finally kicked him out. I was surprised that it took that long. Bah Ba was drinking again, and this, obviously, did not pair well with babysitting duties. The first strike was when my brother came home from work and Jordan was missing. My father was in his room, doing who knows what. "Jordan's here somewhere," Bah Ba told my brother. "I picked him up from school." They searched the house, walked around the courtyard, but no luck. Then my brother received a call from Jordan's school. He was still at the after-school program, waiting to get picked up.

The second strike involved my niece. Goh Goh came home from work, and once again, one of his children was missing, this time, his daughter. Bah Ba was outside the complex, smoking a cig. "She should be upstairs," my father said. "That's where I left her."

"You shouldn't be leaving her at all," my brother said. "She's three."

They, or it's possible just my brother, found her in the play area in the courtyard around the corner from the apartment. She'd wandered outside by herself. There would be no third strike.

THREE AGAINST ONE

The hardest checkmate to deliver is when you're up three pieces to one: a king, knight, and bishop versus a lone king. Even grand-masters struggle with this endgame, some settling for a draw. The tricky part is coordinating the three pieces, to get this motley crew to work in tandem. If they're to win, they must control adjacent squares, forming a wall the enemy king cannot pass. The wall closes in on the king until he's forced to a corner of the board where checkmate is finally delivered. Easier said than done. I'd offer my students a hundred bucks if they could execute this checkmate, but they never could. Just when they thought their plan was work-ing, that they were pushing the king to the edge of the board, the enemy king would once again find a gap in their shoddy wall and slip through to safety.

SINGLE ROOM OCCUPANCY

Bah Ba now lives in an SRO on the outskirts of Chinatown, one room, comparable to a large walk-in closet. He shares a kitchen and bathroom with all the tenants on his floor. I imagine cockroaches, leaking ceilings, cigarette butts crammed into window tracks. Early retirement hasn't panned out for my father. He has to work again. My brother points out the place as we drive past, a dry cleaner on a quiet street.

He doesn't live alone. He has a new wife, a homeland chick, not that much older than me. I'll say this about my father—the guy is resourceful. When he was living with my brother, he stum-bled upon a letter from a childhood friend of my sister-in-law. The friend wanted to marry an American, become an American. My dad figured he fit the bill.

The friend had the same last name as Dai So, which was typi-cal, villagers sharing the same family name. They weren't all rela-tives, but it also wasn't out of the question for villagers to be secretly related. Their families had lived side by side for generations. It was taboo to marry within the village, a risk of inbreeding.

Goh Goh and his wife made plans to visit Macau. My brother had never met her folks. "I'd like to come along," Bah Ba said. "I'm family, too."

That's how my father met his second wife, perhaps a distant cousin of his daughter-in-law.

PRESENTS

We met at my sister's house for Christmas. She moved back to the Bay and lived now with her husband in an apartment minutes from the coast. She was the one who organized our holiday get-togethers. She'd delegate who'd bring what. I brought lasagna, no meat. My sister didn't eat beef, and like me, no pork.

Ga Jeh was all about the holidays. So was her husband. They'd driven an hour north to a tree farm. It was a tradition in his family, cutting down the tree, and my sister had embraced his family's traditions as though they were hers. They'd decorated their tree with ornaments from both of their childhoods.

I was on break from graduate school, my second MFA. I'd jumped immediately into another creative writing program after already completing one, first in New Jersey, now in Houston. I was buying time, another couple of years that I could live a couple thousand miles from my father. Before I'd left June Jordan I'd given a speech at a fundraiser for the school. In front of the audience that included students, parents, and colleagues, I'd announced it'd be my last year at June Jordan. I was leaving to write a memoir, a writer once again. "I tell my students to follow their dreams," I'd said, "so I need to follow mine." Translation: Enough about the kids, what about me!

I'd told Ga Jeh what I'd planned to write, and she gave me the green light. "I don't mind if you have to write about 'that,'" she said. "I remember reading a memoir that had a similar situation and thought, 'How can that happen to people?' but in reality, it had already happened to me. I trust that your book will be an inspiration to others and if they're going through something similar, they'll know they're not alone."

I'd sent her a story of mine that had gotten published. In the story, I question if I should bring up the subject of abuse with my sister. I want to shelter her from more pain. After Ga Jeh read the story, we sat down over tea and discussed the abuse for the first time at length, perhaps the first time she's ever been so willing with anyone. A few weeks later, she scheduled an appointment with a therapist.

When we finished the Christmas dinner, it was time for presents. My sister and her husband gave Jordan and Alana multiple gifts, including stocking stuffers, but Jordan was nine and was starting to be a brat. He'd open a present, take a quick peek inside the box, and, if it was clothes, he'd toss the box aside and move on to the next gift. If it wasn't Legos, it was junk.

The next day, we were at my mother and Willie's house. Jordan would call Willie "Grandpa," and probably because of this, I started to see Willie as my, if not father, stepfather. When Jordan was younger, Willie introduced him to *Chitty Chitty Bang Bang*, and Jordan would watch it on repeat the whole day. He'd make Willie and me join him for the "Me Ol' Bamboo" song. He'd give us each a rolled-up sheet of paper, and we'd pretend it was a bamboo stick. The three of us would dance along to the choreographed routine, high-stepping around the living room, making the silliest faces we could while trying to stay in sync with each other. Watching the way Willie was with my brother's kids—he'd take them out every chance he had—I had to admit we were lucky to have this grandpa in our family.

I called Jordan into the office. "Close the door behind you," I said. "Grab that chair and bring it here." I may not have been a parent, but I'd been a high school teacher for seven years, and if I wasn't taking bullshit anymore from students, I'd be damned if I was gonna let my third-grade nephew get away with his ungrateful attitude.

Jordan sat in the chair, and I didn't even say anything right away. I wanted him to feel awkward. "Why are we sitting like this, Saam Sook?"

"You're not a baby, so we're gonna stop treating you like one. The way you opened Yi Goo Jeh and Uncle Eric's presents was rude. They had to drive to the store, pick out what they thought you might like, stand in line to buy it, bring it home, and then wrap it up. And they bought you a card. They had to write a message for you. It took hours to do all that, just for you, and you didn't even look at their gifts. Hey, look me in the eye when I'm talking."

His eyes shot up.

"Do you know what respect means?" I asked.

"Being nice to people?"

"It's also what you think of someone. If you respect a person, you think they're a good human being. I'm not sure—at least from what I saw yesterday—that you'll grow up to be a person I'll respect. I'm always going to love you, but respect, that's different. I don't have to respect you. I don't respect rude people."

His eyes grew watery, but I continued with the lecture. If I could get a student to cry, it was a good day. Progress was made.

"OK," I said, "now how can you make it up to Yi Goo Jeh and Uncle Eric?"

"Say sorry?"

"That's a start."

GUAYABERA

It was summer, and I was staying at my brother's, visiting from out of state. In the mornings, I'd get my nephew and niece ready for school. Make sure they were fed and dressed in time. When Alana would have a bad hair day, I'd comb and blow-dry her hair. In return, one morning, I let her shave my head with a disposable razor, her little hands wiping shaving cream around my head. Goh Goh would've already left for work and Dai So would be asleep, her nocturnal work schedule.

I'd climb on the cable car with the kids to Chinatown where their summer program was held. When the kids in Alana's class were given nicknames, Alana, who was tall for her age, was named Humongor. My brother didn't find that as funny as me. I'd also pick them up after school. It was risky—Bah Ba lived blocks away.

When we'd return home, Alana would grab her hammer made out of paper and tape. "Beetle!" she'd say. She'd walk around smashing bugs on the floor. My brother, along with Jordan, sometimes would join in using scraps of tissue, the three of them hunched over searching for an insect to squash.

I'd sleep on the sectional. They'd gotten rid of the old sofa from Bah Ba, but our father's taste in furniture was still present in my brother's living room. Goh Goh had made the mistake of allowing Bah Ba to pick out the coffee table. It was an oval lacquered table, cumbersome, too big for the room. I had to squeeze through to sit on the couch. During dinner, everyone else sat on small chairs. I'd broken two of them. One was a tiny plastic one, made for a child. I cracked the seat trying to sit on it. The other chair was a cheap stool, and that flimsy thing fell apart as I was sitting on it.

My brother had turned our father's former room into a dumping ground, mostly relics of Goh Goh's bygone rebate empire. He'd find rebates for electronics, order them online, and sell them for full price. There was hardly space to walk in the room. It was crammed with stacks of boxes, stuff that never sold, also things he'd accumulated over the years but couldn't part with: cassette tapes, video game systems, Bah Ba's old mahjong table, and my brother's childhood desk, the one our father had bought for him, made from maple wood.

It was my summer project to clean out the room. I found in the closest a bag of old clothes, my father's. The bag was filled not of clothes that Bah Ba had left from his last stay, but these clothes were left behind by my father when he'd first moved to Minnesota years ago. They'd remained in the dresser in Mom's room, untouched, but when the old North Beach was about to be torn down, Goh Goh threw the clothes into a garbage bag. It'd been unopened since.

I pulled out from the bag a guayabera-style shirt, something Bah Ba probably had brought over when we emigrated from Hong Kong, when he was younger than I was then. I didn't remember my father wearing the shirt before, or even the shirt itself. It was too stylish for him. I tried it on, but it was too tight. If I arched my back, the shirt would've ripped. This was probably for the best, else I would've kept it. I didn't examine the other clothes. I tossed the shirt back into the bag, slung the bag over my shoulder, and went down to the courtyard. I pictured where I stood in relation to our childhood apartment. The sounds were the same, the hum of the cable car tracks, the electricity surging through the poles of a bus trolley in the distance, but nothing else was familiar. Surrounding me were townhouses, neighbors who were strangers to me. I threw the bag into the garbage chute and listened to it as it slid into the dumpster.

TETHERED

I pass by my father's apartment often, whenever I'm in town. I ride by on the bus, on the way to my brother's house. Bah Ba's neighbors include bars and strip clubs but also an elementary school and a museum dedicated to the Beat Generation. At every stop in that neighborhood, I check out the window to see who's about to climb on the bus. I have to be ready to step off if I see my father, but the chances of me instantly recognizing him are slim. I haven't seen him in a decade. When passengers board, I shield my face.

I walk by his place when I meet up with my homie who works at a nearby hotel. There are other routes to reach the hotel that don't involve having to pass Bah Ba's apartment building, but this way is the most direct. That's what I tell myself. In truth, this path, which places me across the street from my father, must be a guilty pleasure, one I haven't admitted to myself: sneaking a peek at the house of a lost love.

Still, the idea of bumping into Bah Ba terrifies me, in spite of how I put myself in situations to do just that. I don't know how I'd react if I saw him. I might flip out and go off, put hands on my father, or worse, the opposite might occur, some feeling of pity or mercy.

I don't stare at Bah Ba's SRO building. It's on a side street. I glance at it, but knowing that it's there is enough. This is as close as I am willing to get to my father, as close as we'll ever get, unless he finds me first, and that's not likely. I don't believe he's looking for me. He hasn't called or written since I visited him in Minnesota. He knows from my brother that I don't want anything to do with him, and I guess that's all he needs to know.

For my part, I'm not done yet with Bah Ba. Probably never will be. In writing this book, I'd hoped to be freed from my father, that I'd exhaust my obsession with him, but our bond has only strengthened. He'll remain a permanent character in my story. We've become pieces on a board game that will never end.

SPIRIT

They say when an ancestor dies they become a spirit, capable of molding the lives of their descendants. A former girlfriend believed it was her grandma in the afterlife who had brought us together, two lovers joined by a supernatural matchmaker. When we had rocky times, we'd pray to her grandma and ask for guidance.

One day, Bah Ba will leave this world. Declaring that I've disowned him will mean nothing. Spirits don't take orders from the living. He'll follow me around like all good ancestors do. He may hold a grudge against me for what I've written in these pages, and he'll have the power to exact revenge. The ability to shape my story will be in his hands.

POSTMORTEM

Players conduct a postmortem of their chess game once it's finished. The two former opponents now work together as one. They return to key junctures of the game and consider alternative moves. They test the merits of these moves by playing them out and evaluating the resulting positions.

In chess books, moves from a game are recorded along with variations to the main line. This allows the reader, using their own board, to not only reenact the original but also to diverge from the original, to explore an alternate timeline.

TIME TRAVELLED

I was at a jazz club in North Beach with some guy named Fred. Apparently, we were best buds. "We're back in 1985," he said. His mom was playing the piano. We didn't know who she was until later, when we were back at her apartment. Her boyfriend was hanging out with us too. "Yo, these are going to be my parents," Fred whispered to me. I thought I was in a *Back to the Future* remake and that Fred might start disappearing, but we learned the couple already had a wedding planned. All me and Fred had to do was get out the way. We left them alone and hit the streets. For all we knew, that night could've been Fred's night of conception.

We found another club but it was last call. We downed shots of whisky. We stepped outside. It was sunny somehow, a warm heat. I saw my mother up the hill. She was wearing a red scarf and headed our way. We didn't want to disrupt the time-space continuum, so me and Fred ducked back into the club as she sauntered by.

This couldn't be why we'd traveled back in time, to be neutral bystanders. Maybe we'd been sent back to fix something that had gone awry, like Kitty Pryde of the X-Men, who'd also time travelled, but from the '80s. She had to prevent the assassination of a senator by fellow mutants, an event that would eventually lead to a mutant genocide, a dystopian future.

I thought about the year, 1985, what tragedies occurred that I could prevent. It was the year my father began creeping into my sister's room.

I could go to Ga Jeh's school and warn her, but I wouldn't be able to get past her teachers. They wouldn't let a stranger talk to a child in private. I could work my way into the school as a volunteer, but that would take too long. Paperwork had to be cleared.

I decided to find my father. I told Fred I had to do this alone. I waited for Bah Ba outside Tea House. I stood where I could see both exits, the front door and the back door in the alley. My father left through the front entrance. He still had his apron on.

"Bah Ba," I said, "it's Dickson."

He ignored me like I was asking him for change.

"*Tai hah ngoh goh yeuhng,*" I shouted. Look at my face! Look at me, I'm your son.

"You're a man." He stepped toward me, furrowing his brow.

"Don't try to figure this out," I said. I had the feeling that at any moment, I'd be jerked back to my time. "In the future, your kids are going to abandon you, but you can stop this from happening. No, don't leave! Please, just listen. Just listen to me."

And he waited to hear what I'd say next.

* * * * * *

NOTES

8   "My aunt haunts me…" from *The Woman Warrior: Memoirs of a Girlhood Among Ghosts* by Maxine Hong Kingston. Alfred A. Knopf, 1976, p. 16.

8   "You must take your opponent…" from *Chess for Success: Using an Old Game to Build New Strengths in Children and Teens* by Maurice Ashley. Broadway Books, 2005, p. 191-192.

28-29   Quotes from homicide inspector and district spokeswoman from "SAN FRANCISCO/ Hunters Point Killing Called Result of Running Clash between Gangs" by Jaxon Van Derbeken. *SFGate*, 12 Apr. 2005.

39   Deng Xiaoping's evaluation of Mao from *Mao: A Biography* by Ross Terrill. Stanford University Press, 1999, p. 471.

40   Book of sculpted scenes from *Rent Collection Courtyard: Sculptures of Oppression and Revolt* by Revolutionary Chinese Art Workers Group. Athena Books, 2004.

49   Tea House as "arguably the best dim sum restaurant in the country" from "Where the Twain Meet-Deliciously" by Eileen Yin-Fei Lo. *New York Times*, 5 Dec. 1982.

75   Demographics of North Beach Housing Projects from "The Impact of Perceptions on Interpersonal Interactions in an African American/Asian American Housing Project" by Patricia Guthrie and Janis Hutchinson. *Journal of Black Studies*, vol. 25, no. 3, Jan. 1995, p. 383.

116   "The Chinese people have stood up!" from *Selected Works of Mao Tse-Tung: Volume V* by Mao Tse-Tung. Foreign Language Press, 1977, p. 15.

117   "Oppressors are people…" from *Mao Zedong* by Jonathan D. Spence. Viking, 1999, p. 36.

117   Mao generation poem from "Generation Names in China: Past, Present, and Future" by Li Zhonghua and Edwin D. Lawson. *Names*, vol. 50, no. 3, Nov. 2002, p. 4.

119   "The outstanding thing…" from *Quotations from Chairman Mao Tse-tung* by Mao Tse-tung. Foreign Language Press, 1972, p. 36.

119   "If I could drain away…" from *The Autobiography of Malcolm X: As Told to Alex Haley* by Malcolm X. Ballantine Books, 1987, p. 232.

124   Angel Island poem from *Island: Poetry and History of Chinese Immigrants on Angel Island, 1910-1940* by Him Mark Lai, Genny Lim, and Judy Yung. University of Washington Press, 1991, p. 92.

131   Parent survey results from "Children Left Behind Face Tough Road." *China Daily*, 2 June 2004.

131   Children survey results from "Paying the Price for Economic Development: The Children of Migrant Workers in China" by Aris Chan. *China Labour Bulletin*, Nov. 2009, p. 10.

131   The quotes "If I hurt my hands…" and "I used to miss my parents…" from ibid., pp. 14-15.

131   "What's the big deal…" from "Left-Behind Children of China's Migrant Workers Bear Grown-Up Burdens: About 61 Million Chinese Kids Haven't Seen One or Both Parents for at Least Three Months" by Andrew Browne. *The Wall Street Journal*, 17 Jan. 2014.

137   Statistic that ninety percent of sexual assault cases involve left-behind girls from "The Vulnerability of China's Left-Behind Children" by Maura Elizabeth Cunningham. *The Wall Street Journal*, 21 Mar. 2014.

137   "Many of these tragedies…" from "Paying the Price for Economic Development: The Children of Migrant Workers in China" by Aris Chan. *China Labour Bulletin*, Nov. 2009, p. 12.

144   "Just 'cause you…" from *Malcolm X: "Democracy is Hypocrisy" Speech*. Educational Video Group, 1960. Transcript.

145   Asian American magazine was *Giant Robot*, issue 10, 1997.

145-6 "I know you two guys are crazy…" from "Richard Aoki Interview." *APEX Express*. KPFA, Berkeley, 30 Apr. 2009.

146-7 Article about 3F written by Robert Capp. "Taggers, Bangers, and the Battle for SF Graffiti," dated 1993 but went unpublished until self-published on personal website. Accessed 27 Mar. 2013.

162   "The game of chess…" sampled in "Da Mystery of Chessboxin'" by Wu-Tang Clan. *Enter the Wu-Tang (36 Chambers)*, Loud, 1993.

168   "These days…" from *Mao: A Biography* by Ross Terrill. Stanford University Press, 1999, p. 339.

168   Ninety-five percent of cadres redeemable and "touch men's very souls" from *Mao's China and After: A History of the People's Republic* by Maurice Meisner. 3rd ed., Free Press, 1999, p. 307-308.

168   "Bombard the headquarters" from *Mao: A Reinterpretation* by Lee Feigon. Ivan R. Dee, 2002, p. 158.

169   "If the father…" from "The Role of the Red Guards and Revolutionary Rebels in Mao's Cultural Revolution" by the CIA Directorate of Intelligence. CIA, Nov. 1968, p. 15.

177   "Sharing the Blue Sky" campaign from "Paying the Price for Economic Development: The Children of Migrant Workers in China" by Aris Chan. *China Labour Bulletin*, Nov. 2009, pp. 19-20.

178   Eligibility to attend Robeson Rivera Academy from "The Repeat Offenders Prevention Project (ROPP) of the City/County of San Francisco: A Final Evaluation Report" by the California State Board of Corrections, June 2003, p. 7.

201   "His rap style…" from "Nas' 25 Favorite Albums" by Insanul Ahmed. *Complex.com*. 22 May 2012.

212-3 Quotes from *Long Night's Journey into Day: South Africa's Search for Truth & Reconciliation*. Directed by Frances Reid and Deborah Hoffmann. Iris Films/Cinemax Reel Life, 2000.

ACKNOWLEDGMENTS

First and foremost, I would like to thank my sister for her unwavering support through-out this project. Your courage gave me the strength to write this. Thanks to my mom for always be willing to answer questions, including all the random questions about Cantonese. To Willie for his patience and understanding. To my father for giving me permission to use his emails. To my brother for showing me what it means to be a loving father. To my aunts, uncles, and cousins, I hope for your understanding. To my grandparents, who have passed on, we miss you each day. And to our next generation, I wrote this for y'all.

To the homies who've been there from day one of this journey: Maritez Apigo, George Alonzo, Eric Bastine, Sherilyn Tran, Tiffany Saechao, Han Fan. To Ken Ja and Dave Maduli, who I turn to continuously for pretty much everything, next drink's on me. To my oldest and best friend, Koitt Robbins, let's go for another one of those rides. To my brother Rob Santos, rest in power. Wish you were still here so you could read the stories of us and tell me, "That ain't how it happened, man!"

Shout-out to all the students and families I've had the privilege to work with. Keep grinding, keep shining. Rest in power to Javon King, George Hurtado, and Joshua Cameron, stars who had so much more to give. Rest in power to Randy and Keino. We remember.

To Urban Academy, especially my mentor Avram Barlowe, for teaching me how to listen, how to create questions that make a classroom pop, and how to organize the chaos. To the co-founders of June Jordan School for Equity, Kate Goka, Matt Alexander, and Shane Safir, thank you for your visionary leadership and the years that y'all put into laying the foundation. To the other JJSE teachers and staff that I had the honor to work with, so much love and admiration for each of you.

To the Contra Costa College community, especially the Puente Project, for inspiring me with your stories each day. Special shout-out to my Puente partner, Norma Liliana Valdez. You knock it out every time in the classroom and on the poetry stage. To Elvia Ornelas-Garcia for being willing to share joint custody of a program she loves so dearly.

For the gift of time and space to write, thank you to the Millay Colony for the Arts and the Kimmel Harding Nelson Center for the Arts.

To my teachers for their generosity and wisdom, from the MFA program at the University of Houston: Alex Parsons, Antonya Nelson, Chitra Divakaruni, Mat Johnson, Nick Flynn, Peter Turchi, and ZZ Packer; from the MFA program at Rutgers-Newark: Alice Elliott Dark, Jayne Anne Phillips, Rigoberto González, and Tayari Jones; from VONA: Chris Abani, David Mura, Junot Díaz, Andrew Pham; and my very first work-shop instructors who gave my crappy writing so much love, care, and guidance: Elmaz Abinader and Faith Adiele.

Extreme gratitude to the readers who have shaped this book through their encouragement and insightful feedback, especially to Hirsh Sawhney, Armin Tolentino, Leslie Ann Murray, Tracy Lachica Buenavista, Nancy Pearson, Elizabeth Winston, Austin Tremblay, Celeste Prince, Julia Brown, Jameelah Lang, Talia Mailman, Aja Gabel, Michelle Mariano, Claire Anderson, Sara Rolater, Selena Anderson, Tyson Morgan, Thomas Calder, Justin Chrestman, and Jessica Wilbanks. Also, thanks to Ted Closson for adapting my work to comic form.

Special thanks to the editors who have published pieces from this book in earlier iterations: Jennifer Derilo, Roxane Gay, Steven Church, Karissa Chen, David Lynn, and Paul Lisicky.

Deepest thanks to Alison Hawthorne Deming for choosing my work. Forever in debt. Also, Christine Stroud and Alison Taverna at Autumn House Press for their untiring work to put this book in your hands.

And my wife, Jessica Morrow, who wouldn't let me stop believing. You came right on time.

The following essays originally appeared in the journals noted:

"Cross the Line,"
Kartika Review, Fall 2011

A shorter version of "What's in a Name?"
was published as "An Echo," *PANK*, Spring 2014

"The Key to the Combination,"
The Normal School, Fall 2014

"Snowmen," *Hyphen Magazine*, February 2015

"What's in a Name?", *Kenyon Review Online*, Fall 2015

The opening section of "An Unreliable Narrator"
was published as "Sitting on the Toilet in the Alley Is the Hugger
Who Waits for the Drunk Ear Picker to Bring the Red Bean Soup,"
StoryQuarterly, February 2016

2017 & 2018 RELEASES

Apocalypse Mix by Jane Satterfield
Winner of the 2016 Autumn House Poetry Prize,
selected by David St. John

Heavy Metal by Andrew Bourelle
Winner of the 2016 Autumn House Fiction Prize,
selected by William Lychack

RUN SCREAM UNBURY SAVE by Katherine McCord
Winner of the 2016 Autumn House Nonfiction Prize,
selected by Michael Martone

The Moon is Almost Full by Chana Bloch

Vixen by Cherene Sherrard

The Drowning Boy's Guide to Water by Cameron Barnett
Winner of the 2017 Rising Writer Prize,
selected by Ada Limón

The Small Door of Your Death by Sheryl St. Germain

Darling Nova by Melissa Cundieff
Winner of the 2017 Autumn House Poetry Prize,
selected by Alberto Ríos

Carry You by Glori Simmons
Winner of the 2017 Autumn House Fiction Prize,
selected by Amina Gautier

Paper Sons by Dickson Lam
Winner of the 2017 Autumn House Nonfiction Prize,
selected by Alison Hawthorne Deming

For our full catalog please visit: http://www.autumnhouse.org

Teaching resources including lesson plans, essay prompts, and creative writing prompts are also available at **www.dicksonlam.net**.

1. What is the significance of the memoir's title, *Paper Sons*? In what ways is Lam a paper son?

2. How is Lam's mother portrayed in the book? How would you describe the relationship between Lam and his mother?

3. Lam's father is a primary focus of *Paper Sons*, while Lam's sister seems to be a secondary character. What might be the author's rationale for this? Did Lam inadvertently silence his sister by centering the book on his father, the abuser?

4. Writing is a prominent theme throughout the book, from graffiti writing, to Lam teaching writing, to the memoir itself. What power does writing have in *Paper Sons*?

5. *Paper Sons* is organized in short sections. Why might Lam have chosen this structure? How did this affect your reading experience?

6. Think of some common stereotypes of Asian Americans. In what ways does *Paper Sons* challenge these stereotypes?

7. Consider Cynthia Ngewu's statement on the need for forgiveness: "We want to get rid of this burden we are carrying inside, so that we too can feel at peace" (p.213). How does this statement relate to the section "Bandaged Figures"? (p.173-177)

8. "Honesty was a prerequisite for forgiveness," Lam says (p.212). Do you agree with this idea? Is forgiveness only possible with remorse? Under what conditions should we forgive? If the wrongdoing is denied, is it still possible for the victim to find "peace"?

9. In comparing the US immigration policy toward Chinese and Europeans immigrants before the Immigration and Nationality Act of 1965, Lam says, "Citizenship could be extended or withheld, but this choice had nothing to do with notions of legal or illegal; it had everything to do with affirming whiteness" (p.123). Could this same sentence be applied to the treatment of undocumented immigrants today? Why or why not?

10. Why do you think Lam ended the story the way he did? What does the ending reveal about his current feelings toward his father?

* * * * * *